EXTRACTION, GLOBAL COMMODITY TRADE, AND URBAN DEVELOPMENT IN ZAMBIA'S NORTHWESTERN PROVINCE

EXTRACTION, GLOBAL COMMODITY TRADE, AND URBAN DEVELOPMENT IN ZAMBIA'S NORTHWESTERN PROVINCE

An Ethnography of Inequality and Interdependence

Rita Kesselring

ZED

LONDON • NEW YORK • OXFORD • NEW DELHI • SYDNEY

ZED Books
Bloomsbury Publishing Plc
50 Bedford Square, London, WC1B 3DP, UK
1385 Broadway, New York, NY 10018, USA
29 Earlsfort Terrace, Dublin 2, Ireland

BLOOMSBURY and Zed Books are trademarks of Bloomsbury Publishing Plc

First published in Great Britain 2025

Series design by Grace Ridge

Cover images © Jose Luis Stephens via Alamy Stock Photo and Sergey Ryumin via Getty Images

A catalogue record for this book is available from the British Library.

A catalog record for this book is available from the Library of Congress.

ISBN: HB: 978-1-3504-5430-9
ePDF: 978-1-3504-5431-6
eBook: 978-1-3504-5429-3

Typeset by Newgen KnowledgeWorks Pvt. Ltd., Chennai, India

To find out more about our authors and books visit www.bloomsbury.com and sign up for our newsletters.

CONTENTS

ILLUSTRATIONS

ACKNOWLEDGEMENTS

Conducting research is a highly intersubjective practice. The project idea may have been born in my mind, but the long road to this book's completion has been travelled on with many colleagues and friends, who shaped the project's direction, focus and content all along.

With their time, advice and knowledge, Solwezi residents made sure that I have something to say. I can only thank those by name who agreed to be named, but they are representative for all the other persons who kindly engaged with me and tolerated me during my time in Solwezi, teaching me what I later put into my own words:

Fleming and Mary Kakoma; Edward Mwanza, the late Lewis Mumba and Collins Tembo from Shekina Engineering; Charity, Dave and Raford; Freddie and the boys; Naomi Simwanza, Adriada Daka, Justin Mbashila and all the other staff members of Solwezi Municipal Council at the time of my research; Monde Sitali and Simon; Chaiwa Njovu; Mutinta Williams, Mr. Kapashi and Mr. Sebo; Kennedy, Chola, Joe and friends; headwoman Kalepa, Chief Mumena, Chief Mukumbi and Chief Mujimanzovu; the entire Solwezi Urban Baseline Study team; Eliack Shikamo, Zangi Kamangala and Oliver Fotah; Roman; Lena Preuss and Albert, Sabine Mantsch, Daniel Nickel, and Jennifer Chibamba Chansa and Samuel Lungu.

I also thank mine managers and employees and their families for allowing me in and making time for interviews and conversations.

During the almost two years of field research, the Dag Hammarskjold Institute for Peace and Conflict Studies (DHIPS) at the University of the Copperbelt provided an academic and engaging home for which I have to thank Owen Sichone, John Bwalya, Ignatius Mukunto, Robby Kapesa, Lisa Sawomba, Greyford Simaloli and Chola Waluzimba.

I was lucky enough to be welcomed into a partly established but largely new and generous generation of scholars researching the Katangese and Zambian Copperbelts. Exchanges with many of them, in Zambia and elsewhere, was always very insightful and affirming: Hélène Blaszkiewicz, Alexander Caramento, Jennifer Chibamba Chansa, Hikabwa Chipande, Donatien Dibwe dia Mwembu, Alastair Fraser, Kristien Geenen, Jan-Bart Gewald, Enid Guene, Stephanie Lämmert, Emma Lochery, Miles Larmer, Thomas McNamara, Duncan Money, James Musonda, Patience Mususa, Margaret O'Callaghan, Iva Peša, Francesca Pugliese, Benjamin Rubbers, Sishuwa Sishuwa, Christian Straube and Paul David Wilkin.

A force that pushed and drove this book's transregional content was the most enthusiastic group of scholars and activists bringing the project 'Valueworks: Effects of Financialization along the Copper Value Chain' to life: Ganga Jey Aratnam,

Tinenenji Banda, late Maio Bulawayo, Christian Busse, Gregor Dobler, Aurora García, Hanna Haile, Anna-Sophie Hobi, Marja Hinfelaar, Ellen Hertz, Katja Hujo, Alice Kohli, Stefan Leins, Edna Litana-Kabala, Sabine Mantsch, Joachim Merz, Dale Mudenda, Barbara Müller, John Lungu, Wilma Nchito, Manenga Ndulo, Horacio Ortiz, Yvan Schulz, Simone Wasmann and Wiebke Wiesigel. Many more contributed to the project's aim in conversations and at conferences and workshops: Isolda Agazzi, Andrew Bowman, Filipe Calvão, Juvience Chalwe, Thaulo Chewe, Liliana Doganova, Dunja Herzog, Opa Kapijimpanga, Yann Mingard, Laura Miti, Zebbies Mumba, Chris Mweemba, David Ngwenyama, Christopher Nkhata, Chisomo Phiri, Pamela Towela Sambo, Cassandra Vet and Natascha van der Zwan.

Returning to Solwezi with ten master students from the University of Basel in early 2018 and witnessing their openness for Solwezi and its residents was most rewarding.

My activist home has been the Swiss Apartheid Debt and Reparation Campaign and its members committed to Swiss business' international accountability and liability. For reliably challenging conversations, I want to thank Aurora García, Anna-Sophie Hobi, Barbara Müller, Vreni Schneider, Urs Sekinger and Daniela Zimmermann.

I have written the first version of the book while employed as a senior lecturer and researcher at the chair of anthropology, University of Basel, and could finish it only due to the sustained support from the chair, Till Förster, and my many colleagues at the chair, the Departments of Social Sciences and History, and the Center for African Studies. I have been shaped as an anthropologist by Till Förster's seriousness in combining empirical depth with analytical rigor, and his enthusiasm for both has since long shaped my outlook on our common discipline. For one year, the Princeton Institute for International and Regional Studies (PIIRS) was a most pleasant and productive workplace thanks mainly to Jeremy Adelman, Nicole Bergman, Guillaume Calafat, Meng-Hsuan Chou, Tolga Demiryol, Joseph Prestel and Kristin Surak. I finalized the book in my current intellectual home, the School of Humanities and Social Sciences at the University of St Gallen, which also provided the funds for open access. Zeno Adams from the School of Finance became my trusted conversation partner on commodity markets. Nick Wolterman and the team at ZED/Bloomsbury enthusiastically took on the book project and calmly helped turning it into a book.

Funding for time away from teaching and administration and for academic collaborations was provided by the Forschungsfonds and the Stay on Track program of the University of Basel for two terms of field research leave and teaching relief, respectively; by SARECO (Swiss-African Research Cooperation) for a workshop in Solwezi with the DHIPS; by SNIS (Swiss Network for International Studies) for the two-year project 'Valueworks'; by the Freiwillige Akademische Gesellschaft (FAG) for the guided field course with MA students; and by the Fung Global Fellows Program for a one-year stay at PIIRS in Princeton.

The person whom I cannot thank enough and who has been with me at most of the book project's stops, including in Solwezi for six months, is my husband

Gregor Dobler, an often intellectually intimidating comrade and father to our daughter who joined us when this book started to take shape and our son who came to us more recently.

Parts of chapters were published as early drafts in *Energy Research & Social Science* (Chapter 5), *The Journal of Modern African Studies* (Chapter 6), *The Extractive Industries and* Society (Chapter 2) and in a Routledge volume (Chapter 2).

INTRODUCTION

'It's like another country!'

One evening in August 2017, Fleming Kakoma and I chatted on his plot in the Saviye area in Solwezi town, the urban centre of Zambia's mostly rural Northwestern Province. He and his wife Mary had just returned from several days of work at their family field a few kilometres outside of town. A retired teacher, Mr. Kakoma works in an agricultural program run by the Corporate Social Responsibility Program of Kansanshi Mine ten kilometres north of his plot. Kansanshi Mine was Africa's largest copper mine by output at the time. Its owner, First Quantum Minerals Ltd. (FQM[1]), is based in Canada and the sixth largest copper producer in the world. The mining giant also owns Africa's now largest copper mine, Sentinel mine, which is situated near Kalumbila town just 140 kilometres west from Kansanshi Mine, and next to which it will soon open what is poised to be the largest nickel mine on the African continent, the Enterprise Mine (see Figure 1).

This new mining hub sits at the centre of geopolitical and economic interests which have come into full force now: Not far away in the Copperbelt Province to the east, an area well-known for its long history of industrial copper mining, KoBold, a Jeff Bezos and Bill Gates-backed exploration and mining company, announced its find at Mingomba mining site in early 2024. KoBold also partners with the Canadian firm Midnight Sun Mining to explore deposits just south of Kansanshi Mine and Solwezi town. Pioneering the use of artificial intelligence to search for critical raw minerals such as copper, cobalt, lithium and nickel, KoBold's investment ties in with most recent geopolitical interests in a region where the United States, Europe, China and since recently also the Middle East compete for access to critical minerals in the Zambia-Congo Copperbelt. The European Union's and the United States' investments in the renewal of the century-old Lobito corridor, a railway line from Lobito harbour in Angola to Kolwezi, a Congolese mining city just north of Solwezi, and a planned extension into Northwestern Zambia, is seen as a major pushback against China's influence in Central Africa.

In that sense, Solwezi, a town sitting next to an old albeit throughout the twentieth century mostly dormant mine that re-opened during the 2000s global commodities boom, forebodes what is yet to come for many old and new mining places in reaction to the current – some say the foreseeably longest – run for

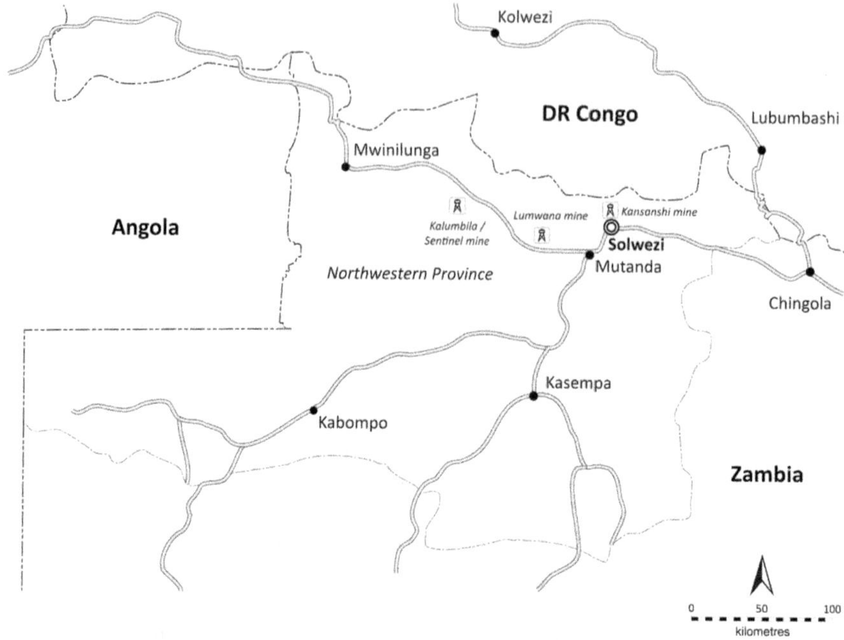

Figure 1. Solwezi and other towns in Northwestern Province, Zambia, with its three largest mining projects. Map by the author.

critical minerals. Mr. Kakoma and I had known one another for three years. That evening, I visited him to catch up since he had not seen me in a while. I had lived in Solwezi's residential compounds for one and a half years but had now moved to the mine's private compound reserved for its management and expatriate workers, the so-called Golf Estate for research purposes (see Figure 2). After some weeks living on the estate, it was good to see Mr. Kakoma, and hearing him talk about the maize and peanut harvest gave me a much-needed sense of normality. 'So how is it there?', he eventually asked, referring to the gated community of the Golf Estate. I told him that it was a bit strange. People were preoccupied with themselves and did not look beyond the fence. Mr. Kakoma, who had never been inside the estate, nodded, and assisted me in finding the proper words: *It is like another country!*

In retrospect, his analysis contains what has become the central theme of my book: I want to understand why interdependent places linked by myriad uneven connections still appear as separate and unconnected, and I want to show what consequences that specific way of ordering of the world has on people excluded from the world's 'golf estates', figuratively speaking.

Solwezi is the capital of Zambia's Northwestern Province, which borders the Democratic Republic of the Congo (DRC) to the North and Angola to the West. The town lies in a relatively sparsely populated area characterized by slash-and-burn agriculture in scattered villages and small towns. Solwezi's history as a town goes back to the colonial extractive project in the waning nineteenth century (see

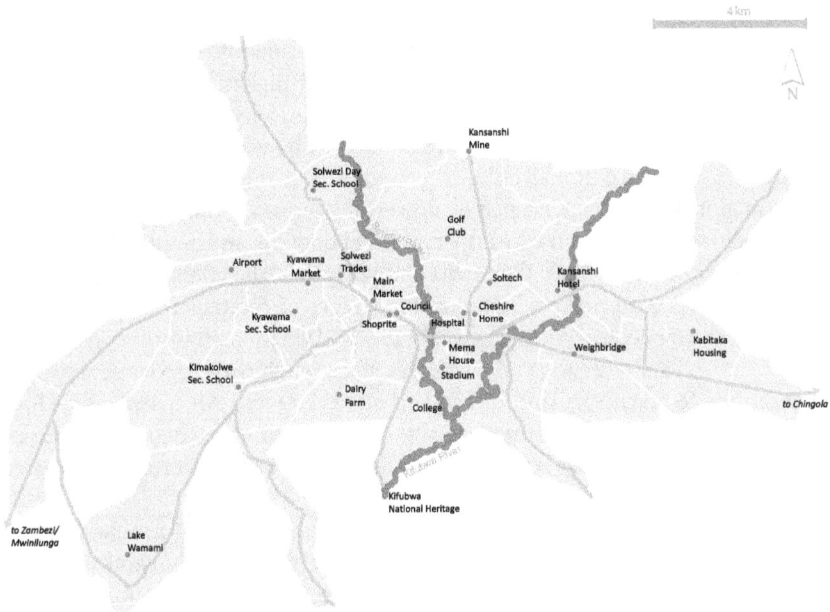

Figure 2. Map of Solwezi town with landmarks. Reprinted by permission from Preuss und Schmidt-Eisenlohr (2016, 38).

Chapter 1). Today, it is a rapidly growing mining town, simultaneously home to the continent's largest copper mine and a gateway to the even newer frontier developments further west. Despite limited employment opportunities, the town's reputation as a new mining hub and the economically dominant place in Zambia attracts a huge number of migrants. Population figures have almost quadrupled since Kansanshi Mine reopened in 2001 from 70,000 to 266,000 in 2015 or quintupled to 332,623 in 2022.[2]

When I first came to Solwezi in 2013, I wanted to understand the urban dynamics of a mid-sized town. In a new mining town, I figured, infrastructural changes happen at an extraordinary pace that would enable me to observe and analyse urban management and building practices. I knew about Solwezi's longer history as a small mining centre and was conscious of its global connections through copper extraction. Yet I still conceived of Solwezi as my field site and my unit of study. I often said in conversations that I wanted to understand 'how Solwezi residents are affected by the mine's presence'. By framing my topic in this way, I realize now, I obscured it rather than clarifying it. The seemingly innocent sentence accepted a number of conceptual divisions I should have questioned instead. As I defined it in the beginning, my topic was urban life in Solwezi. The mine, while important to understanding urban life, was an outside factor influencing it. I looked for the *real* Solwezi in the compounds, in the farming homesteads and in the shared flats of mineworkers, not on the mine's Golf Estate or in the mine managers' offices.[3]

Yet, what I found changed my research project and my perspective. It still took me a long time to see that the image I had of Solwezi and my definition of 'the field' reproduced the very separation of the world that makes extractivism possible, though (see also Gómez-Barris 2017, 5–6). This separation comes in many guises. My own way of reproducing it was shaped by what I saw as a progressive perspective on international political economy. On the one hand, we have the forces of global capitalism, shaped by powerful interests in the Global North, who spend their nomadic lives feeding upon poorer countries and marginalized people. On the other hand, we have the towns and villages of the Global South and their inhabitants trying to make a living on the fringes of capitalism: in places where capitalist labour becomes a privilege of the few, and where capitalism's consumption chances are a distant dream, endowed with just enough reality to let people prefer its promises to an unsure and difficult-to-achieve revolt. An inseparable chasm separates the two worlds. If they meet, the rich North constructs economic and social enclaves in the poor South, or poor Southerners live as foreigners tolerated as long as their cheap labour power is in demand.

I still think that this perspective is essentially correct. Yet formulated in this oppositional way, it cements a conceptual divide that is an integral part of its reproduction. It transforms the mine in Solwezi into an outside force external to the town; conversely, it transforms Solwezi into a place that is somehow more real, if less powerful, than the enclave of the mining compound. This conceptual separation is a subterfuge that obscures what should be obvious: that in reality, the mine is *as real, as present and as local* as the town. It is not an external influence on the real Solwezi; it *is* the real Solwezi. The existence of the conceptual divide is an important feature of my field, but instead of taking it for granted in defining the field, I must question it, show its workings and consequences and describe a world shaped by its constant reproduction.

Once we understand that the mine's Golf Estate and the compounds of Solwezi are equally real and equally local, and once we ask instead why they *appear* as different worlds, Fleming Kakoma's description of the Golf Estate suddenly takes on a larger meaning. We find the separation between both worlds mirrored on a larger scale. The United States, Europe, my home country Switzerland: these might be enclaves of order in a world of poverty and insecurity, but they belong to the same place. Their order and wealth are unthinkable without their connections to other regions.

Switzerland is host to the largest commodity trading houses. My research shows that all copper mined at Kansanshi Mine and at least half of Zambia's entire production – regardless of where the mine has its headquarters – is bought by trading companies based in Switzerland: by Glencore, by Trafigura or by the Swiss trading arms of other international companies. In Zambia's official statistics, Switzerland accounts for 40–50 per cent of Zambia's total export earnings (Central Statistical Office Zambia 2023, 17). Moreover, these companies control a large part of Zambia's and Southern Africa's logistics and service sector connected to mining: transport, surveillance, certification, trade, finance and assurance of copper exports. And finally, they also increasingly act as lenders to publicly owned enterprises in countries like Zambia.

Most of this is not visible for ordinary Zambians (nor for the Swiss, for that matter). Services connected to mining rather than mining pits themselves are much easier to ignore (and much more difficult to conduct research about), but they are just as key to global value chains and crucially affect the unequal distribution of profits in the mining sector. If we include services, we realize how important Swiss companies actually are for mining in Zambia, and how important countries like Zambia are for Switzerland's wealth, its order and living standard.

In the words of a Princeton colleague: Switzerland is the golf estate of the world. The walls around it are kept in place by our unquestioned knowledge that wealth and order belong there (here), just as poverty and insecurity belong here (elsewhere). The aim of my book is to show that both wealth and poverty, both order and insecurity, are defining features of the same order, not intrinsic qualities of separate places. In the variant I am writing about, this order is usually called extractivism – 'the rapid and widespread removal of resources for exchange in global capitalist markets' (Jacka 2018). I want to understand Switzerland and Zambia just as I want to understand the Golf Estate and Solwezi's compounds: as features of the same larger place, kept apart by artificial separations.[4]

The order of things

But who makes this order and how is it reproduced? Asking *whose order?* allows me to not only identify the planning, negotiation and implementation power of the different actors but to also analyse how different aspects of a specific order can be presented by the actors involved as either orderly or disorderly. In this book, I thus approach governance practices through the heuristic lens of 'order-making'. I briefly illustrate what that means by building on the introductory vignette.

Asking any Zambian who knows Solwezi town what the main characteristic of the town was, almost everyone would respond: 'Solwezi is a dusty town' and put on a disapproving face. Indeed, during half of the year, almost everything is covered by a layer of red dust, mainly because very few of the busy roads are tarred, and that soil erosion drastically increases when forest vegetation cedes its place to a town's pathways and courtyards.

The second judgement about the town Solwezi's residents share is mentioned immediately after the first: 'Solwezi is disorderly' – or, for others, 'chaotic'. This impression, as well, has clear foundations in the town's physical features. Only a fraction of the roughly 50,000 houses are built according to municipal standards. Infrastructure often does not work as it was intended to work. At the onset of the rainy season, the dust is washed from trees, roofs and cars, and Solwezi looks green and lush for a few days; once the rain sets in, in earnest, however, roads turn into streams and people have to walk extra cautiously to not slide on the mud. The few tarred roads get undermined, even more potholed and frequently washed away in places. In these days, in particular, most residents feel their town should be more orderly. All agree that the most orderly area in town is the gated residential area for the mine's management and senior, white employees and their families: the Golf

Estate. It is neatly planned and green throughout the year, the houses are solidly built. The two hundred residents have plenty of space, and the greens are nightly sprayed against mosquitos.

Yet, this contrast between apparent 'order' and 'disorder' visible within Solwezi is symbolic. The Golf Estate does not lie in another country. The 'order' of the mine and the 'disorder' of the town exist in relation to each other and are two sides of the same coin.[5] Both form integral parts of the same order – the extraverted order of extractivism which, be it based on agriculture or on mining, is the dominant feature of most African economies (Castel-Branco 2014; Greco 2020).

We see the same relation of 'order' and 'disorder', of their interdependence as well as their co-constitution, on a global level: between 'chaotic' Zambia and 'orderly' Switzerland. Minimally processed minerals are transported out of the country and the continent, using electricity, roads and other types of infrastructure paid for by the Zambian state through unsustainable international loans (or, as the Zambian musician Pilato expresses it: 'They borrow, we pay.'). A large part of the profit goes to Switzerland and to other tax havens. There is no chaos in this arrangement and no disorder. *This is the order of things.*[6]

Any kind of order needs to be created and reproduced in daily, habitual practice. Solwezi residents make order – different kinds of order, of course – every day through such practices. On top of building a town and maintaining its social relations, they must cope with insecurities of planning produced by resettlements, environmental degradation and economic imbalances caused by the mine. Similarly, commodity traders, state officials, parliamentarians, CEOs and corporate social responsibility representatives create order. This does not imply that all actors have the same amount of power to influence and change the order as it exists, but it does mean that all are implicated in the creation and reproduction of order. Indeed, understanding governance as the outcome of social practice between different actors (Förster and Koechlin 2011, 8–9) requires us to approach all groups of actors – state and non-state, private and corporate, informal and formal etc. – with the same ethnographic, non-normative standards. In a mining frontier where investors are typically far more resourceful to change governance processes than the 'local' population and the local state, the analysis of corporate governance practices and their impact on everyday life is particularly important (Behrends and Hoinathy 2017).

From such a perspective, urban governance and planning (both formal and informal) are an important hinge between resource extraction, infrastructural change and people's embodied knowledge and agency. This connection is tangible both locally and globally: On the one hand, Solwezi is an ordinary town, a secondary city, thus an urban centre that 'may not compete on the demographic, economic and infrastructural level with megacities within their national or regional territories' (Sanogo and Ammann 2017, 6). With that, it shares many commonalities with other African, post-colonial cities and towns (Pieterse and Parnell 2014, 9–15); just like other of these towns and as every urban centre across the globe, it also has developed a *specific* form of urbanity (Robinson 2006). On the other hand, Solwezi is as much an urban place as the world's metropolises

(Bell and Jayne 2006). It occupies an important role both towards other urban centres in the country – the Copperbelt towns, the capital Lusaka and the border towns – and the transport nodes and harbour cities in Southern and East Africa, and towards Zug, Switzerland; Perth, Australia; and London, UK. Hence, the study of a town is necessarily always a study of interdependence as an aspect of urban life (Sennett 2012) and as a mode of connection to global processes. A town's role in a global network or urban centres cannot sufficiently explain its unique style of urbanity, and vice versa. The book must therefore be both, a study of a town *and* a study of its global entanglements.

Yet, how can we do justice to both, the local and the global? Certainly, other scholars have tried to deal with the tensions and connections between places with great geographical distance or strong conceptual differentiation before me.

Dependency and articulation

Scholarly analysis of global dependencies goes back to the time of decolonization. The early 1960s was a time of change and hope in the Global South; many countries finally gained independence and pursued, in the spirit of modernization theory, small and large infrastructure and development projects. The 'Third World' tried to catch up with the 'developed' Global North. The reasons for this disparity and the necessity of reparations were of course not lost on Africans, as Frantz Fanon wrote at the time:

> Latin America, China, and Africa. From all these continents, under whose eyes Europe today raises up her tower of opulence, there has flowed out for centuries toward that same Europe diamonds and oil, silk and cotton, wood and exotic products. Europe is literally the creation of the Third World. The wealth which smothers her is that which was stolen from the underdeveloped peoples. The ports of Holland, the docks of Bordeaux and Liverpool were specialized in the Negro slave trade, and owe their renown to millions of deported slaves. So when we hear the head of a European state declare with his hand on his heart that he must come to the aid of the poor underdeveloped peoples, we do not tremble with gratitude. Quite the contrary; we say to ourselves: "It's a just reparation which will be paid to us. (Fanon 2005)

It is in this historical and political context that world system and dependency theorists wanted to explain the production of global inequalities in both colonial and post-colonial times (Arrighi and Drangel 1986; Hopkins and Wallerstein 1977).[7] Their neo-Marxist analysis brought out the fiercest critiques of the then dominant positivist modernization theory. Their key argument is relational: 'underdevelopment' in the 'periphery' is not the absence of development, but has itself developed jointly with, and as a direct consequence of 'development' in the 'centre'. The 'world system' is thus a structure of economic interaction where socio-economic difference creates a hierarchy. The actors – states – through their interaction are constitutive of the system themselves and partake in the emergence of the overall structure as core, semi-periphery and periphery economies. In his work on Brazil's export-oriented sugar production, Andre Gunder Frank (1967) concludes that the more ties between the periphery and the metropole there are, the greater development in the 'periphery' is forestalled.

Both world system and dependency theorists thus attempt to understand the impact of capitalism on the Global South. Arguing that resource-rich and commodity-consuming countries are intimately – and asymmetrically – linked, they understand capitalism defined primarily at the level of exchange (Laclau 1977, 43–6). Ever since, scholars have further developed theories of (nation-state-cantered) inequalities in the global arena, some with a focus on their emergence, reasons and conditions, others on the different forms (Go 2008), and most of them with an international (state) relations approach or, as the earlier scholarship, from an macro-economic perspective.

Around the same time, French Marxist anthropology also developed an interest in colonial and post-colonial interdependencies of African and European/metropolitan economies. In *Maidens, Meal and Money* (1981), Claude Meillassoux shows how Côte d'Ivoire's cacao industry dramatically changed Guro society and migrants' lives, but also communities in the savannah. Women remained in the villages to care for the children and elders with the additional burden of taking on men's work. Men in turn did not earn enough on the plantations to make up for their absence at home because cacao's prices were determined on the international markets. Women thus had to work more and harder than ever before. Meillassoux shows that the *articulation* between different modes of production allowed people in the Global North to enjoy cheap cacao products and coffee at the cost of people in West Africa, and women in particular. For Claude Meillassoux and for other economic anthropologists like Pierre-Philippe Rey, Emmanuel Terray and Harold Wolpe, articulation became the key concept to explain the production and reproduction of pre-capitalist domestic production. Unlike dependency theories which focus on relations at the macro level, the Marxist-structuralist school shows the entanglement of seemingly autonomous elements in terms of production and at the socio-economic meso and micro level. From that angle, domestic production stops being an autonomous mode of production but is 'a form of the reproduction of labor power within capitalism' (Berman 1984, 409).

For this book, articulation is the most promising concept to work with. At the most abstract level, articulation is understood as 'any practice establishing a relation among elements such that their identity is modified as a result of the articulatory practice' (Laclau and Mouffe 2001, 105). Key here is that two elements enter a relationship with one another and are both being changed as a result of that. In its application by Marxist theorists, articulation has had a number of shortcomings, though. Already in the 1980s, Bruce Berman critiques it as an essentially 'rigid' concept infused with a 'teleological structural determinism' (1984, 409). Articulation, according to him, is seen as a 'static and self-reproducing relationship that, once established, continuously and unproblematically, serves the 'needs' of metropolitan capital. … These indigenous societies are thus treated as essentially passive receptors of external forces, acted upon but having no active effect on the process' (Berman 1984, 409).

Malawian economist Thandika Mkandawire raises a similar point in relation to world system and dependency theories and its more recent variants. He argues that they adopt a perspective that starts and ends in the North; or, in Samir Amin's (2010) words, *Eurocentrism* is 'structural' and not only cultural as Edward Said (2007) showed. According to Mkandawire, developmentalists and their critics alike hold fast to the idea that the North 'was entrusted with the task of developing the South' for it 'to catch up' (2011, 7). Contrary to that view, he argues, development has always been an emancipatory project for Africans, a fact neither dependency theories nor the world system perspective take into account. In other words, even for critical theories analysing global connections, the South primarily serves as proof that the North is exploitative and powerful.[8] To illustrate this with Solwezi in Northwestern Zambia: if one is primarily interested in the metropolis, Solwezi is relegated to the 'periphery' and thereby appears as little more than a place of articulation for global dynamics; dynamics that are predictably shaped by capitalist extraction and relatively independent from local agency.

The inability by the dependency, world system and articulation scholarship to deal with its Eurocentric perspective and the relationship between structural determinism and human agency was of course responded to (albeit never satisfyingly answered) in anthropology already in the 1980s and ever since. James Scott's work (1985) was important to start this discussion, but it was the post-colonial scholarship in and of the Global South such as the scholars Dipesh Chakrabarty and Gayatri Spivak who have consistently decentred the Global North. In hindsight, what followed from there – globalization studies of the 1990s and the 2000s – seemed to have depoliticized the discussions led by dependency and articulation theorists *where something seemed to be at stake*. Once everything was deemed 'globalized', domination, dependencies and the seeds for resistances were more difficult to pin down.

Naturally interested in the 'global' since its beginning, anthropology nevertheless managed to make some key contributions to globalization studies since the early 1990s (Behrends, Park and Rottenburg 2014, 9–10; Lapegna 2009; Loimeier et al. 2005; Marcus 1995; Ribeiro 2019). Ethnographic studies showed how people adopt, often creatively, 'global' ideas, goods and practices (Appadurai 1990; Hahn 2011; Spittler 2002). Wary of assigning too much power to the 'global', theories emphasizing creativity and agency argue that people respond selectively and situationally to influences from 'outside'; 'localizing' them into their own lifeworlds. Methodologically, the description of life in a specific place meant to single out elements that did not seem to neatly fit into the local arena, attributing them to the 'global' sphere. Ideas of development, peace corps volunteers, consumer goods, capital investment, infrastructural enclaves, to cite but a few, have all been treated in this way.

Privileging the local over the global suits the discipline's methods and our urge to complicate a simple story. An anthropology overly committed to people's agency and creativity or the localness of a place, however, runs the danger of constructing a conceptual chasm between 'local agency' and 'global structure'. Such an implicit conceptual divide assigns different degrees of 'localness' to what after all are all elements in the assemblage of one locale, and it introduces both a dichotomy (local versus global) and a hierarchy between them. This often results in a situation where the 'global' is not carefully researched and therefore poorly understood as a site where power imbalances are produced (Çağlar and Schiller 2015). Especially when focusing on the Global South, anthropology runs the danger of implicitly equated the 'global' with 'the global North'. In consequence, 'the global South' appears as less global – if more strongly affected by global connections – than the Global North.[9]

Yet, leaving the 'global' under-analysed obscures the production and reproduction of forces which are not placeless flows, but take shape under the concrete condition of a locale. Global connections are not 'a done deal' (2005, 271), as anthropologist Anna Tsing reminds us, not unchangeable structural forces hovering above the local level: 'Capitalist forms and processes are continually made and unmade; if we offer singular predictions we allow ourselves to be caught by them as ideologies' (2005, 76). In contexts that pit locals against global forces, 'the dichotomy between global force and local response" (Tsing 2005, 271) often appears stark enough, and mining frontiers frequently belong into that category' (e.g. Behrends and Hoinathy 2017; Werthmann and Grätz 2012). Every such dichotomy, however, unintentionally contributes to a further mystification of the behemoth and the cementation of its real power (Abu-Lughod 1999, 417).

Asymmetrical interdependence

Despite the critique, from the brief introduction into the connections between Zambia and Switzerland above, it is obvious that the basic tenets of world-system approaches and dependency theories still hold true today for Zambia as for most resource-rich countries in the Global South, and that theories of articulation and social reproduction still have much to teach us. Most profit in global production networks is still appropriated outside of the regions of extraction. Dependency therefore remains a key feature of articulation in late-capitalist modes of production.

For this book, I therefore draw on these theories but try to avoid the many described pitfalls. My aim is not only to show that local dynamics matter in the South, but that the Global North, as well, is more than a static global force. There is as much agency (and creativity, for that matter) in the making of the global as in any specific locale. Indeed, the global force's existence is in itself the result of ongoing practices of appropriation, adaptation and exploitation – much of which happen in the Global South but the conditions for which are made in the Global North. As suggested by Michael Burawoy (2001, 149), the global can and ought to be studied from two standpoints: from its experience and from its production.

In this book, I use the term *asymmetrical interdependence* as an analytical lens. With it, I do not attempt to develop a new theory. The thesis of interdependence is neither new nor mine. What I try to do is to present it with new care and detail and in response to new socio-economic constellations and actors in this late-capitalist world. I use it to describe the relationship between urban centres and the role of resource trading and service provision in global production and supply chains, but the applicability may not be limited to that. It may be useful for any analysis of how regions or clusters are unequally articulated through people, things, ideas and capital. Using the term interdependence, I want to emphasize three aspects:

Firstly, analysing global relations as interdependence should contribute to a more decolonial framing of our understanding of the world economy. Today, we realize that defining the Euro-Anglo world as 'the centre' may hide more than it shows. Not only have new economic centres in the Global South emerged and global production networks have produced much more than one-way streets between a core and a periphery. They also involve multiple and varied, constantly changing economic relationships shaped by a variety of actors such as states, traders and unions (Alimahomed-Wilson and Ness 2018). More importantly, debates about decoloniality have made us freshly realize the extent to which ascriptions of power serve to stabilize that power and hide its construction. As Sabelo Ndlovu-Gatsheni points out, 'How can a continent like Africa, which they say is not developed, continue to finance and support the good living of those in the industrialised North?' (2017, 35). Debtors are certainly in the South and creditors in the North, but the relation established by debt is one of mutual dependence that makes attributes like 'underdeveloped' unnecessary. In that sense, as Ndlovu-Gatsheni suggests, dependency theory can be a departure point for theories on decoloniality. Such theories include societal aspects of dependency and violence that go far beyond economic relations (Fanon 1967). Finally, the project of decoloniality is language-sensitive. Scholars and policymakers casually call Zambia's economic model 'extractive'. With her notion of 'the extractive zone', Gómez-Barris (2017, xvi) critiques the deeply colonial paradigm inherent in such geographies. Viewed through the lens of asymmetrical interdependence, it is more thus to the point to call Zambia's economy 'extracted' and Switzerland's 'extracting'.

My use of the term 'interdependence' should secondly open up the possibility of an analysis that is less deterministic and linear than dependency and articulation theories have suggested. 'Durable inequalities' (Tilly 1999) need to be produced and continuously reproduced. This fact at the same time presents the possibility for change. Thinking of global relationships in terms of interdependence should encourage us to ask for the mechanisms that both connect and disconnect different regions and actors – such as trade, investment and logistics services – and force us to explain their reproduction rather than assume their continuity. This focus on what are often called 'intermediaries' in the global production and supply chain literature (Yeung and Coe 2015, 42, 50) takes up the meaning of *s'articuler sur qc / autour de* (to be connected through a joint / to rotate about something) in its literal sense and helps us to ask what group of actors facilitate the articulation of two entities.

And finally, my use of the term 'interdependence' should attest to my conviction that global interdependence could be symmetrical. 'Another possible is possible'

(Escobar 2020, 1). It does not have to be extractivist, and it does not have to assign as widely diverging chances to people in different regions. We could easily imagine economic relations in which every party has the same degree of dependency on the other, and where everyone has the same exit costs.[10] Moyn (2018) makes a similar point for debates about human rights. He argues that this debate has been dominated by the notion of sufficiency rather than equality. Assigning equality rights instead of defining what is strictly necessary to the poor would offer a path to sustainable sufficiency for all. It would imply an emancipation of the 'have nots' from 'the haves'. Adapting Moyn's concept to the economic context, I would argue that a thorough understanding of asymmetrical interdependence could be the starting point for actually redistributing decision-making power – instead of merely regretting that some people have 'too little' of it.

Symmetrical ethnography

The book starts in Solwezi, and I privilege the town and its inhabitants in my writing. If I want to take interdependence seriously, I must move beyond the conceptual divides which structure the field of practice, show how they are reproduced and analyse their consequences. Switzerland is not an enclave; its wealth, as well, is continuously generated in and through countries such as Zambia. What is at stake here is not just a global centre's influence on a local lifeworld, but their mutual dependence on the globality of the other. To show how asymmetrical interdependence works in practice, I had to search for ways to write a *symmetrical* ethnography. It is an answer to Macarena Gomez-Barris's question: 'How do we attend to the complexity of extractive zones without reproducing coloniality?' (2019, 153).[11] The book and the way it is presented must therefore be seen as a response to current global asymmetries. As the flipside of asymmetrical interdependence, symmetrical ethnography is a necessary intervention.

In the social sciences, the notion of symmetry is mostly associated with Bruno Latour's 'symmetric anthropology' which he coined in the early 1990s. In *We Have Never Been Modern* (1993), he proposes to turn the gaze with which Western scholars had looked at the 'other', the non-modern, also towards the supposedly modern. We should thus apply an ontological symmetry in terms of methodology, judgement and gaze. For him, this meant to study that which arguably made the Western world modern, namely its science. He later expanded this project of symmetry beyond the *Anthropos* from the human to the non-human (2005). More recently, in a conversation with Carolina Miranda, Latour pondered about the emergence of what he sees as a 'new symmetric anthropology' in times of (the cognitive realization of) the Anthropocene – an experience common to everyone – putting forth the notion that the North can learn from the 'others' (2017). Pushed to explain his understanding of symmetric anthropology and to address the scholarly critique that in his work he had ignored power relations, Latour answered in the same conversation: 'Of course it is never balanced at first. But that's the link between the two meanings of "symmetric anthropology": to generate, at first artificially, a symmetric balance so as to then register the asymmetric in power relations. It is called an instrument!' (Latour and Miranda 2017, 336).

My approach in this book turns the project of symmetry, I believe, on its feet again: I describe asymmetrical power relations ethnographically across spaces that have been *artificially* disconnected with the aim to create an entry point for action that makes the world more symmetrical. It is thus in none of the two meanings proposed by Latour (turning our gaze towards ourselves; learning from the others) that I use the concept of symmetry in my work. Neither do I believe that applying the same lens, scrutiny and vocabulary for everyone is a point that still needs to be made in anthropology, nor can I propose a lesson that the South can teach the North. Instead, my concept of symmetrical ethnography rests on three pillars: (1) where we look for knowledge, (2) how we present the data and (3) how we link analysis to joint action. While I developed this specific notion as a guiding concept for the book to capture urban positionalities in the global political economy and the mutual but unequal dependencies between and within urban centres, its applicability may be wider and beyond the topics covered here. In what follows, I address the three pillars where pursuing a *symmetrical ethnography* has consequences in general by explaining the specific consequences it has had in the research and writing project at hand: firstly, research methodology, secondly, writing and the organization of this book and, finally, the book's relationship to public action.

Firstly, doing *symmetrical ethnography* in an asymmetrical world means to ask the questions from a deeply ethnographically informed position and balance real asymmetries with symmetrical attention to the production thereof. This meant to try to get into the mine near Solwezi town and to go to Zug, one of the urban clusters of global commodity trading in Switzerland. Importantly, attending to the places of the production of asymmetries ought not to come at the cost of less thoroughness to a specific locale. To some extent, Claude Meillassoux has done that, too. As he states, 'it was through acquaintance with the world of the African migrant workers in France that the problem of their exploitation was posed in a critical way. Our research, which had begun in African villages, led us to the squalid and overcrowded dormitories of Paris suburbs where the very same men that we met in their places as proud peasants were converted into anonymous proletarians' (1981, ix–x).

This book is based on 693 pages of densely typed field notes documenting around 600 days spent in Solwezi District (including Solwezi, Kansanshi Mine, Kalumbila town and Sentinel Mine) between 2013 and 2018[12] as well as two short stays in Zug, Switzerland (2020 and 2021) and some research time in London, UK (2023). In 2023, I participated in a master course on commodity trading at the School of Finance, University of St. Gallen. As part of my research, I further produced 12,468 photographs, 52 audio recordings, 4,641 photographed pages of minutes from Solwezi municipal council meetings, 126 tracks and 581 points of GIS (geographical information system) data, hundreds of documents, and copies of contemporary and archival material. In addition, I participated in and received permission to use the raw data of the first baseline study of Solwezi town undertaken by the town council and the provincial water provider, advised by GIZ, which comprises 29,772 entries on individual households in Solwezi town.

These are some of the numbers behind this book and a manifestation of my attempt to understand situated action, sociality and governance in a mid-sized town. Although an archive in itself, these numbers and the data behind them are worth little without their links in my experiences and my bodily knowledge acquired over these years. What ties all my objectively accessible data together is my participation in the contexts that generated them. 'Thick participation' (Spittler 2001) gave me access to 'thick knowledge', which includes knowledge which is not easily expressible through language (Dobler 2015; Förster 2001; Kesselring 2017a).

The bulk of my ethnographic research happened in the years from 2015 to 2017, the years when the global resource boom started to turn into a bust. In 2015, the Zambian economy started to feel the consequences of China's declining demand for natural resources, and the downturn in global copper prices triggered the closure of a mine (Luanshya) and the decision to put others on maintenance (Mopani Copper Mines). The three mines in Northwestern Province however remained open, reducing instead of ceasing investment. The same happened during the global Covid-19 pandemic in 2020–1; while other companies were quick to stop production (see Chapter 5), FQM kept its operations running.

Returning to Zambia multiple times enabled me to get a perspective on medium-term changes in the town and simultaneously helped to earn the trust of and gain privileged access to many interlocutors. I participated in the lives of town residents (unemployed youth, small-scale miners, employed miners, farmers, market women, etc.). But I also followed those who by profession shape the built outlook of the towns such as planners, architects, artisans, surveyors, the mayor, the town clerk and the staff at the local planning department. I undertook a two-month 'internship' at the Department of Planning at the municipal council which offered detailed insights into planning processes and everyday governance, attended meetings across suburbs and milieus (town council meetings, traditional ceremonies, trainings offered by the mine's corporate social responsibility department, residents' assembly …), and lived on the mine' Golf Estate for two months (for the ethnography, see Chapters 4, for the ethics and my positionality, see Chapter 6).

To my surprise (in comparison to my previous research experience in South Africa), it was quite easy to become part of a variety of milieus and groups with different sets of powers, even though they are themselves not necessarily connected to each other – the most obvious example being the exclusive Golf Estate. I retrospectively realize that I practiced what Laura Nader initially meant with the term 'studying up' (1972), namely 'link[ing] ups and downs' (Hertz 2014, 64). While my access to the white mining community can partly be explained by my being white (although this is no guarantee; it took me many years to get deeper access and I was eventually blocked from further conversations, see Chapter 5), the ease with which I could spend the morning with artisans and the afternoon with state officials at the council was still remarkable. I was often encouraged to look at the other side of things and did not feel forced to be with one group in exclusion to others. I also became knowledgeable about spheres to which many of my research partners did not have access to (the town council, for instance); a position I tried to use generously without jeopardizing people's trust.

Participation in everyday life in Solwezi over time provided access to social situations that often remain inaccessible to researchers, and enabled conversations with several elusive actors. While I was always open about my research interests, I did not enter a formal agreement, such as a confidential disclosure agreement, with the mine. For the internship at the council, I applied with a letter of application explaining my research interest to the town clerk. I thus always tried to keep my independence as a researcher. This was particularly important to me when it came to mining and trading companies. I certainly tried to understand corporate actors' perspective and to generate good ethnographic data about them, but unlike many other researchers, I never agreed to submit to controls of the use of data or conditions for access (Appel 2019a; Salverda 2019). This implies that I take full responsibility for the data I use and for the way I present corporate actors. The section 'Capture of both Researcher and Value' in the first pages of Chapter 6 offers a thorough reflection on my research ethics and my positionality vis-à-vis the corporate actor and how it changed over the period of my research. I describe in detail how I gained access to the mine, the housing area Golf Estate as described in Chapter 4, its managers and directors, and how this abruptly changed. As this aspect of my research may be particularly interesting for some readers, the section is written in such a way that it is understandable even without the knowledge of the other chapters.

First and foremost, I tried to be a good ethnographer and to keep scholarly integrity in divisive and asymmetrical contexts. Scholarly integrity and scholars' 'commitment to objectivity', however, has two sides, as Stuart Kirsch points out: 'while intended to bracket out external influence on research, [objectivity] may also discourage scientists from evaluating their political responsibilities in relation to the larger consequences of their work' (Kirsch 2020, 8). Good ethnography is not 'objective', but it lays out the challenges and struggles one necessarily has to go through in order to arrive at a nuanced picture of social and power constellations. Faced with uneven power structures, the ethnographer has the mandate to point them out. If she shirks that responsibility, her analysis of a social situation will not become more objective but simply less accurate. In this book, I strive to be an ethnographer who is liable for both 'accuracy and justice' (Boltanski 2011; Hertz 2016, 154).

In their review of an anthropology of mining, twenty years after Ricardo Godoy's (1985) call for anthropological studies on the production process as a whole, Ballard and Banks (2003) challenged the pertinacious 'romantic ideal of the solitary scholar'. An ethnography of mining, they argued, lies beyond the competence of an individual researcher and ought to include transnational coalitions including NGOs, think tanks and community activists (2003, 307). This is certainly even more true for a study like this that follows value creation beyond the mining site. As part of her study on fracking in the United States, Sara Ann Wylie (2018) also sees collaborations with scientific and activist partners as the necessary path to push for accountability and repair of social and environmental damage. In the course of this book project, I was invited to and created alliances that are transdisciplinary and international and that became both a corollary to and a necessary part of my project (see Acknowledgement and Conclusion). A large part of the content for Chapter 5 was co-researched with another scholar. Still, what I can offer in this book necessarily remains a fragment of a larger whole.

In its first aspect, *symmetrical ethnography* is thus the practice of where we look for knowledge. Its second aspect is how we compose and present the narrative. This book is an ethnography of a globalized place that has fallen under the spell of capitalist extraction – an ethnography that privileges the perspective of the town's inhabitants, but that also analyses the ways in which the town is impacting on by the Global North and in turn instrumental in producing and maintaining its wealth, power and mode of production. Articulation is not happening in the air; it is happening in a concrete place. I thus study the global as seen from Solwezi – not as an exotically creative local place, not as the spectacular expression of capitalism's power at its frontiers, but as an ordinary town.

While this is the perspective the book takes, the structure is all but conventional. The book is divided into two large parts. In the first part, I focus on Solwezi, and in the second, I examine Solwezi's interdependence beyond regional developments. This second part was (and remains) a trade-off. I would have naturally filled it with personal stories of my interlocutors and write about people's everyday lives in Solwezi town. This however would have only cemented the conceptual division between the Global South and the Global North I described at the onset of the book. Writing ethnographically symmetrically dictated to explicitly address asymmetrical interdependence and have it reflected in the structure of the book. As a result, the different chapters (see Chapter overview below) are based on a variety of methods and employ rather different analytical methods. The narrative break between Chapters 3 and 4 is intentional to make the conceptual division but actual articulation tangible to the reader.[13]

The use of photographs is part of this aspect of symmetrical ethnography. Generally, the choice of photographs must adhere to the same standard of symmetry as the text. About a fourth of the figures in this book originate from my participation in urban life, and only a small part was taken in the 'golf estate', both literal and figurative, thus using a ratio similar to textual emphasis and focus. The viewer will however notice a difference in quality between these two sets of photographs. Some of the residents of Solwezi with whom I have had trusting relationships were happy to be depicted in this book. In contrast, the 'golf estate' constitutes a less trusting corporate environment. As a result, my photographic documentation of this aspect is much more distanced and less intimate. I thereby protect those who granted me access to the corporate world, and myself, from repercussions.

With the Conclusion: On Being Concerned, I introduce and respond to the third aspect of *symmetrical ethnography*: its relationship with public action. Drawing on bell hooks's (2001, 143) 'making community wherever we are', I explore lines of resistance to and lines of action against asymmetrical interdependence. I reflect on why successful joint action across conceptual and material boundaries is so difficult to achieve. I subsequently examine some examples of resistance against the ways in which the 'extracting' industry is organized in Zambia and Switzerland, and across the two. I highlight (at first sight unexpected) similarities between Solwezi and Zug, such as urban enclavement, high migration population, lack of sustainable planning for ordinary residents, elite land capture and a rent polity dependent on extractivism. While people in the Global South and the Global North are undeniably differently concerned – 'affected' – by global extractivism, two further meanings of *being concerned*: to relate to (similarity) and to have a responsibility for (interdependence) may be starting points for joint activist action. Such practices of 'making community' are radical because they go against all odds. The feminist notion of 'commoning' may be helpful to enter such symmetrical practices across conceptual boundaries because it invites to image alternatives to commodified, financialized, racialized and corporatized spaces.

Chapter overview

While the search for symmetry is manifest in the book's focus and its overall structure, the image of interdependence is sustained in all chapters throughout the book: The first three chapters zooms in on the history of the place and its urban planning and into the everyday planning practices of the population of Solwezi Town. Chapter 1: 'Copper's promise from Solwezi to Zug' addresses the city's centennial history in conjunction with Kansanshi Mine, and the current context. I examine migration patterns related to the mine, but also urban development and population changes detached from the mine. I draw my insights from archival documents such as population statistics since the beginning of the twentieth century, historical photographs, reports on work in the mines, hand-drawn maps, political framework conditions and price developments for copper. Most scholarship on mining towns, historically and contemporary, analyses urban change through the lens of the mine. In contrast, I treat the two histories as interconnected but also in their own right. I thereby decentre the mine by asking 'What happens in town?', putting into practice the book's claim for interdependence. The chapter shows that only recently have the town and the mine become more strongly entangled. This has paved the way for an unproportionate impact of Kansanshi's re-development since the 2000s on urban communities, foreboding the currently dominant disengaged form of resource extraction in the Central African region.

The presence of natural resources does not 'naturally' result in uneven development, as many variants of the 'resource curse' theory insinuate.[14] Instead, the role resource extraction plays for a country is the outcome of distinct political and economic processes under very concrete conditions. In Zambia, a large part of these struggles plays out in the capital and the ministries of finance and mines (Bebbington et al. 2018, 148), but the precise effects global extractivism has on an urban centre are also influenced by local state authorities. They are responsible for land acquisition and land rates, for urban planning and for resettlement and compensation processes. Chapter 2: 'The council' focuses on Solwezi's municipal council – including both civil servants and elected councillors – as the steady actor in town and shows its daily work of governing the town. Drawing on ethnographic research in the town's planning department, I show that the re-development of the mine and the increased in-migration have had considerable impact on the work of the municipal council. The chapter applies the lens of interdependence by examining how corporate and state governance intersect – albeit asymmetrically – in the everyday running of the town. In their daily work, civil servants try to cushion the impact of global extractivism on urban governance by applying long-learned standard practices of governance and bureaucracy under dramatically altered conditions. With case studies into taxation, town planning and political representation, I show how residents' responsiveness regarding their duties vis-à-vis the local state has decreased while local authorities' accountability towards its citizens and its capacity to provide services for the urban population have declined.

Chapter 3: 'The house' responds to the widespread perception that Solwezi, whose number of residents has quadrupled within fifteen years, is 'unplanned'. I accompany urban residents – artisans, planners, architects, homeowners and caretakers – in their building practices and show that the general perception of chaotic, uncontrolled growth and unplanned development at the town level sits at odds with individual and collective aspirational practices focused on building a home. Solwezi may look like an unplanned town, but this look is the outcome of rather a lot of planning and investment. By investing their labour-power into the construction of the urban, Solwezi's urban communities perform *reproductive labour*. Urban development undertaken primarily by residents absorbs shocks to a global extractive system resulting locally in casualization, unemployment and indebtedness, and offers a cushion for miners and their families to fall back to for housing, goods, services and care. Solwezi residents are dependent on the presence of the mine, but the mine is even more dependent on residents' unpaid labour for its mode of production to work. Residents' everyday reproductive labour must thus be read as a mode of production that stands in a relationship characterized by asymmetrical interdependence with life on the Golf Estate in particular and the North-based centres of the global extractive industry at large.

Chapters 4–6 of the book extends the framework to make visible the structures of asymmetrical interdependence which characterize Solwezi's embeddedness in the wider world. Chapter 4: 'The golf estate' describes the other side of urban life of the same coin: the gated housing area for the mine's management and expatriate employees and their families. The chapter presents a rare ethnographic account of life in such a secluded area of 200 FQM employees. I show how estate residents' preoccupation with making a community inside the fence (walking, running, partying, doing sports, gossiping, caring, etc.) helps to create and reproduce a conceptual divide between those inside and those outside, thereby cementing a global division of labour structured along racial lines and ultimately substantiating conceptual differences between the Global South and the Global North. Despite its functional integration, living on the estate requires little engagement with the world on the other side of the fence, with Solwezi town and with Zambia more generally. The mining company, headquartered in Canada but with strong Southern Rhodesian / Zimbabwean roots, privileges whites over Blacks for leading positions and prefers white South Africans over other whites. Further, the mine's management facilitates family life in order to 'stabilize' an expatriate workforce, a practice that translates into the production of white privilege to a degree unseen in this region.

Given its place-bound nature and the massive socio-environmental and economic changes at mining sites, the 'extracting' industry is often narrowly construed as limited to the site of extraction. In reality, the industry's impact is much wider and covers regions far beyond the mine. To offer a more complete – and symmetrical – picture of Zambia's privatized mining sector and foreign investment, Chapters 5 and 6 focus on infrastructure and development. In the chapters, I follow the value chain and, gradually moving away from Kansanshi's mine site, examine the structures (roads, electricity, tax, services, etc.) which the mining industry needs to ensure a smooth and 'cost-effective' extraction and transportation of minerals to the end producer or consumer.

Chapter 5: 'Infrastructure and power', adopts a regional perspective and presents two case studies into spatial governance against the context of the extractive industry's recent extension into the Northwestern Province. Using electricity distribution and electrical and road infrastructure as examples, I show that the mining industry's infrastructural power – to negotiate for, plan and implement infrastructure for its own use – affects Zambians far beyond Solwezi town. Corporate power exacerbates the state's existing planning challenges and prevents constituents to ask broader questions about distribution and access. This also has a South-North and thus an interdependent dimension: public infrastructure serving the extracting industry is paid by Zambian taxpayers through infrastructural loans.

Chapter 6: 'Trading inequality' follows copper on its journey from Solwezi to world markets and shows where profits flow. In this chapter, the interdependent relationship between Switzerland and Zambia is at its most obvious; the Swiss wealth is based on its articulation with Zambia's extracted mode of production. Between their extraction and their use in global industrial production, commodities are financed, insured, moved, stored, cleaned, weighed, blended, bought, sold, certified, tracked – to mention just a few downstream activities. Service providers such as trading firms, transport and shipping companies, financial institutions, certification and software providers are as important agents of commodity extraction as mining companies, but these segments of global production networks figure less prominently in the literature. I show how Swiss companies active in these sectors have the capacity to order value chains to their benefit, controlling essential parts of copper's global production network and generating a great amount of profit on the way. Getting access to such kind of information is notoriously difficult. In the chapter, I not only show how companies capture value but also show how they attempt to do the same with researchers.

The 'Conclusion' offers ethnographic and document-based insights into the local economy of Zug, Switzerland, and its beneficiaries, discontents and critics.

As mentioned above, it follows actual and potential lines of solidarity between Zambia and Switzerland on the basis of shared experiences in terms of similarity or differently situatedness in the same global order. The book ends with the hope that 'making community' (hooks 2001) can lead to responses to intense commodification, financialization and alienation that overcome separations created by these very processes and that proposes political alternatives.

Chapter 1

COPPER'S PROMISE FROM SOLWEZI TO ZUG

Zambia's mining towns were the subject of early anthropological research on urbanization, industrialization and migration from the 1940s onwards. Scholars of the Rhodes Livingstone Institute (RLI) and later the Manchester School focused on the interrelation between mining and urbanization processes in the studies they conducted only some 150 to 200 kilometres east from Solwezi town, in the Copperbelt towns. At the time, life in mining towns was mostly looked at through the predisposed lens of 'mining'. In their analysis of the emergence and 'stabilization' of the urban, the RLI scholars privilege the mine, describing urban life as life in a mining town primarily. Up until today, this bias can be seen in mining scholarship: facets of urban life not dominated by mining tend to disappear from view (notable exceptions for the region are Larmer et al. 2021; Mutale 2004). Solwezi town has also already fallen victim to this 'mineral narrative' in scholarly work. The region around Solwezi is typically described as the 'New Copperbelt' (Chansa 2020; Kapesa and McNamara 2020; Negi 2010) or as 'an extension of the Copperbelt' (Macmillan 2012, 545). Solwezi's history, however, cannot be compared to the Copperbelt towns', nor is it a reiteration of their history seventy years later. First, Kansanshi was the first commercial mine in the Rhodesian and Congolese Copperbelts; second, it never developed into a large and continuously operating commercial mine like the Copperbelt mines; and third, Solwezi has never been planned and built as a mining town as the Copperbelt towns had been. Solwezi town is a curious cross between an old, early twentieth-century and a new twenty-first-century pair (mining) town.

In this chapter, I briefly outline both the town's and the mine's histories.[1] Taking urban dynamics seriously even when the mine's story stalls prepares the ground for the ethnography in the subsequent chapters. As any mining town is more than the product of urban life, its regional history and national politics of rent distribution, but the outcome of its articulation with the global mining economy, I also introduce Switzerland's role in Zambia's mining sector, in particular the history and growth of the Swiss trading and service hub.

Zambia

Zambia has a long history of commercial mining, a history which has always been global (Bebbington et al. 2018, 223): in private ownership during British colonial rule in the first half of the twentieth century, followed by three decades of public ownership under the independent country's one-party rule (Caramento 2023), and, since the late 1990s, again in private ownership with the largest companies headquartered in Switzerland (until January 2021), Canada, China, India and the United Arab Emirates (since December 2023). Zambia's mineral resources are the foundation of the profits made in mining's global value chain, but throughout the twentieth century and until today, the country has not been able to increase its share of these profits. Under the colonial regime, the country's population had little say in the attribution and redistribution of the wealth generated. After decolonization, Euro-American investments were increasingly withdrawn or channelled through tax havens, depriving lower-income countries of tax revenues (Ogle 2020). Many of Zambia's state assets, including all mines, were re-privatized in the 1990s in a constrained environment of liberalization and deregulation (Craig 2001; Simutanyi 1996). Zambia, like many countries in the Global South, has gone through and suffered from IMF-imposed structural adjustment programmes. Liberalization of the mining sector did, however, not help the Zambian state to increase the share of profits remaining in the country. In addition, the state was unfortunate enough to majority-own the mining industry in economically depressed years, and to be forced to sell them shortly before the next global metal boom of the early 2000s. As the lengthy process of privatization of Zambia's mining sector was completed, global copper prices started to rise, and Zambia experienced a revival of the mining sector and a construction boom. Both politically and economically, Zambia's mining sector is generally attractive for direct foreign investment.

Currently, Zambia is the world's sixth largest copper producer. The extractive sector accounts directly for 10 per cent, indirectly for up to 50 per cent of its GDP, for 77 per cent (2021) of exports (agriculture accounts for approximately 10 per cent of total GDP); and in 2021, mining contributed 39 per cent to government revenue (up from 18 per cent in 2015) (Zambia EITI 2023). With the aim of enhancing productivity (in relation, among others, to deeper deposits, harder rock mass, decreasing ore grades) and reducing risks and costs (e.g. Sánchez and Hartlieb 2020), the number of workers needed has decreased from above 60,000 in the 1970s to approximately 24,000 direct employees with the nine largest mines today (Zambia EITI 2020, 100; Fraser and Lungu 2007, 20).

In an increasingly financialized global economy, capital owners' share in profits has generally grown to the detriment of both workers and states (Krippner 2012), and commodity markets in particular are financializing faster than other economic sectors (Adams and Glück 2015). Zambia's economy is no exception to this trend (Gewald and Soeters 2010; Mudenda, Bulawayo and Ndulo 2018), and the ensuing redistribution of profits leaves fewer resources for the country's economy and its citizens' livelihoods. Today, Zambia is dependent on global liquidity, exposed to foreign financial flows and dominated by foreign-owned banks (Kvangraven,

Koddenbrock and Sylla 2020, 17). It is locked in unfavourable trade agreements with, for instance, the EU (Money, Frøland and Gwatiwa 2020; see also Elsby 2020), while South Africa plays an important role as 'the gateway, which interlinks the continent globally' (Scholvin 2020, 9). High expenditure on infrastructure and a debt spiral have led to debt default at the end of 2020 (see Introduction). Zambia has failed several times to introduce nationalization policies (Larmer 2005), and its attempts to capitalize on the most recent commodity boom are largely restricted to a limited revision of the mining tax regime (see Chapter 5, footnote 14).

In May 2019, under Edgar Lungu's Patriotric Front (PF), Konkola Copper Mines (KCM) in Chingola and Chililabombwe owned by Vedanta Resources was placed under provisional liquidation and subsequently, 49 per cent of its smelter division was sold in January 2021. In the same month, Zambia Consolidated Copper Mines (ZCCM), until then a 10 per cent shareholder of the mines, acquired Mopani Copper Mines (MCM) from Glencore and FQM for US$1 and US$1.5 billion debt, which Glencore has borrowed from its subsidiaries and associate companies over the years. Until the debt is repaid, Glencore would be the only off-taker of Mopani's copper, thus remaining a key player in Zambia's mining industry. These two moves by the Lungu administration were hotly debated and it remains to be seen whether the Zambian state acquired the Copperbelt mines in a favourable moment.[2] For the adjacent communities, the question of who is responsible for the cleaning-up of decades-long pollution is also at stake (Kesselring 2021b). In 2021, the 'new dawn' government under Hakainde Hichilema and the United Party for National Development (UPND) assumed power. A foreign-investment-friendly (and, for the mining companies, more predictable than his predecessor) administration, it resolved the conflict between ZCCM and Vedanta and allowed the company back in as majority stakeholder of KCM in 2023, a decision confirmed by a court in Lusaka in 2024. In terms of the Mopani Mines, ZCCM looked for a foreign (minority) investor to help implement necessary investments for two years. In late November 2023, to the surprise of many observers, the government selected the United Arab Emirates' investor International Resource Holdings (IRH) as the new equity partner in Mopani Mines. IRH, which has recently expanded its operations in Africa's mining industry, completed its 51 per cent acquisition of Mopani Mines in March 2024.

The Northwestern Province, a previously marginal region, and the Solwezi District in particular, became the target area for the largest foreign investments in Zambia in decades. Today, the region is the country's most important province economically. While the Zambian population grew by 3.4 per cent in average and while urban areas in Zambia even recorded a decline in growth rate (3.5 per cent) between 2010 and 2022, the Northwestern Province, the least densely populated province in Zambia, had the highest annual growth rate (4.8 per cent) in the same period (Central Statistical Office Zambia 2022, 11–12). This is largely due to Solwezi District with its average annual growth rate of 8 per cent and Kalumbila District with 8.1 per cent in the same period (Central Statistical Office Zambia 2022, 25). Its large-scale open-pit copper and nickel mines are surrounded by one rapidly growing town, Solwezi, in Solwezi District, a largely unplanned sprawling urban centre, Lumwana, and a new company town, Kalumbila, both in Kalumbila District (see Figure 1).

Solwezi town and Kansanshi Mine

The very existence of Solwezi as a town goes back to the colonial extractive project. In the late nineteenth century, European prospectors 'discovered' the Kansanshi copper reserves and started to commercially exploit what had been mined by Africans since at least the fourth century (Musambachime 2016, ch. 3). Mobile political associations up to the eighteenth century and later territorialized chieftaincies in South Central Africa entertained copper-based networks of trade and production (Gordon 2021), and the remains of Kansanshi's old pits provided the best archaeological sources for this period (Bisson 1980, 242–7) until they were destroyed by the expanding open pit.

Colonial extraction in Kansanshi started in 1905. Ten kilometres south of the new mine, the colonial administration of Northern Rhodesia established Solwezi, a tiny administrative centre as a control post overseeing mining activities in what was then Kasempa District (comprising roughly today's Kasempa, Mwinilunga and Solwezi Districts). Like many other colonial administration posts, the old town centre is still referred to as the *boma* today by residents but also by government more broadly.

The first phase of commercial mining, roughly from 1905 to 1914, coincided with the establishment of European control over this part of Northern Rhodesia and in a period of political and demographic change in the region, partly generated by the mine's labour needs (cf. Gewald 2015). Kansanshi Mine knew a short phase of success, but after the rich copper reserves in the Zambian and Katangese Copperbelts were discovered in the 1910s and 1920s, it struggled to compete with the new mines and their higher ore grades. Nevertheless, there was hardly any year through the twentieth century without any mining, processing or exploration activity at Kansanshi (Kesselring 2021a). Commercial interest in the mine never ceased, and the ore bodies were always considered as having great potential – a potential which just now, for several reasons, could not be fulfilled. Low grade and harder access compared to the Katanga and later the Zambian mines, the World Wars, economic recessions, mine flooding, too little processing capacities, difficult connections to the line-of-rail, remoteness of the area as seen from the Copperbelt – all of these served to explain why economic viability was just out of reach for the moment.

In contrast to Kansanshi Mine's variable history, urban life in Solwezi town was characterized by strong continuity. Over the century, Solwezi steadily grew into a secondary town and a regional hub (for a detailed history, see Kesselring 2021a).

This made Solwezi an outlier in a province characterized by out-migration for much of the century. Solwezi grew steadily because it benefitted from a geographical position at the eastern end of the province where many stopped temporarily or permanently 'en route to the Copperbelt' (Johnson 1980, 75). The pace of urban growth picked up from the 1980s due to growing mobility and multilocality within

Zambian households and extended families. Changing lifestyles, new consumption patterns and increasing integration into translocal social institutions necessitated access to cash income and to urban infrastructure, while economic decline and job scarcity made full-scale urban life more difficult to sustain. In this situation, many families had members spread across different economic and social spheres (Crehan 1997; Moore and Vaughan 1993; Pottier 1988), and more people moved to urban areas even without clear income perspectives there.

In many ways, then, Solwezi developed like many other secondary towns in Southern Africa. A clear indication that the town's history has been partly independent from the mining industry is its balanced gender ratio over at least the past fifty years. In contrast, Zambian Copperbelt towns, like most mining towns across the globe, had a skewed gender ratio due to male-dominated in-migration attracted by the mining industry for much of the twentieth century (Kesselring 2021a, 149; Macmillan 1993, 686–7; Parpart 1986, 53).

With the lower importance of the mine also came a relative lack of infrastructure compared to the Zambian and Katangese Copperbelt towns. While these towns began to look like a 'mini welfare state' from the 1960s onwards (Bebbington et al. 2018, 136), the mining industry in Solwezi contributed very little to the town's development and its infrastructure throughout the twentieth century. The mine mostly built permanent housing for its expatriate staff. Until the 1970s, the Black labour force was mostly housed in temporary compounds at Kansanshi Mine, while white workers and white employees enjoyed comfortable living conditions in the 'mine village' southwest of the mining site. Apart from the administration compound, outlying mission stations and one or two shops, this enclave housed the only people of European descent living in the area. A few 'white spaces' provided opportunities for white administrators, prospectors and expatriate mine employees to meet: the European Rest House, the *muzungu* club and the few trading stores in town, and the Kansanshi Mine Social Club at the mine village which is shown in Figure 3 with the only swimming pool in the district and the possibility to watch movies on the mining site (Wilkin 2012).

While Solwezi residents' lives remained separate from that of the better-off mining employees, the mining project nevertheless changed the social structure of the town. Under both colonial-private and postcolonial-public ownership, Kansanshi's hiring practices divided labour between 'local, un-skilled' and 'skilled' workers; the latter mainly came from the Copperbelt towns. Since independence in 1964, these colonial categories have been reproduced, and under the current, reprivatized ownership of Kansanshi Mine, they have stabilized as a sentiment and a practice, so that the division between 'locals' and 'in-migrants' at least in parts intersects with class divisions. One element of this, and the one most visible in the spatial set up of the town today, is the re-emergence of racial segregation linked to employment practices. Kansanshi Mine once more pursues a highly gendered and racialized staff recruitment, building both on the global division of labour in contemporary capitalism and on the specific history of the mining history and its labour markets in apartheid and post-apartheid Southern Africa (see Chapters 4 and 5).

Figure 3. Mine village today, Kansanshi Mine, Solwezi, August 2017. Photo by author.

Only in the past twenty years have the mine's development and the town's population growth correlated in scale and pace: From 2001, Kansanshi turned into the most productive copper mine on the continent, and the town's population has grown fourfold to about 266,000 residents in 2015 (Preuss and Schmidt-Eisenlohr 2016) or almost fivefold to about 332,623 residents in 2022.[3] As a result, migratory movements changed direction: the town now attracts people from the Copperbelt and elsewhere who seek work in this new regional mining hub. Town and mine have become much more entangled than they ever were in the past century.

Fleming Kakoma, whom I introduced at the opening of the book, has experienced the massive increase in population first-hand. His trajectory is exemplary for the experience of many families from the Solwezi district, although his family is certainly among the better-off people in Solwezi (at least if we take the Golf Estate to lie in a different country). He grew up in a small town in the Solwezi district and went to Solwezi Technical Secondary School. He schooled with the time's local elite, such as Chief Mumena, a traditional leader for the kiKaonde-speaking people. He knows Solwezi's mayor well, and the ward councillor is his neighbour. Like most voters in Northwestern Province, he supports UPND, a party in opposition for two decades and ruling party since 2021. In 2003, two years before the re-development at Kansanshi Mine began, he was allocated a plot of agricultural land by the chief of the area, Kapijimpanga. The Kakoma family's plot was integrated into the urban area in 2010. Slightly elevated and with a good view, immediately south of the mine's Golf Estate and close to the *boma*, plots in the

Figure 4. Areas and compounds in Solwezi town. Reprinted by permission from Preuss und Schmidt-Eisenlohr (2016, 43).

Saviye area are today sought after and pricy (for the different areas and compounds in Solwezi town, see Figure 4). Renting out their house along Independence Road, the main traffic artery in town, the family built a residential house on their plot. The house is connected to piped water but not yet to the electricity grid. Relations to neighbours are good, except perhaps for some young people who, Mr. Kakoma thinks, 'are partying too much'. The planned wall fence might bring some privacy and tranquillity. He and his family work hard to keep their standard of living.

Because of such experiences, Solwezi is often described as a 'booming new mining town', but that definition hides rather more than it reveals. It is certainly true that Solwezi is booming in terms of population increase. Most of the population growth is due to in-migration. Many young men first move to the town on their own, temporarily leaving their families behind. Young women, as well, come to Solwezi on their own in search of work. For them, family members or friends who are settled in Solwezi provide a temporary home. (For more on Solwezi's demography and lines of differentiation across town, see Chapter 2.)

Many of the new arrivals make Solwezi their home over time and manage to build or rent a room or a house of their own. As a consequence, the town's built area has greatly expanded into all directions. Vast new neighbourhoods have developed, often leaving official town limits behind, and extending into the surrounding 'tribal' lands. In previously settled areas, both overall density and spatial differentiation have increased. If many migrants turn Solwezi into their home, most of them also maintain regular contacts with friends and families in other towns and villages or live in households extending over different localities (see also Udelsmann Rodrigues et al. 2021, 9). These connections offer a fallback option if town life becomes economically unsustainable, but they also are part of a permanently dual way of living that straddles the urban and the rural and undermines the easy oppositions introduced by earlier generations of anthropologists – between 'rural' and 'urban', 'tribal' and 'detribalized', and 'traditional' and 'modern'.

Mine workers only make up roughly 3 per cent of Solwezi's population. Some are moving here from the Copperbelt without finding employment. Many mineworkers have come on short-term contracts and still consider the Copperbelt towns their main family home. They often maintain a home in a Copperbelt town and share a house in Solwezi (and often sleep in shifts in the same bed). The largest part of Solwezi's population does not have a direct connection to the mine. Many of those with steady employment indirectly depend on the mine – working for mine suppliers or for outsourced service companies providing cleaning, building, gardening or security for the mine. Others live on their own or a relative's civil servant salary, on income from small independent businesses (like hostels, carpentry shops, second-hand clothes stalls, car repair or panel-beating workshops). Most, however, get by through a combination of inner-household redistribution and informal economic activities: buying and selling agricultural and other produce, cultivating a garden in town or a piece of land outside Solwezi, sometimes engaging in casual jobs.

Residents come from all over Zambia and the neighbouring countries, making up a rather diverse population in terms of language and ethnic affiliations. Bemba speakers from the Copperbelt towns not only dominate the Zambian workforce in the mine, but their language has also become the lingua franca in many spheres of urban life (Martin 2018). The differences in status and income due to demand structures in the mining industry have created some tensions between Bemba speakers on the one hand, and kiKaonde-, Lunda- and Luvale-speaking Zambians, the majority residents in the Northwestern Province, on the other (Kapesa and McNamara 2020). More and more Swahili is spoken by migrants from the Katangese Copperbelt.

Kansanshi Mine under FQM

The current owner of Kansanshi Mine, Canada-based First Quantum Minerals Ltd. (FQM), is the second owner after Zambia's privatization of its mining sector. FQM's shareholders include the Chinese state (Jiangxi Copper Company Limited; 18.39 per cent), the US Capital Group (10.84 per cent), Fidelity, BlackRock and Vanguard, among others. Cyprus Amax Minerals Corporations acquired majority ownership of surface leases and selected assets at Kansanshi Mine in 1998 after it undertook some diamond drilling at the Kansanshi site in 1997.[4] When FQM bought Cyprus' 80 per cent share in Kansanshi in 2001, ZCCM (now ZCCM

Figure 5. Main pit, Kansanshi Mine, March 2015. Photo by author.

Investment Holdings, ZCCM-IH) retained its 20 per cent share.[5] (FQM offered multiple times to buy ZCCM's stake in Kansanshi Mine. In 2022, ZCCM's dividend rights were converted into royalty rights.) With the takeover, Kansanshi Mining Plc (KMP) obtained all surface rights to develop and operate and a large-scale mining license for twenty-five years from 1997. The license allows for the exploration and mining of copper and other minerals and applies to an area of approximately 21,593 ha. The open-pit mine went into production in 2005 (see Figures 5 and 6). With new technology, the low grades of Kansanshi's ores ceased to be a comparative disadvantage; the ore structure merely continues to pose a challenge (and sometimes a puzzle) to geologists.

For the construction phase, labourers from the area (typically kiKaonde- or Lunda- and Luvale-speaking) were recruited, but soon most workers came either from the Copperbelt Province or from further away, equipped with grades and experience in mining. This dashed expectations of local residents and led to collective grievances and ethnic tensions (Kapesa 2019; Kapesa, Mwitwa and Chikumbi 2014), which also prevented strong unionization and furthered intra-union accusations of tribalism (Kapesa and McNamara 2020).[6] As a completely mechanized open-pit mine, Kansanshi today employs a small operations workforce of 3,252 direct employees (in 2021) (Zambia EITI 2023, 90) and 4,003 contract workers. Kansanshi Mine contributed 32 per cent to total Zambian government revenues in 2021 (Zambia EITI 2023, 87). That large percentage is indicative both of Kansanshi Mine's output and of the state of Zambia's economy.

Until recently, Kansanshi Mine near Solwezi used to produce around 260,000 tons of copper annually out of two pits (Main and Northwest), which made it the

Figure 6. Crusher, conveyor belts and smelter, Kansanshi Mine, July 2015. Photo by author.

sixteenth largest copper mine globally and the largest copper mine by output in Africa. Due to lower grades and water accumulation in the pit, its output decreased in the past two years, and it was overtaken by Sentinel Mine next to Kalumbila town, FQM's second mining project which produces approximately 250,000 tons per year, increasing tendency. In 2022, First Quantum Minerals opened Kansanshi Mine's third pit southeast of the Main pit (SE Dome) and launched Enterprise, a new nickel mine as part of its Trident Project in Kalumbila. These two projects had been in the pipeline for several years with the company waiting for what it considers a more predictable political and economic environment. Today, FQM is the world's sixth largest copper producer.

Operations at Kansanshi are based on conventional drill-and-blast, shovel-and-truck mining techniques. It has two tailings storage facilities, one on the south and one, opened in 2012, on the east side of the license area. A copper smelter was commissioned in 2014 and achieved commercial production in 2015. Over the course of several years, Kansanshi expanded to the east for waste dumping, towards the west for the smelter and in its southwest for its 'game management area' and college. Villagers were displaced and resettled to New Israel and Kabwela. In addition, the mine acquired land in customary areas at the western end of Solwezi town for an economic zone called Kipenda, at the eastern end of Solwezi for the gated housing project Kabitaka, and in the northwest for a new access road to its smelter. Several companies hold copper, cobalt, gold, nickel and uranium prospecting licenses adjacent to FQM's, among them Rio Tinto. These license areas partly cover built-up parts of Solwezi town and are situated in Chief Kapijimpanga's, Chief Mujimanzovu's and Chief Mumena's areas.

It is difficult to precisely assess Kansanshi Mine's impact on the environment, primarily because the company holds a factual monopoly on such data. Recently, the South Africa-based NGO Southern Africa Resource Watch (SARW) conducted a study (2020) on environmental degradation due to mining in Solwezi and came to conclude that the mine fails to treat hazardous waste and did too little to prevent dust from the tailings and other effluents from its smelter and concentrator from reaching adjacent communities and to prevent the leaching of toxic chemicals into waterways, used downstream by Solwezi residents.

First Quantum Minerals and its subsidiaries have been implicated in legal proceedings and arbitration cases in Zambia. One dispute was between ZCCM-IH, the state-controlled mining investment firm, and FQM (UK) Ltd, wholly owned by FQM, around a fraud allegation in relation to Kansanshi Mine. ZCCM-IH, the 20 per cent shareholder of Kansanshi, argued that FQM took out a loan from Kansanshi at non-commercial interest rates, using the loan for an investment outside of Zambia to the disadvantage of ZCCM-IH. FQM claimed that the money borrowed from Kansanshi had been used to set up the Kansanshi Smelter wholly owned by Kansanshi. ZCCM-IH brought the case before the Lusaka High Court on 28 October 2016 against First Quantum Limited, FQM Finance Limited, Philip K.R. Pascal, Arthur Mathias Pascal, Clive Newall, Martin R. Rowley and Kansanshi Mining PLC, and it led a Notice of Arbitration on 26 October 2016 in London (UK) against Kansanshi Holdings Limited and Kansanshi Mining PLC. Early May 2017, FQM approached Zambia's Attorney General to ask ZCCM-IH to suspend its criminal proceedings in the Lusaka High Court, especially against some of its directors who threatened to be charged individually (and arrested when entering Zambia), and to allow for commercial arbitration. Subsequently, then president Lungu told ZCCM-IH to drop its fraud case against FQM and some of its directors and to settle the dispute out of court. There will thus be no test case on alleged malpractice, transfer pricing and switching tax concessions from one project/subsidiary to another. In other matters, the Zambian Revenue Authority billed FQM with a tax claim of approximately US$7.5 billion (penalties and interests) in 2018. It alleged that the Kalumbila Mines incorrectly classified imported goods as mining machinery, thereby avoiding customs duties ranging from 15 per cent to 25 per cent (i.e. potentially trade misinvoicing) over the course of five years. Most of the penalties were waived by the government in 2019, though. Critics allege collusion between FQM and the PF administration and call on the Anti-Corruption Commission to investigate (Charles 2024).

Despite the country's wealth in natural resources and the new extracting hub in the Northwestern Province, 29 per cent of Zambia's population are currently estimated to face high levels of acute food insecurity (IPC 2020). Solwezi District has been classified as 'stressed'[7] in 2020 due to a combination of below-normal and erratic rainfalls, high maize prices, an outbreak of the army worm and reduced remittances due to Covid-19.

If – as a thought experiment – we divide Kansanshi's annual copper production equally among Solwezi's residents, each person would receive one (metric) ton of copper per year, priced at an average of around US$8,000 a ton. According to the Jesuit Centre for Theological Reflection (JCTR), which monitors the cost of living in Zambia, a family of five from Solwezi (the second-most expensive town in Zambia) needs roughly US$350 per month to buy basic food and essential non-food items, or US$840 per person per year.[8] In other words, a ten per cent increase in the copper price could pay for the basic needs of Solwezi's entire population. Even if copper prices rise, as they have done after an initial drop in the early pandemic months of 2020, very little of the additional income in reality trickles down to Solwezi's residents. Most of the profit generated from Zambian resources leaves the country, and much of it ends up where I have grown up: in 'the golf estate of the world'.

The Swiss commodity trade sector

At first glance, Solwezi seems to have very little to do with Switzerland. Glencore, the Swiss commodities giant, owned mines in the Copperbelt until recently, but Northwestern Province is dominated by the Canadian companies First Quantum and Barrick Gold. No Swiss company has an office here, no Swiss NGO is active in Solwezi, and besides my students from Switzerland I have never met another person with a Swiss passport in the town. Yet all copper from Kansanshi Mine – and at least half of Zambia's entire production – is bought by trading companies based in Switzerland: by Glencore, by Trafigura or by the Swiss trading arms of other international companies. This explains that Switzerland accounts for 40–50 per cent of Zambia's total export earnings (Central Statistical Office Zambia 2023, 17).

Such companies also control a large part of Zambia's logistics and service sector connected to mining (see Chapter 6). When scholars describe how unfavourably Zambia is integrated into the global economy, they usually concentrate on mines and mine ownership. Mines are very localized, massively visible and difficult to ignore, and they draw much scrutiny. Services connected to mining are much easier to ignore, but they are just as key to global value chains and crucially affect the unequal distribution of profits in the mining sector (e.g. Heintz 2006; Milberg 2004). If we include services, we realize how important Swiss companies actually are for mining in Zambia. Among other things, they are crucial for transporting, storing, surveying and certifying, trading, financing and assuring copper exports. Through this role, they have been successful in appropriating a high share of the value created by the mining sector.

Banks, as well, are key elements for stabilizing asymmetrical relation between the Global South and the Global North. In 2020, Zambia became the first country to default on its sovereign debt as a result of Covid-19, yet even before the pandemic, the situation was difficult. Expenditure on health and education has continuously declined since 2016 – both proportionally and in real terms – as debt servicing has taken up a continuously growing part of the national budget (AFRODAD and JCTR 2020). Most creditor institutions are based in the UK and the United States, but the Swiss banks Credit Suisse, Pictet, Graubündner and Zürcher Kantonalbank also own their share. UBS was one of the ten members of the team representing creditors in the unsuccessful negotiation with the Zambian government for a push back in interest payments in 2020. In June 2023, a debt restructuring deal with the IMF and official creditors was reached in principle, and Zambia is in the process of securing a deal with its private creditors. Bond holders benefit from this situation (Jubilee Debt Campaign UK 2020).

Zambia is by no means unique in being on the receiving end of Swiss global business acumen. This becomes clear from even the most cursory glance at global trade statistics. It is estimated that Switzerland-based traders currently cover between a fifth and a fourth of the global commodity trade, with rising tendency (Tille 2017). Around 60 per cent of metals, 35 per cent of crude oil and 50 per cent of wheat traded globally are bought and sold by companies based in Switzerland (Federal Council of Switzerland 2018, 13; Lannen et al. 2016, 2), even if few of the commodities physically enter the country.[9] Approximately 900 companies headquartered in Switzerland are active in the trading sector, with clusters in Zug, Geneva and Lugano. Some of them, especially the larger companies, are also increasing their interest in the related logistics sector, including financial and legal advice, ship brokerage and certification. The three clusters have developed some distinctive expertise: Geneva is leading in oil and soft commodity trading, Zug in trading metals and Lugano in gold trade. The largest and most prominent firms are Vitol, Glencore, Trafigura, Mercuria, Gunvor, BHP and Cargill. Out of the ten largest multinational companies headquartered in Switzerland across all sectors, seven are trading houses (excluding Nestlé, among others also a trader). The commodity sector generated 33 billion Swiss francs in 2015, and 82 billion Swiss francs in 2023, for the first time overtaking the finance sector's contribution to Switzerland's GDP (8.9 per cent) with 10 per cent.[10] According to the Federal Office of Statistics, the transit trade sector employs approximately 10,000 persons (Federal Council of Switzerland 2023, 1; see also Eggert, Ferro-Luzzi and Ouyang 2017; Public Eye and Missbach 2017).

If Switzerland's global share in commodities trade has rapidly risen in recent decades, that rise builds on structures grown over at least the past 150 years. The rise and power of the Swiss transit trade can be explained by a combination of Switzerland's 'neutrality', its government's approach of active and intentional non-involvement in the economic sphere, while providing the favourable currency, customs and tax policies that facilitated Swiss merchants' global entanglements (Haller 2019, 375–6). If the political and economic spheres have remained relatively separated, personal entanglement between the economic and political elite has been tight (Haller 2019, 377).

Since the mid-nineteenth century, 'cosmopolitan', 'discreet' and 'social conservative' Swiss merchants pursued global trade mainly in soft commodities (Haller 2019, 380; see also Franc 2021). Until the mid-twentieth century, the exact size of Swiss transit trade was difficult to assess. Since it was not covered by trade statistics gathered when goods physically crossed national borders, transit trade largely evaded public scrutiny (Haller 2019).

From the 1960s onwards, Swiss governments offered tax incentives to international business in a competitive race to the bottom, both internationally and between different Swiss Cantons. The ensuing internationalization of firms considerably changed the Swiss trading landscape and diminished the role of family-run Swiss companies, many of whom closed down from the 2000s onwards. Today, the 'Swissness' of the Swiss commodity trading hub is thus less of a question of a company's origins and history. It is primarily a question of the location of its headquarters, which provides access to Switzerland's favourable regulatory and institutional environment. Hanspeter Uster, a lawyer and long-term critic and a one-time councillor of Zug, called the canton a 'total service provider' (Schmid 2020, 1:16:40 hour), in reference to both the type of companies it attracts and to the canton's extensive provisioning to them and their (expatriate) employees.

As will become clearer over the course of this book, its importance in the global service sector brings Switzerland into a direct functional relationship with Solwezi. To render this relationship, which is obscured by the same conceptual divides that let even the Golf Estate appear as 'like another country' to Solwezi residents, visible is the main purpose of this book.

Conclusion

Any mining town is much more than its mining compounds: it is the outcome of the interaction of the global mining economy, national politics of rent distribution, regional histories and the urban communities living in it. The histories of Solwezi town and Kansanshi Mine show that the relation between the two has constantly changed. While the town's founding goes back to the mining project, the town has grown continuously and with its own dynamics of in- and out-migration, sometimes connected, sometimes disconnected from the mine, which often lay dormant. Solwezi's history has been intertwined with the history of the mine without being determined by it. Today, Solwezi's urban communities are minimally integrated into the mining project – and thus often maximally affected.

These are dynamics that speak of a disengaged form of global extractivism, something we see across the globe. In Zambia and beyond, replacing an often paternalist welfare system with corporate social responsibility (CSR) programmes rolled out in the communities adjacent to the mining ground (on this shift, see Hertz and Schulz 2020), companies' most direct impact is through labour. But even this composition has dramatically changed with the shift to increased automated mining and companies' ability to sustain operations with a smaller workforce, more so in new mining areas where mines are designed as completely automated and partly digitized from the beginning (cf. Arboleda 2020). All of this does not automatically mean that a mining town's population cannot benefit from the mine – yet it is something we have become used to. In scholarly and everyday lingua, this is called the 'resource curse'. The next chapter tries to show the mechanisms through which the urban population is systematically deprived of most benefits from the mine's profits. I show the working of extractivism in its most ordinary, bureaucratic and typically hidden or ignored place: in the municipality's offices and the council chamber.

Chapter 2

THE COUNCIL

'Please wait a bit longer'

I drove up Solwezi's Independence Road, part of the main east-west highway in Northwestern Zambia that connects the Copperbelt Province in the east to Lumwana, Kalumbila, and Mwinilunga in the west (see Figure 7). Lucky to find a parking spot in the *boma*, the town centre, I stepped out of my car and walked into the old council building. The sound of the road mingled with noise from the construction site for the new council offices, already underway for several years. It was a normal day of my time as an 'intern' with the municipality's Planning Department in 2015. The area around the council building was already crowded with visitors who used these early hours in the hope of finding officials in their offices and the computer systems working. I entered my office, meant for two people, but now occupied by five. The room was already packed with at least ten 'clients', and many others were waiting in line in the corridors.

One colleague was busy revising a compensation scheme for an area in which rural residents were, with good cause, dissatisfied with the compensation the mine had paid for their loss of built structures and land. Another one wanted to print a form, but the entire council had run out of toner cartridges. A third colleague prepared for that day's audit committee meeting, and the fourth wrote a presentation for the town clerk. Shortly after my arrival, the department's head entered the office in alarm, exclaiming: 'The people from the African Development Bank are here! Wasn't the meeting supposed to happen tomorrow?' – and left again. I got dizzy. How could my colleagues manage to complete even the smallest task in this environment? It was just a normal day at the council, though, and somehow, the line of 'clients' slowly moved forward.

When it was his turn, an elegant elderly man explained that he had come to collect the site plan he had requested a while ago. One of my colleagues responded that they still worked on it and that he would need to wait 'a bit longer'. The man complained: 'In those days, you were so quick and efficient. But today, you are slow.' The civil servant defended himself: 'Ah, but then we were 2,000 residents. Now we are 15,000 … 15,000 million!' Everyone chuckled at his helpless hyperbole and his obvious inability to say how many residents the town had (in fact, no one

Figure 7. Truck carrying copper concentrate on Independence Road, Solwezi, August 2017. Photo by author.

can). One of the waiting people muttered, mildly annoyed, that the answer was always the same – 'Please wait a bit longer.'

In his disapproval about the quality of service delivery in Solwezi, the elderly man is no exception. Hardly any Solwezi resident is satisfied with the municipal service provision, and many voice their disapproval in more searing tones. The Municipal Council and its administration appear to many as incompetent and unwilling to address important problems. Council officials, on the other hand, usually shrug off such critique, sometimes explaining how limited their resources are in the face of rapid change.

This chapter is my attempt to take the council and its attempts at regulation as seriously as residents' disapproval, and to analyse the scope of urban governance in Solwezi town. This field has found surprisingly little interest in the scholarly literature on mining towns. Most of the research on the latest rise of extractivist projects in Africa focuses on the new, easily identifiable actors, the mining companies or on civil society's resistance to them. If local authorities and their role come into the focus at all, the topic is quickly dealt with by blaming the 'resource curse' and extending its logic from the national to the local level.[1] Local authorities appear in the debate as rather insignificant: powerless against the mining companies, and largely unable to represent and stand up for their constituencies.

In Solwezi, there is an incredible amount of everyday work invested by local authorities in trying to deal with a massively altered environment. Over the past fifty years, Solwezi's Municipal Council has been *the* steady actor. The municipality receives 1 per cent of mining royalties (primarily through land rates), which is a considerable part of its total revenue, and it must deal with the mining company daily. Despite many practical limitations, it has the power to set some of the conditions for the mining company's operation vis-à-vis its hosting town: it can sell land and set rates, can regulate infrastructure and integrate the mine into urban planning, and can supervise and influence the quality of resettlement and compensation processes. The council tries to take up these responsibilities in its everyday workings. What its attempts and sometimes their failures reveal about the impact of extractivism on a local polity is the focus of this chapter.

Solwezi has somehow fallen off the radar even of scholarship on Zambia.[2] For most authors, the town is simply an opposition stronghold (which it was until 2021 when UPND assumed power) and a place with a logic to itself: 'unlike the old Copperbelt, Solwezi has shown no signs of emerging urban politics that link to the national level' (Bebbington et al. 2018, 146). I want to change this perception and give Solwezi's governance the attention it deserves.

In what follows, I first give an overview of Solwezi town, its compounds and their unequal access to infrastructure, using data from my ethnographic work and a corpus of georeferenced data generated as part of the *Solwezi Urban Baseline Study* (SUBS), an exceptional and comprehensive household survey conducted in 2015 with the financial and operational help of the German cooperation GIZ (Preuss and Schmidt-Eisenlohr 2016). I participated in the study both as an observer and as an advisor to the interviewees, young Zambians, going from plot to plot and filling in some 30,000 questionnaires.

After this overview, I briefly portray Solwezi's Municipal Council. The second part of the chapter then presents the three case studies on the impact of extractive industries on practices of statehood. The first case study is on taxation and revenue collection. I show that the presence of the mine has made the council's work easier since it allows it to periodically collect additional revenue. This makes officials more comfortable and less accountable. In other regards, however, the mine constantly interferes with the council's tasks. The second case study shows how the mining company's capacity to realize its own spatial planning diminished the council's scope of action and authority. The third case study shows how the elected Municipal Council and its accountability towards its constituents is affected by the considerable in-migration triggered by the mine's employment policies. As the town's population becomes more diverse, voting patterns and ideas about representation are gradually changing. I will show this with an analysis of the 2016 elections, in which I participated as a locally appointed election observer.

All three case studies show how, in different municipal realms of local governance – financial, economic and political – the council has not addressed the challenge of governing a new situation differently, tending to proceed with its habitual, bureaucratic activities as it did before the mine reopened – under dramatically altered conditions.

As a consequence, foreign direct investment has changed statehood on the local level – 'the imagination of the state and the practices that relate to the state as an image and an institution' (Förster 2012, 8). Local authorities' accountability towards its constituencies has declined, and residents have become less responsive with regard to their duties vis-à-vis the local state (such as taxes). This has eroded the local authority's significance and its governing capacities. In some domains, other actors have stepped in; especially in the 2000s when the mine negotiated for land, and still today for specific expansion projects, local chiefs have regained the position of important power brokers. The overall image of urban governance that emerges from the chapter thus does not contradict theories on the resource curse but, by focusing on contingency, allows us to understand the consequences of a powerful external economic actor in a much more differentiated manner. While secondary towns in Southern Africa equally face a dramatic shortage of resources and infrastructure to keep up with urbanization rates, the situation in mining town – and towns with a large foreign investor more generally – is particular in that the government's authority is challenged by and becomes heavily interdependent on a competitor with state-like power to influence urban life and state governance, as well as the relationship between the local state and urban residents.

Solwezi town

Since the early 2000s, Solwezi's built environment has rapidly changed. The town constantly expands into the formerly agricultural lands around it, while in more established neighbourhoods, residents often subdivide their plots, sell parts of them to new migrants and reinvest the money in new housing structures (see Figure 8). The municipal council finds its attempts to administer and plan the town and to provide the necessary infrastructure constantly overturned by rapid change and a chronic lack of funds, and the situation is exacerbated by the mining company's financial power to selectively implement the infrastructural projects it needed for smooth extraction (see Chapters 5 and 6). Independence Road, one of the few tarred roads in town, is almost always congested, mainly around the first Shoprite supermarket in the *boma*, the town centre, and a couple of open markets, while the few traffic lights are routinely down due to power cuts.

To cater for the increase in population, the Municipal Council has negotiated for land held under traditional tenure and opened new areas for residential and industrial use. Under that regime, the council sells individual plots to the public, thereby keeping some degree of control over the planned developments. Individuals can however also acquire leaseholds over land outside the narrow municipal boundaries from the traditional authorities (see Figure 9 and Chapter 3). In these peri-urban areas, the council does not normally impose coherent planning; access roads are lacking, and a church may easily stand next to a bar. The Solwezi Urban Baseline Study (SUBS) found that there are 29,750 plots within the new town boundary, which roughly correlates with Central Constituency (see section Solwezi Municipal Council). On average, each plot hosts 2.3 households, amounting to a total of 69,500 households and 266,000 people living in Solwezi town in 2015 (Preuss and Schmidt-Eisenlohr 2016, 61) and 332,623 in 2022 (Central Statistical Office Zambia 2022, 20) (see Figure 10).

The use of land depends on the area of town. Commercial and industrial land use are clustered along Independence Road (N5) and Kansanshi Road, and in the *boma* around the council and provincial administration buildings is largely used commercially. The most prominent of these are shopping malls built between 2008

Figure 8. Notice board at Solwezi Municipal Council where owners and dealers offer plots for rent or sale, October 2015. Photo by author.

and 2016: the South African owned supermarket chain Shoprite (Negi 2014), the two malls Solwezi City Mall and Kapiji Mall and, on Kansanshi Road, Botswana-owned chain store Choppies. Two high-end hotels, Kansanshi Hotel and Royal Solwezi, mostly cater for contractors and visitors to the mine. Over the years, Solwezi has also attracted investment in retail services and banking.

The largest part of Solwezi town is however made up of residential areas, so-called compounds (see Figure 4), which the town's population looks upon as separate and identifiable neighbourhoods. Although many compounds have become denser through the subdivision of plots, the compounds still vastly differ in density. As a rule, the western compounds of Solwezi are more densely populated than those in the centre and on the eastern side. Not only density but also the size of plots varies considerably. The council grades compounds into low-, medium- and high-cost areas. This evaluation defines the respective size of the plots in an area. The differentiation further exacerbates differences between the compounds. For instance, the compound 'Urban' dramatically differs from the adjacent compound 'Kizhinge-Zhinge' where the number of residents per plot is not only higher but the plots are also considerably smaller.

The availability of infrastructure in compounds gives additional information about differentiation across the urban area. Generally, residents in the older, more central parts of town have privileged access to a variety of services. Residents in the older, more central parts of town have privileged access to a flush toilet, which can but does not have to correlate with access to (faulty and unreliable) piped

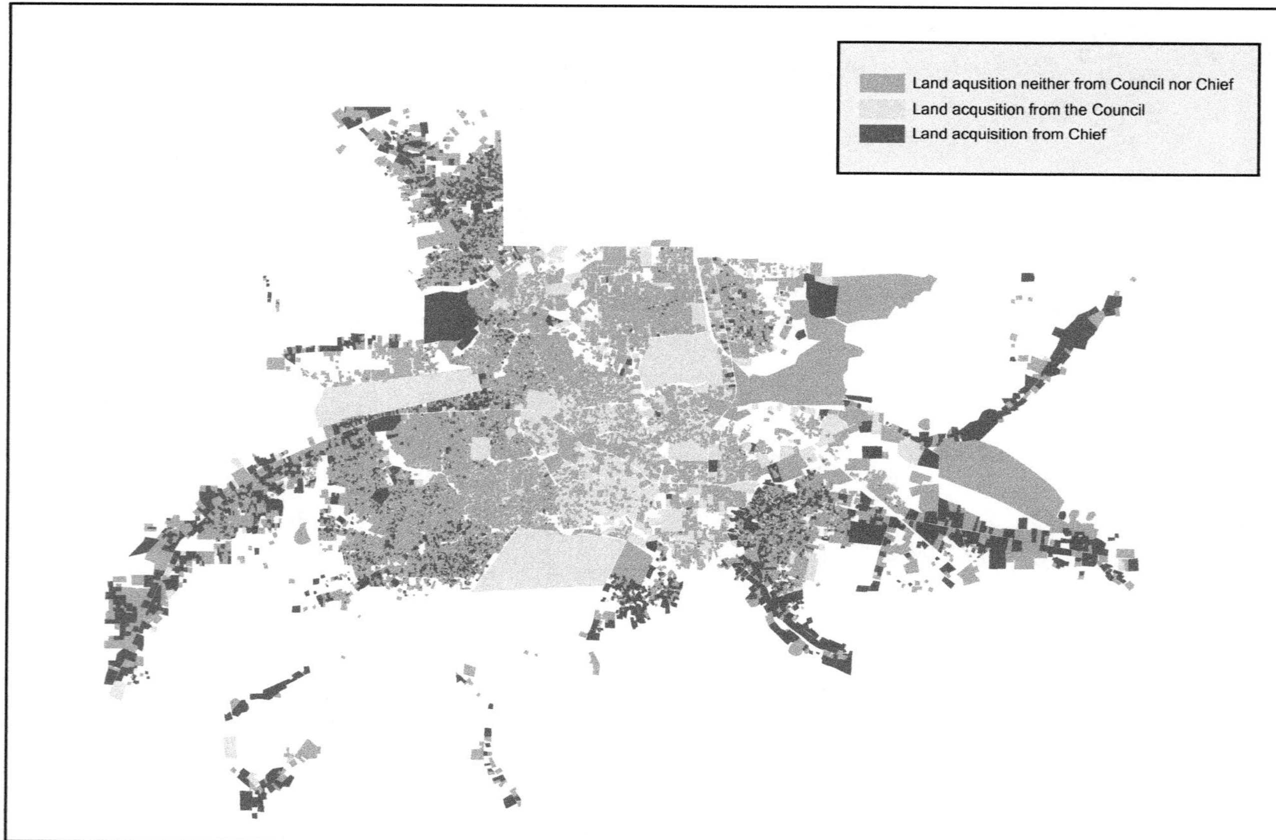

Figure 9. Map of source of land acquisition, Solwezi town (Map by author produced on the basis of data from the Solwezi Urban Baseline Study. Reprinted by permission from Preuss und Schmidt-Eisenlohr (2016).

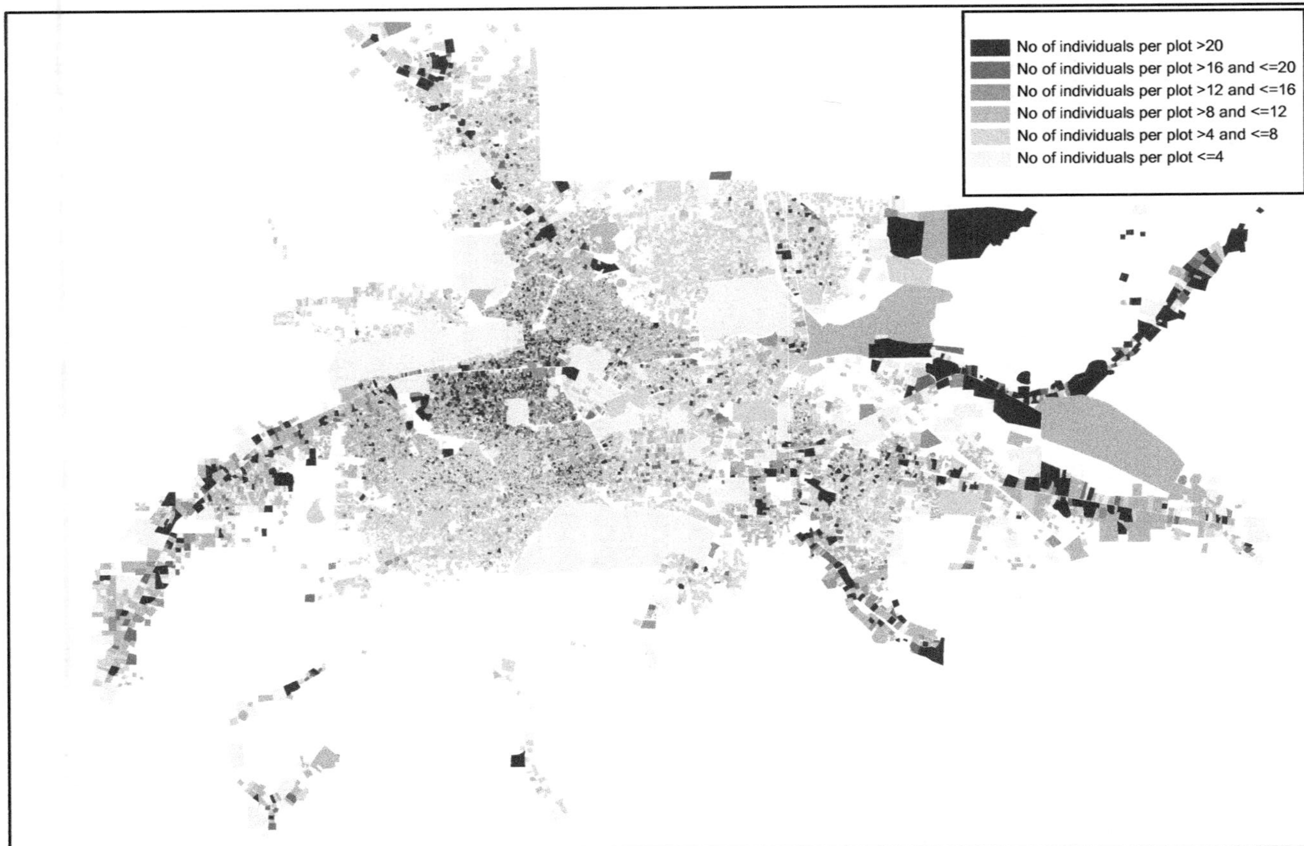

Figure 10. Map of number of individuals per plot in Solwezi town. Map by author produced on the basis of data from the Solwezi Urban Baseline Study. Reprinted by permission from Preuss und Schmidt-Eisenlohr (2016).

water, a service provided by the parastatal NWWSC.[3] Figure 11 shows the type of water sources residents have access to. Residents closer to the *boma* and the area around the secondary school in northwestern Solwezi benefit from water infrastructure that was built several decades ago, while newer compounds have never been connected to piped water or the electricity grid. The map also shows that households use several different water sources. Some have a water source on the plot – tap, boreholes or hand-dug wells – while others must walk to their source of water: water kiosks, sources on neighbouring plots, community wells or a stream.

Just like water, most services are distributed unevenly across town. For instance, rubbish is only collected in households that pay the disposal company, while most families burn or bury their rubbish on their plots. Electricity is a privilege for the more affluent (see Chapter 5).

Compared to the town's size, very few Solwezi residents directly depend on Kansanshi Mine. Zambia has no mandatory local content measures, and the mine mostly contracts foreign-owned suppliers and service providers, whose presence has little impact on local value addition (Caramento 2020, 1). Kansanshi's corporate social responsibility programs, as well, only benefit a fraction of Solwezi residents (Southern Africa Resource Watch 2020), but almost every inhabitant experiences the direct and indirect externalities of mining: land encroachment, environmental degradation, increasing costs for goods and services and the negative impact on the municipality's planning capacity (see section Infrastructure).

The growth of urban settlements into customary land has partly weakened the influence of traditional authorities as the custodians of rural and communal land. At the same time, chiefs and headmen assumed a central role in land deals with small and large foreign investors. Before formalization or privatization of land, their consent needs to be sought, a process which gives the traditional authorities leverage (and income). Chiefs' power has been strengthened in the course of previous administrations across Zambia (Green and Norberg 2018). In many cases, the strengthened role of the traditional authorities has exacerbated rather than curbed social inequality and insecurity of land tenure (Sitko 2010). I heard the phrase that 'the chief is not protecting us' numerous times. Headmen in the name of the chief sell land to newcomers and families later struggle to expand their (family) villages to build for their newly married children.

In Solwezi, despite the disconnect between foreign-driven investment and the older local elite, some established families – such as the Kalepa, Hazell, Mulemba, Mumena, Saviye, Mukumbi, Sondashi, Kayumba and Kapijimpanga – managed to appropriate business opportunities and make the boom profitable for themselves. Most of them are either part of the traditional authorities or belong to families that have held political (opposition) positions in the provincial and local government. With direct access to state resources and information or, in the case of the traditional leadership, positioned at entry points for negotiations with the mine for land (Cheelo 2008), they could monopolize information and access, offer their services or seize on developing opportunities. The ensuing elite land capture helped driving the selective commercialization of land (Sitko and Jayne 2014).

Figure 11. Distribution of water sources in Solwezi town. Map by author produced on the basis of data from the Solwezi Urban Baseline Study. Reprinted by permission from Preuss und Schmidt-Eisenlohr (2016).

Seen from a global perspective, Solwezi residents are at the reproductive end of global extractivism, as I will argue in the next chapter. Looked at from inside – from differentiated access to key infrastructure to the formation of elite groups – consumption patterns and possibilities for upward mobility vary greatly along the intersections of ethnicity, social and political capital and gender, though.[4]

Solwezi Municipal Council

Solwezi Municipal Council (SMC) is the elected authority charged with governing this vast and rapidly changing urban area. It is responsible for planning the town's development, for implementing the plans on the ground and generally for guiding urban growth into predetermined channels. Its efforts to do so, however, regularly fail. The most recent development plan for Solwezi District dates back to 1964. Two later attempts to get a new development plan was approved in 1978 and 1990 – both failed. Hence, to this day, the council works with the utterly outdated 1964 document and with an integrated development plan that was drafted in 2009 but never officially approved by the central government. (This 2009 plan greatly expands the township boundaries into the area of Kapijimpanga Chieftaincy and more or less covers what is now Central Constituency. Consequently, the Ministry could not approve the plan without the signature of the reigning chief. The current chief Kilolo Ng'ambi was embroiled in a succession battle since his predecessor's death in 2008 and, until its resolution through a Supreme Court ruling in October 2018 (Kaaba 2019), was not authorized to sign off any official documents.)

To understand everyday urban governance, a few words on its organization are necessary. Zambia has a total of 109 districts, which are governed by four city councils (Lusaka, Livingstone, Kitwe and Ndola), 13 municipal councils and 92 district councils. Solwezi currently is classified as a municipality; it has been preparing for city status since 2015. SMC oversees all local government matters for Solwezi District, which, up to 2016, covered three constituencies – Solwezi East, West and Central. Solwezi town is situated in the Solwezi Central constituency. Solwezi East is a largely rural constituency, while Solwezi West hosts the Lumwana and Sentinel/Kalumbila Mines, which have triggered the growth of two new urban clusters. During my research, the boundaries of Solwezi District changed per Statutory Instrument No. 39 of 2016. The district was subdivided into three new districts, namely Kalumbila District (formally Solwezi West), Solwezi District (formally Solwezi Central) and Mushindamo District (formally Solwezi East). The current Solwezi District thus primarily covers the urban settlements, and its revenue base shrank from three mines to one, Kansanshi.

Until 2016, SMC consisted of three Members of Parliament (MPs) for the district, two representatives of the local chiefs and twenty-two elected councillors. Since 2016, the council consists of one MP, one representative of Chief Kapijimpanga's chieftaincy, the mayor and five elected councillors (for the Kamalamba, Kapijimpanga, Kimasala, Sandang'ombe and Tumvwanganai wards). Councillors work part-time and are accountable to the electorates of their respective wards.

The full council meets under the mayor's chairmanship, with senior administrative staff in attendance.[5] Councillors chair the standing committees, whose meetings are not open to the public (but were for me).[6] The committees' decisions serve as recommendations to the full council.

On the administrative side, the town clerk is the council's chief executive officer. He or she is assisted by the departmental heads for Administration, Finance, Engineering Services, Planning and Housing, and Social Services. In contrast to the elected councillors, the administrative staff are full-time, salaried officials who oversee the day-to-day implementation of the council's services. The Ministry of Local Government and Housing (MLGH) is responsible for overseeing all local government in Zambia. With the enactment of the Local Government Amendment Act No. 6 of 2010, the Local Government Service Commission was established with oversight from MLGH. The commission is mandated to hire, fire, promote, demote and discipline officials. Any official appointed by the Local Government Service Commission is subjected to a system of rotation intended to prevent corruption. Hence, state officials are often unfamiliar with the culture of their workplace and may even struggle to understand the language spoken by their 'clients'.

Under the terms of the Local Government Act, a council may levy taxes, borrow money, manage and own housing projects and control a wide range of public services, such as roads, water, power and health facilities. Moreover, it receives several national grants, including the Constituency Development Fund, through the MLGH. In November 2013, the government approved the Revised National Decentralization Policy. The strategy, enacted from 2015 onwards, is 'decentralization through devolution' of power and of certain functions to the councils, including fiscal decentralization. It is meant to give citizens more authority and power in decision-making with respect to local matters. In reality, SMC has been rather overwhelmed by this new policy, mostly because of a lack of financial and human resources to take on its extra functions.

Taxation and revenue collection

Against this background, I can now turn to the ways in which extractive investments influence the legitimacy, capacity and authority of the local state. I first examine discussions and proceedings in the council chamber concerning taxation and revenue collection from the mine (mainly property rates) and ordinary landowners. The numbers may seem dull, but their discussion offers a key insight into decision-making processes at the local state level.

During the SMC's full council meeting of 13 July 2015, which I attended, the minutes of the last Finance, Human Resources and General Purposes (FHRGP) Committee meeting were discussed. In that meeting, the FHRGP Committee members had debated the 2015 budget estimates.[7] For the fiscal year of 2015, the approved revenue estimates were ZMW 78,608,825 (approximately US$ 7,860,000 at the time), out of which approximately ZMW 30 million were scheduled to come from local taxes (the largest portion of which are property rates).[8] The 2015 budgeted expenditure estimates were ZMW 89,020,569, leaving the committee with a projected budget deficit of ZMW 10,411,743 (approximately US$1,040,000). The full council deliberated on the matter brought forward by the committee and eventually resolved that the item should be noted but also, in the words of the minutes, that the 'management should consider the possibility of covering up the budget deficit by surcharging Kansanshi Mine a penalty fee and a service charge for the illegal development of the Smelter and for the construction of the Smelter Road'.

To understand this solution, some context is needed. In what way was the development of the smelter and the smelter road 'illegal'? In 2015, Kansanshi Mine had applied to the council to transform an area of roughly 2,500 hectares from customary tenure to freehold title. As required, the application contained a Form II stating the chief's approval of the alienation. The council was then supposed to fill in a Form III to confirm that the land was under the jurisdiction of the chief and that no other legitimate claims on the land existed and pass on its recommendation to the Commissioner of Lands. The problem with this particular application was that the application for conversion (and approval of structures) only reached the council after the fact. When it submitted the application, the mining company had already – without securing the necessary authorization – constructed a copper smelter and the access road leading to the smelter on this land.

What follows are my notes of a discussion between elected councillors and appointed officials during the council meeting that was not recorded in the minutes:

Councillor 1: Council lawyers should help us and slap them [Kansanshi Mine] so that they stop doing illegal things!

Councillor 2: The avenues they are using are not right. Give them the land they already occupy but charge them ZMW 8,000 per plot. And charge them a penalty so that they feel it. They should repay every plot. Let's propose a penalty.

Councillor 3: The chief can only hand out 250 hectares, can't he? Let's go physically on the ground.

Town clerk: We do an inspection, get the drawings (which we don't have) and then decide on the penalty.

Councillor 4: They are so corrupt. They don't consult the local authority, instead they consult others [that is, the President]. Let's enter into a lease with these 2,500 hectares.

In the end, the Municipal Council used the illegality of the mine's actions to raise missing funds. This solution is symptomatic for the chances and pitfalls the mine's presence offers to local government. The presence of the mine – temporary and unsustainable by definition – offers a relatively easy solution to the most pressing financial problems and regularly allows for stopgap measures. This, however, increases the administration's dependence on the mine. It makes it more difficult to develop structural and sustainable solutions to the problems of revenue collection. As the example shows, the financial dependency of the council on the mine also gives the mining company increased leverage to ignore the council's rulings and figure in the ensuing fines.

These dangers were not lost on the councillors. In the case mentioned above, officials and elected councillors agreed, but the budgetary allocation of revenues from the mining companies is a recurrent point of disagreement between the two groups. The mining sector pays roughly 98 per cent of its rates and taxes to the Zambia Revenue Authority (ZRA), but property rates and some annual business fees are paid to the local authorities twice a year. For the fiscal year of 2015, SMC received ZMW 25,985,900 (approximately US$ 2,500,000) for property rates – ZMW 14,936,900 from KMP and ZMW 11,049,000 from Lumwana Barrick (Zambia EITI 2017). To put this in context, this sum is a little less than half of the total revenue the council collected in the 2014 fiscal year.[9]

Because it constitutes such a fundamental and substantial part of the annual budget, the revenue collected from the mines is discussed as a separate item and budgeted separately. When the Finance Committee tabled its half-yearly 'Utilisation Report on Funds Received from Extractive Companies in Solwezi District from January to June 2015' to the full council on 13 July 2015, this sparked a lengthy and heated debate. This time, there was a clear division between the elected councillors and the officials, led by the town clerk.

Basically, the report outlined that, out of the ZMW 13,028,450, the council spent ZMW 2.6 million on salaries, ZMW 2 million on the repayment of a loan, ZMW 1.8 million on the construction of the new civic centre, ZMW 1.3 million on vehicles (including a mayoral vehicle) and insurance and ZMW 800,000 on councillors' allowances.[10] It was the issue of salaries that triggered the heated debate:

Councillor 1: I would like to see a new item like 'Funds from the mines should not be used to pay salaries'.

Town clerk: When we are budgeting as a Council, taxes, fines etc., we put everything in one basket. The first we then pay is manpower. Let's not adopt this item, it is not helpful. Let's leave it at the point that we will control better the funds flowing into manpower.

Councillor 2: Let the departments do their work and collect taxes and levy. Let's adopt [my fellow councillor's suggestion] as an item.

Councillor 3: Only when the mine pays, the checks are moving. The TC [town clerk] should budget how much we collect ourselves. People in Zambezi [another rural district in Northwestern Province], they are paying their workers, there are no mines.

Town clerk: There is no fear that we can't manage this place without the mines. But don't make this into a policy, this does not make sense. Let us maximize on the collections of the revenue from the bus station for instance. We are building a new station now and people will pay the fees.

In the end, the full council did not adopt a new policy outlining how the revenue from the mines should be used. However, the debate showed a clear divide between the elected councillors, who were unhappy about what they saw as overreliance on that revenue, and the appointed officials, who denied such dependency. The political wing of the council suspected that the municipality would be unable to manage the town without the mines' rates. They argued that structural costs, such as salaries, should not depend on the mines' payments (although they said nothing about the mayor's vehicle or their own allowances). They accused the officials of neglecting general revenue collection while they waited for the half-yearly windfall money. The elected councillors thus argued against fiscal indiscipline and an unsustainable use of rent revenue.

In many ways, the councillors were correct. In what follows, I will show that the council was indeed lax in the collection of revenue, even when it had the chance to broaden its revenue base dramatically with a new valuation roll.

All landowners are required by law to pay property rates to the council. The amounts payable is determined as follows: the value of the land and the value of any improvements to that land are added together to generate a 'total rateable value', which is multiplied by the assessment rate defined by the responsible council. Only owners whose properties are captured in the valuation roll are required to pay the rates.[11] According to the Rating Act (chapter 192 of the Laws of Zambia), the valuation roll is supposed to be revised every five years by a government valuation surveyor, appointed by the Minister of Local Government and Housing. In the Solwezi District, the old valuation roll dated back to 2010, and the valuation surveyor prepared the 2015 valuation roll in 2016.

In the full council meeting of 12 December 2016, the Director of Finance presented his report on the new valuation roll. According to the new valuation roll, including some adjustments due to the division of Solwezi District and the consequent loss of Kalumbila town and Sentinel and Lumwana Mines, the new Solwezi District (formerly Solwezi Central constituency) would receive land rates from 4,415 entries.[12] The old valuation roll had just 2,416 entries.

The modest increase in the number of (primarily residential) entries does not correlate with the reality on the ground. The Solwezi Urban Baseline Study, as mentioned above, gives a more realistic picture of the number of plots. It counts 29,750 plots within the proposed new township boundary, many of them the result of the subdivision of existing properties (Preuss and Schmidt-Eisenlohr 2016). By accepting the new valuation roll, the council tolerated and cemented smaller land revenues and missed the opportunity offered by the new valuation roll to address old failures, such as ignoring houses without house numbers.

The consequences of this failure were covered by taxing the mine. At the same full council meeting, members approved new rates to be levied for the different categories of properties. The only rate increase the council approved was imposed on mining property, where the multiplier was increased from 0.025 to 0.04. Based on the new valuation roll and the new rates, the council's revenue rose from ZMW 33,610,480 under the old valuation roll to an estimated ZMW

38,594,765 und the new one, out of which the Kansanshi Mine would have to contribute 65 per cent.[13]

Apart from failing to capture all titled and occupied land in the valuation roll, inefficiency in revenue collection has been a concern of the Council's management for many years. In 2014, for instance, only 52 per cent of the total revenue estimate was actually collected. In December 2016, the council was owed ZMW 15.7 million for rates and ZMW 32 million for other revenue sources. In the above-mentioned full council meeting, the Director of Finance thus took an unprecedented step by requesting the councillors' help in the collection of revenue:

> As a measure, management appealed that the honourable councillors assist in the sensitization of the residents in wards to pay their bills so that the budgeted activities could be achieved in the year 2017 and years to come … [A]ll the landlords had an obligation to pay the rates twice a year … However a number of landlords had not been fair in the sense that when they rent out their houses they receive reasonable rentals but do not, out of the rentals, pay anything to the Council.[14]

Collecting revenue from ordinary landowners is certainly challenging due to a lack of financial and human resources, sprawling settlements, an insecure tenure situation, multiple claims of ownership and often the physical absence of landlords. The mining company, in contrast, can be relied upon to pay its local rates (albeit while simultaneously, and successfully, opposing any increase in the national taxation and royalty regime much more important to its bottom line).

As Solwezi town continues to grow, most of the town's revenue comes from just one taxpayer – the mine. Kansanshi Mine's contribution to the total property rates paid to the municipality was even higher than the 65 per cent quoted above if we factor in non-payments by many other commercial, industrial and residential actors. Ordinary residents and small businesses are either not on the valuation roll, and thus not required to pay rates, or manage to avoid payment by ignoring bills and dodging revenue collectors.

As a result of the council's lax revenue collection, residents who find it easy to evade taxation have little leverage to claim better service provision. Similarly, elected councillors have little incentive to heed the town clerk's appeals and ask their constituents to pay their rates. When a council relies on just one or two large players for most of its income, its responsibility towards ordinary resident shifts. This not only affects accountability towards those citizens but increases the council's dependence on the mines. Solwezi is thus turning into a rent-seeking local polity, mirroring developments at the national government level. Martin, Mehrotra and Prasad (2009) recently argued for renewed scholarly attention for taxation because it 'enmeshes us in the web of generalized reciprocity that constitutes modern society' (2009, 3). The case of Solwezi shows that we also need to be attentive to forms of civil *dis*-engagement as a result of tax policies and revenue collection practices.[15]

Infrastructure

Kansanshi Mine covers a large proportion of the district's total area. Due to the nature of open-cast mining, a large tract of the district's land has been transformed from customary to state land, and regional and national forest areas have been decommissioned. But the mining complex also contributes to massive spatial changes outside its license area. In what follows, I elaborate on one infrastructural project spearheaded by Kansanshi Mine which not only changed the environment by its mere presence but also triggered socio-spatial change beyond its concrete surface: the smelter road whose illegal implementation triggered the exchange in the Municipal Council quoted above. I will argue that the mine's selective interference in the town's set-up, coupled with the council's dependence on the mine, has resulted in a situation where the local authorities have handed over traditional state tasks to a corporate actor. Due to their uncontrolled and uncoordinated implementation, infrastructural projects as the smelter road also have a negative impact on the council's accountability vis-à-vis its constituents.

Solwezi town has one primary road, Independence Road, which cuts through the centre of town. The trucks that carry Barrick Gold's copper, mined at the Lumwana Mine, and FQM's copper, mined at Sentinel Mine, drive right through Solwezi town. They not only block other traffic and endanger pedestrians and marketeers selling their produce along the road but they regularly get stuck in traffic jams themselves. With the prospect of processing both Sentinel's and Kansanshi's copper concentrate, and given the paucity of smelter capacity within Zambia, FQM's Road Division built a new copper smelter on the Kansanshi license area between 2014 and 2015. At the same time, it constructed the smelter road to reroute trucks coming from the western mines straight to the smelter, so they did not have to enter Solwezi town centre (see Figure 2). Since the smelter started operating in March 2015, it has processed most of Sentinel's copper concentrate into anodes (with small portions processed at Mopani Copper Mines). Some trucks from Barrick Gold's Lumwana mine still cut through the centre of town, but the smelter road has dramatically reduced traffic, noise and pollution in Solwezi. Today, a few hundred trucks thunder along the new road each day. To conform to Zambian regulations, there is a 100-metre-wide road corridor to avoid accidents when truck drivers lose control of their vehicles. The road was recently handed over to the Zambian Roads Development Agency for public use.

More than eighty households had to be resettled for construction of the road to proceed. Farmers' losses included agricultural land, cultivation potential, annual and perennial crops, fruit-bearing trees, two homesteads and many non-residential structures such as sheds, wells, temporary farm shelters and so on (URS Scott Wilson Zambia 2013, 77). Most of these farmers' homesteads or houses are in adjacent villages, but many temporarily live on their farms when harvesting. Due to the lack of a national resettlement policy at the time, the mine, through its CSR Department, implemented international standards of resettlement and commissioned consultants to carry out an Environmental Impact Assessment, part of which was a Resettlement Action Plan. Both were approved by the Zambia Environment Management Agency, and the resettlement process was rolled out in parallel to the construction of the road. In my multiple conversations with the mine's supervisory (white) employees whom I temporarily shadowed when they enacted this two years-process, I could sense the heightened awareness for the need to act as representatives of a 'responsible actor' (Rajak 2011; Welker 2014) to, not at least, prevent bad press. (The smelter road resettlement process followed several rather disastrous earlier resettlements, something employees freely admitted.)

The mining company plans the town for its own use. In the case of the smelter road, the result of a decongested Independence Road was welcome, but it also entailed many costs for the town and the council; costs that the company did not care about as soon as outside its technocratic framing of the project and that the council could not take into account because it was not leading the process. The company's mitigation measures only targeted the consequences in the immediate environment of the road, its consequences were however much larger.

A new road always changes the environment. It influences how people perceive the surrounding areas and it is invariably adopted in various – often unforeseen – ways (Dalakoglou and Harvey 2012; Harvey and Knox 2015; Beck, Klaeger and Stasik 2017). The smelter road was no exception. For a small number of farmers, the road turned out to be a blessing since it facilitated easier access to their fields. Others made the most of the dramatic rise in real estate values in the area by selling their plots of land. However, most of the farmers living or farming adjacent to the road had mixed feelings, at best, or saw their livelihoods destroyed, at worst. They complained of thieves who stole their harvests during the night. Population density in the area rose immediately and continues to do so. And, for many, the CSR Department's resettlement packages – which included some training and limited assistance for the first year after resettlement – introduced a regime which pitted them against those residents who did not enjoy these benefits, contributing to fights with old and new neighbours alike. Moreover, the assistance was insufficient to compensate for the loss of time and labour they had put into the land. Finally, parents feared for their children's safety, as they now had to cross the busy new road to get to school. The road also had consequences far beyond the road: it laid waste to the council's own spatial planning. The council had initially planned a new residential settlement – the Humphrey Mulemba Villa Park – at the junction of the smelter road and the T5, but it was unable to proceed with this amid rapid informal settlement and a dramatic rise in land disputes.

For the mining company, the smelter road was simply a transport corridor. It was not interested in the additional changes that its construction precipitated, and it gave them little thought during the planning process. The planners merely looked for a route through a relatively thinly populated area so they would not have to resettle too many residents and farmers. However, while the road's course was chosen simply with a view to increasing profits and bypassing the busy *boma*, once it was built, the local people and the council started to be affected by it in multiple – often negative – ways.

By pursuing its own logic of infrastructural development in an urban setting, the mine engaged in town planning – a task that should be fulfilled by the Municipal Council. In the area around the smelter road, the company's actions helped to delegitimize the council's authority. Its CSR Department focused on the farmers who lived along the road (with a narrow understanding of the effects of a new piece of infrastructure – a technocratic approach that was approved and supported by the central state organs) and thus singled them out for special treatment. The road, which was built purely to increase a corporate actor's profits, and the accompanying resettlement programme shifted the residents' attention from the council to the mine, and it remains fixed there to this day. If the directly affected farmers need more assistance, they ask the mine for help; if they have a boundary dispute in the resettled areas, they turn to the mine and its state-of-the-art GPS database. In other words, statehood has been reconfigured by a piece of infrastructure that was designed to aid disengagement with the population and speed up extraction and processing. (A recent so-called debt swap between the company and the council in which Kansanshi committed to undertake urban roadworks in exchange for tax relief should also be read in this light.)

The case of the smelter road shows that the Municipal Council struggles to regulate because the mine is quicker, and because it needs the funds from the fine. Planning for the local authorities is a complex task that includes social, political and economic aspects. In contrast, the mining company can act one-dimensionally and technocratically and can thus see the construction of a piece of infrastructure through to the finish.

Voting patterns

The key mechanism linking the Municipal Council and residents are of course elections. Solwezi has been an opposition stronghold throughout its history, a sentiment that only increased since the Patriotic Front (PF) came to power in 2011 and arguably ignored the region even more than previous administrations. More recently, due to in-migration, the party in power (until 2021) has gained some leverage, though. This shows how the mine's presence can change the structures of statehood indirectly, by way of voting patterns.

For the 2016 general elections (presidential, mayoral and parliamentary), I was accredited as an election observer and thus gained access to Solwezi's polling and totalling stations. These were Zambia's fifth elections in ten years, partly as a result of the deaths of presidents in office and consequent by-elections. Earlier in 2016, the president had signed a constitutional amendment which stipulated that the president should be elected by a majority of the national vote. In August 2016, Zambians went to the polls to elect a new president and Parliament and to vote in a referendum on the amended Bill of Rights. The incumbent PF party urged its supporters to vote 'yes' in the referendum, which needed the support of more than 50 per cent of all eligible voters to pass.

Residents in the Northwestern Province, dominated by kiKaonde-speaking groups, are not represented in any of the 'ethnoregional' blocs distinguishing the competing parties – Movement for Multi-Party Democracy (MMD), Patriotic Front (PF) or United Party for National Development (UPND) (Hern 2020, 89). In the 2011 general elections, Solwezi District's constituencies voted for the incumbent MMD which lost the election to the PF under late Michael Sata's lead. In the 2016 elections, which I analyse in more detail here, Solwezi's constituencies voted for UPND, the opposition party that lost the national elections to the PF now under the lead of Edgar Lungu. Erin Hern, a political scientist, explains this shift from MMD in 2011 to UPND in 2016 as follows: 'Without a strong ethnoregional connection to either party, and facing a dismal record of service improvements under the incumbent, the opposition party was a better bet in the face of the ruling party's record, *despite a lack of ethnoregional ties to the UPND*' (2020, 90). She also interprets the 2016 voting results in Solwezi's constituencies as 'swinging hard' to the opposition UPND (2020, 89).

Staff and officials overseeing the voting process experienced considerable pressure amid allegations of fraud and vote rigging. The outcome of an election process that was 'mired in controversy from beginning to end' (Wahman 2020, 283) had a significant, dividing effect on the country and the main opposition party UPND has not stopped to reject the results (for more on the 2016 elections and its aftermath, see Banda et al. 2020).

While the general shift from MMD to UPND is important to explain, I would like to put focus on a less visible but equally important fact: the results at a couple of the thirty-six polling stations (and one in particular) indicate that voting patterns are gradually changing. Kansanshi polling station in the Kamalamba ward was housed in a tent outside the mine's license area and was designed to allow Kansanshi employees to vote either before or after their shift, but local residents could use it, too. It had 1,100 registered voters, and the turnout was 64 per cent. At all other stations in the constituency, the numbers for male and female voters were quite balanced. However, 84.6 per cent of the registered voters at Kansanshi were men, which supports the assumption that a majority of mineworkers voted there.

In the parliamentary elections, 289 votes were cast for the ruling PF party and 396 for UPND, with just 3 ballot papers rejected. Similarly, the UPND candidate received 372 votes in the mayoral election and the PF candidate 298. Finally, 319 voters gave their presidential votes to the PF and 383 to the UPND, with 3 ballot papers rejected.

The referendum did not come close to reaching the necessary threshold across Zambia, but in Solwezi Central 9,972 people voted 'yes' while 7,393 voted 'no'; thus, a majority followed the ruling party's advice to vote for the constitutional amendments. However, support for the PF's position was much more pronounced at Kansanshi, where 403 people voted for and only 170 against the proposals. This was the clearest expression of a pattern that was visible throughout the town: areas with large numbers of mine employees and newly arrived jobseekers showed a strong tendency to support the ruling party. Solwezi, in other words, moved closer to the voting pattern on the fiercely contested Copperbelt, where the PF and the

UPND were about equal, even though many internal migrants left Solwezi on election day to vote in their hometowns.

After a long day of voting and an even longer night of counting, a young, female official at Kansanshi polling station revealed to me that she had come under intense pressure from PF agents when counting the ballot papers: 'I don't know about those in remote areas – the women – how they handle them [the PF agents]. They really pushed!'.[16] Hinting at the general neglect of the province by central government, she said she hoped the UPND would win, because, 'if the PF wins again, Northwestern will be a bush'. Ultimately, the incumbent PF candidate, Edgar Lungu, won the presidential election, but otherwise Solwezi District voted in UPND candidates across the board, with every Member of Parliament, every councillor and the mayor all voted in by opposition supporters.

Despite the rapid growth of its urban population, Northwestern Province still had the second-lowest number of registered voters among the country's ten provinces during the 2016 elections. However, Solwezi Central accounted for a fifth of all of Northwestern's registered voters (81,344) – a significant number from a national perspective. Hence, Solwezi is no longer a minor, peripheral town. It is an important urban centre that the political parties cannot ignore. The arrival of considerable foreign investment has not only attracted the attention of the central state and the ruling party but has also changed the agency of the council and its relationship to its constituencies. Constituencies have become more diverse and governance more challenging for the local authorities. In contrast to the rapid changes in population, by and large the Municipal Council continues to represent the original residents, while the administrative staff, as elsewhere in the country, tend to arrive from across the country.[17] In the final section, I will explore what this entails for the relationship between statehood and the extractive industries.

Conclusion

When Solwezi was founded as an administrative centre in the early 20th century, the town was deliberately established around ten kilometres south of the mine. Today, Solwezi town has grown to cover that distance, with new houses built right up to the electric fence to the mine's license area. But still, Solwezi town and the mine seem at first sight to be separate and disconnected entities. The mine's premises (the mining site, the Golf Estate, the housing complex Kabitaka) are gated and privately controlled enclaves in the urban landscape, with high fences and strict access controls. The physical 'disentanglement' (Appel 2012b) of the mine from the urban life around it, however, hides various kinds of real-life interdependencies between residents, the municipality and the mining company. Looking at changes in taxation, infrastructural power and political representation in three case studies, I have charted this triangular, interdependent relationship.

Throughout the twentieth century, the municipal administration could successfully ignore the mine, and the mine was indeed largely disconnected from urban life in terms of infrastructure, labour and capital (see Chapter 1). After the reopening of Kansanshi Mine in the early 2000s, this parallel-but-separated coexistence came to an end. The massive scale of the resulting foreign investment, the economic importance of the mine for the town's budget and not least its huge power to set its own agenda and implement its own plans with cavalier disregard for existing regulations have turned the mine into an important factor for urban governance. As the paradoxical result, the impact of the mining company on urban life has grown considerably just as the share of mine employees in the town's population decreased.

The Municipal Council attempts to provide effective urban governance in a situation of rapid change and with very limited means. Its attempts have always been hampered by its limited capacity, but they are made more difficult by direct and indirect effects of the mine's presence.

The first direct effect of the mine's presence is that it offers an easy way out of financial difficulties. The possibility to use the mine as a stopgap measure to mitigate structural deficits leads the council to neglect urban governance reforms that would, over the medium term, increase its capacity. The council practices a rent-seeking economy that relies on revenue from the mining companies and mirrors national development on the local scale. As a result, residents can avoid paying rates, feel less connected to and less obligated towards local authorities and have fewer reasons to hold them accountable for their actions. This, however, does not remain unchallenged. We have seen that there is a chasm between elected councillors and appointed officials with respect to their views on the use of income from the mine for municipal service provision. Trying to represent their constituents, however, councillors are often torn between short-term and long-term goals. They do not want to anger their voters and make life more difficult to them by increasing rates and taxes – a situation in which, once again, increasing the mine's rates is an easy way out that prevents structural change.

The second direct effect of the mine is that it severely limits the municipality's power to make and implement its own regulations. This aspect may be counter-intuitive after I stated the state's easy access to funds from the mine. This, however, is precisely what makes the relationship between the local state and the mine not only interdependent but also asymmetrically so. The mining company unilaterally alters the spatial set-up of the town by investing in specific infrastructural projects that serve its needs. It commandeers a planning authority legally reserved for the state. The pace and power of the mine's technocratic planning leave the Municipal Council with little option but to react and mitigate the consequences. This consumes a lot of its worktime even if it is not necessarily visible in the minutes or uttered as such in the council chamber. The mine's extractive infrastructural projects thus undermine the council's legitimacy while simultaneously adding to its tasks.

Further tasks linked to the mine's presence loom ahead: the fact that there is literally no space between the mine and the town along some parts of the electric fence guarding entry to the mine means that the risk of environmental damage through mining operations has increased considerably, for instance for villagers who farm downstream from the mine's tailings under which flows a tributary to

Solwezi River (Southern Africa Resource Watch 2020). These indirect effects, as well, increase local governance problems and have the potential to bind governing capacity in specific areas.

In some domains, the presence of the mining company has also indirectly weakened the municipality's capacity for urban governance. The mine's massive expansion and the parallel growth of the town have led to a competition over land between the local authorities and the mining company. This has not only created new conflicts between ordinary residents but also strengthened traditional authorities in relation to the municipality. Like elsewhere in Southern Africa, large investors' land needs have increased chiefs' leverage towards both the foreign investor and the local state.

Finally, at the political level, the presence of extractive investors and the ensuing in-migration have started to affect voting patterns and thus very soon likely political representation in a region that has traditionally supported the opposition. The demographic changes triggered by the mine's recruitment policies and the influx of jobseekers have given the ruling party an entry point into what has long been an opposition stronghold, as was demonstrated in the 2016 elections. If the trend continues, it is also likely to change the relations between Solwezi and the more rural regions of Northwestern Province.

Many of these effects on urban governance indeed conform to the notion of a 'resource curse', but in my eyes, that sweeping label is of limited use. By lumping together the effects of very different causes under one term, speaking of a 'resource curse' obscures the real-life paths on which the mining company's presence translates into weaker governance and obfuscates possibilities of change. Rather than an inevitable curse, I see a lack of synchronicity in the town's development and the expansion of the mine, coupled with the investors' capacity to produce relative order to ensure smooth extraction. The result of this uncoordinated situation is profound: governmental regulatory capacity declines in relation to the mine's, and probably in absolute terms, too. In other words, the local authorities' significance and range are indeed eroded due to the extractive industry. Calling this a 'curse', however, undermines the daily work in which many people try to cushion the impact of global extractivism on urban governance.

Speaking of a resource curse, especially when seeing it as inevitable, also neglects the conditions under which the 'curse' comes to be effective. Zug, one of the urban clusters of the Swiss commodity trading hub (see introduction, Chapters 1 and 6 and Conclusion) has the means and the choice to shift its municipal priorities and transform the town into a service-oriented polity. There are externalities such as the increase in rent, pressure on land and, according to some, a badly planned urban landscape (see Conclusion). In Solwezi, the externalities of the town's integration into the global economy are much more consequential and detrimental. Unless the country assumes a different position in the global economy, the council simply must deal with the foreign investor – under conditions shaped by structural adjustment reforms and increasingly by indebtedness.

The council also must deal with national politics, a factor that I have so far neglected. Many political forces intervene with an open discussion of urban planning between elected councillors and civil servants. For an opposition town like Solwezi, the main influence comes from 'political functionaries', as UPND-member Luckson Mulumbi expressed it in a conversation in August 2017. He was a long-time member of a local youth organization, Youth Alliance for Development (YAD), and had recently entered public politics. In 2017, he became the first chairperson (mayor) of the Council of Mushindamo District (after the election of a PF candidate was nullified by a court), the new district east of Solwezi District. In areas like this 'where it's 150% opposition', Mulumbi said, the institution of the district commissioner (and to a lesser extent of political appointees at the provincial level), an appointee of the president, becomes 'a tool, sometimes for suppression, sometimes for creating an environment and impression that these guys are not working; are not delivering'. Before elections, the situation can become 'a type of war'.

These are not promising signs for open, democratic processes at the municipal level (but it may change now that the opposition party UPND is in power since 2021). Besides residents, civil society organizations (for civil society activism in Solwezi, see Hobi 2019), unions and other regional, national and international actors, the council will however remain central in demanding the town's fair share from the extractive industry. Many facets of the political economy of a mining town, in particular issues of land and land rates, infrastructure, resettlement and compensation processes, are negotiated between elected councillors and appointed officials, who listen selectively to their constituencies, NGOs and central government or to powerful economic actors. Despite regular political interference (and more recently frequent defections to the governing party) and strong national, international and corporate forces, the council chamber must be seen as one key space where we might see a counterforce to resource extractivism.

In the difficult attempt to mitigate consequences of a situation they have not been responsible for creating, different local actors assume diverse positions. Above, I have examined some of the lines of conflicts within the council. As Spencer (1971, 174) wrote with regard to 'Aberton', an industrial town in the north of England in the 1960s:

> [T]he committee meeting emerges as a focal point in the decision-making process … While there is an explicit 'master–servant' relationship maintained between [council members and career officials] and any issue is finally decided solely by the council members, the latter depend on the officers for technical advice and guidance and the pressures towards certain decisions are by no means one-sided.

In Solwezi, civil servants generally work hard but are not well equipped to deal with the challenge; many of them simply do what they do best and what they learnt in previous postings at other local authorities in very different circumstances. 'Councils', Audrey Richards writes in her introduction to *Councils in Action* (1971), 'are governed by conventions and persist in time' (1). Indeed, when reading Solwezi's council minutes from the 1980s to today and attending full council meetings, I was struck by the continuity of the topics that were discussed in these meetings. The Municipal Council's extraordinary resistance to change might be read as an expression of local agency; more likely, it expresses the persistence of routines of governance even where the routines are ill-suited and the officials ill-equipped for the new task.[18]

Chapter 3

THE HOUSE

'Solwezi is unplanned!'

Edward Mwanza takes some building sand in his hand and scatters it on the ground. 'This is how people build here. They just put up something.' Mr Mwanza is the head of a small construction firm. He is worried about the quality of houses in Solwezi's low- and middle-income residential areas, called compounds. The density in the compounds has continuously increased over the past twenty years. Plot owners expand old homes, allow family members and recent arrivals to build their own house on the plot, put up cheap rental structures for miners and work seekers, and often sell parts of their plot to finance their own aspirations. Many, according to Mr Mwanza, build their houses too quickly and too cheaply.

With his company Shekina Engineering Zambia Limited, Mr Mwanza is one among many artisans who try to make a living from Solwezi's construction boom. He was a supervisor for a subcontractor of Kansanshi Mine until 2013, when workers demanded an increment and the firm instead finished their contracts. The name *Shekina*, glory in Hebrew, expresses hope and faith, as Mr. Mwanza explained to me: hope for a new beginning, for business success and for fair working conditions. Coming from the Copperbelt town of Kitwe, with family origins in the Eastern Province, he lives with his wife and their children in a rental house in Messenger Compound, an old area of town which grew and densified quickly in the past decade (Figure 12).

Shekina struggles to win public tender bids. Getting contracted by the mine is immensely difficult for a small, Zambian firm, and Mr. Mwanza and his colleagues put their hopes into the town council. Finding an entry point into public procurement has been a challenge, though: 'I want the council to give us even a small job, the job of constructing toilets at the market. We are pushing for that one. Each time when they advertise, they require a reference from the previous job. If you don't have it, you have problems.' The difficulty to win bids as a new bidder was confirmed to me by a council employee, giving ward councillors' pressure to perform as one reason: '[For a bidder], it is very crucial to work with politicians. Because when we try a new one, and it fails, then politicians say: why didn't you chose this one we know that he delivers, he is established.' While applying for bigger jobs, Shekina has mostly done piecemeal work. 'We earn just 1,000 or 2,000

Figure 12. Children resting and playing, Messenger, Solwezi, September 2025. Photo by author.

Kwacha [approx. US$10–20)] for one job. You know, people complain when it comes to building. Everyone will say: "No, me, I am suffering. Can you assist me?" So, we understand, and we do the job for little money' – and, what he did not say explicitly, as a result often work with poorer quality than they would prefer.

Comparing the construction method in residential compounds to the randomness of cast sand, Mr. Mwanza is in good company. Indeed, many people living in the compounds share his sentiment. As a characterization of the town, the words 'Solwezi is messy' come second only to 'Solwezi is dusty' (see introduction). Even those charged with planning and supervising the town's built environment agree. Having spent several months as an intern of the town council at the planning department, I became well familiar with the planners' frustration about Solwezi's urban environment and learnt of their own explanation for it: 'Residents misbehave!' According to civil servants, Solwezi residents build houses indiscriminately and below standard and prevent proper planning processes from happening by ignoring the fact that infrastructures like roads and water pipes need space and must be planned in advance. To them, residents are unruly and disrespectful of the municipality's role by passing over bureaucratic processes. At one point in a committee meeting I attended, the mayor became so frustrated that he shouted: 'These people are making our town dirty!'

Solwezi's messiness is one of the few points on which compound residents, civil servants and mine managers agree. To the white-collar employees of Kansanshi Mine, the town is variably an 'eyesore', a 'mess' and a 'shantytown'. One manager living on the gated Golf Estate freely admitted to me that he would not want to live in town: 'It's a dysfunctional town.' Another long-time manager told me: 'Sometime after we bought the mine [early in the 2000s], we offered the council to bring in an expat town planner; but they refused. See what has come of it. It's wasted!'

From a bird's perspective, for instance, on google satellite(-12.183059041367212, 26.404795833368595), one's eyes immediately focus on the mine, the largest infrastructural change in the past twenty years. Overshadowed by it, however, the spreading of new residential areas turns out to be as massive a change. Between 2001 and 2022, Solwezi's urban population has quintupled, from 70,000 to 322,623 inhabitants, and it has most likely grown ever since. Four out of five residents have recently arrived in town. Most of them are what the development jargon calls 'mining-affected', that is hit by displacement, soil erosion, receding ground water levels and air, water and noise pollution. They live in new and rapidly densifying compounds which spread into land held under customary tenure (see Figure 13 and previous chapter). People moving to Solwezi have been attracted by the economic hopes triggered by the redevelopment of the mine in the early 2000s, even if chances of finding formal employment at the mine or elsewhere are incredibly slim. Most people's chances to make a living do not lie in the formal economy, but rather in the precarious economic possibilities of everybody else who has moved to Solwezi during the past decades.

As a whole, the mine's influence on urban housing is small. As described in the previous chapter, apart from its own extraction-related investments, the corporate investor is hardly involved in urban development. Kansanshi Mine does

Figure 13. People walking home after a downpour, Urban Extension, Solwezi, January 2018. Photo by author.

not provide housing to ordinary workers but pays them a living-out allowance instead. Apart from some corporate social responsibility programmes, the company leaves the urban space and its governance to the municipality. In other words, extractivism *indirectly* shapes urban environments, in that it produces differentiations among places which has consequences for people's choices and chances.

The local state's influence on urban development is also much smaller than in urban centres in the Global North. Despite the administration's efforts to formalize urban planning, most planning and building activities happen without any official approval of land acquisition and building plans. Figure 14 depicts the stage of formalization of the town's roughly 30,000 plots in 2015. Approximately 80 per cent of all plot owners put up structures without holding a title deed to the land. To acquire land, be it from the council, from an individual or from the chief, requires funds and endurance, frequent follow-ups, and considerable reading and writing skills. Ordinary residents often hesitate to formalize land they have privately acquired. While formalization is legally obligatory and increases tenure security, its costs are high, and sanctions for non-formalization have been rare in the past. The town's land administration is both slow and strongly bureaucratic. Residents feel that regulations are opaque and randomly applied, and that even those who understand and comply with the regulations have no possibility to demand accountability from the administration. Furthermore, because of commercialization and preferential treatment of an elite, patches of formalized land routinely sit next to not-yet-formalized stretches of land, and tentacles of titled land reach far into customary land (see Chapter 2); the resulting patchwork, as well, makes people feel that it is perfectly normal to build on land one is not bureaucratically entitled to.

How then does such a town grow? Who builds it, who decides on its order – and what *is* its order? As I will show, the making of the urban is largely driven from 'below', by house owners and residents. A large portion of Solwezi residents continuously invest their hopes and aspirations and most available money in making a home and a house. Their main aim is to have a home, and they pursue this aim under two specific conditions that result in quick informal growth and cheap residential structures. First, most families face economic insecurity and a general unequal financialization (manifesting in a lack of access to affordable credits and mortgages[1]) which hinders them to follow through their building plans in one go and without alterations or concessions. Second, the local state has little capacity to regulate urban development through its institutions, despite civil servants' strong claims.

The perception of chaotic, uncontrolled growth and unplanned development at the town level sits at odds with the individual perspective focused on the plot and the house. Building a house indeed needs a lot of careful long-term planning and foresight and of economic and social investment. It is witness to the individual tenacity in sticking to a long-term decision and ordering one's priorities in relation to it. If Solwezi looks like an unplanned town, that look is the outcome of rather a lot of planning and investment.

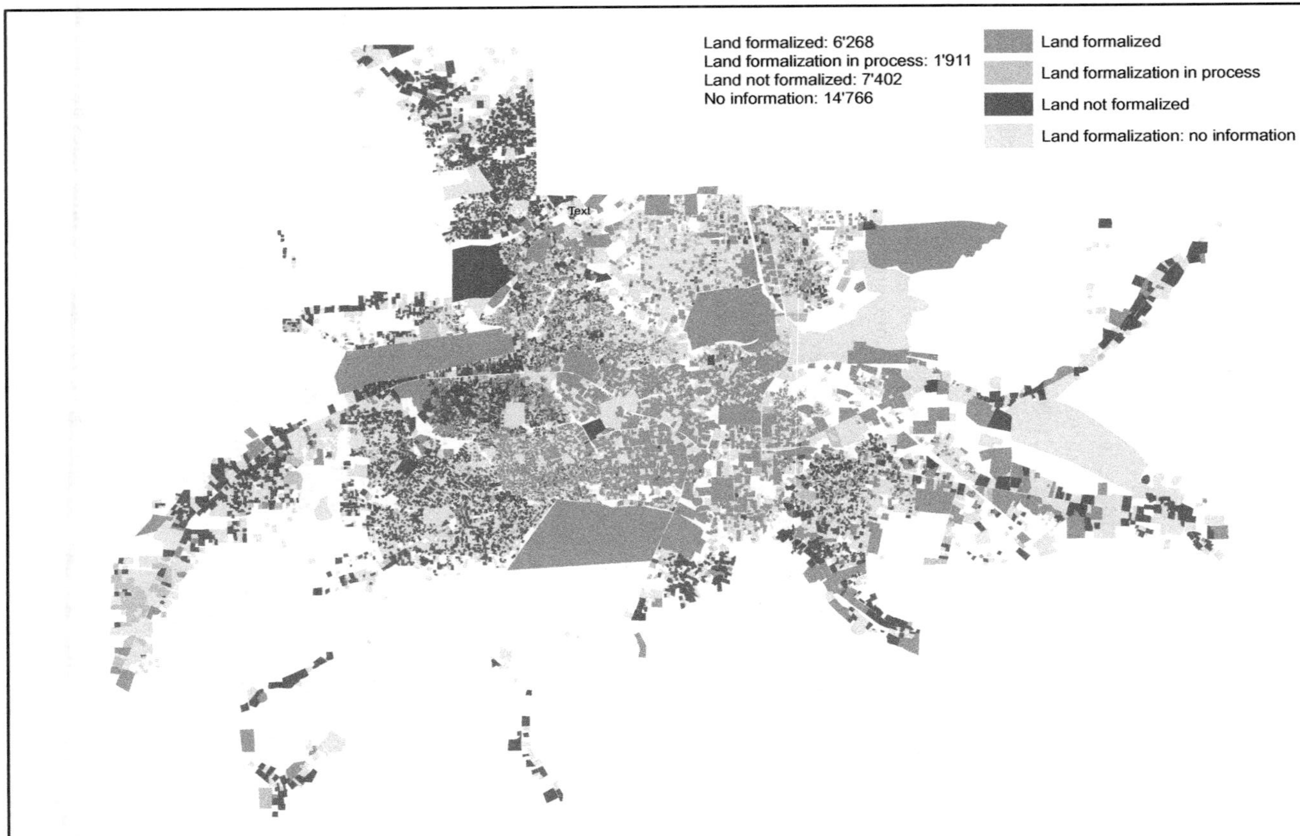

Figure 14. Stages of land formalization in Solwezi town, Northwestern Zambia. Map by author produced on the basis of data from the Solwezi Urban Baseline Study. (Preuss und Schmidt-Eisenlohr 2016).

As I will argue towards the end of this chapter, while mine managers see its outcome as a nuisance, the inhabitants' investment directly benefits the mining industry. By investing their labour-power into the construction of the urban, sometimes paid, often unpaid, Solwezi's urban communities perform *reproductive labour*. Feminist economists have long drawn attention to the necessity of reproductive labour for formal sector economic actors, but they have mostly cantered their analysis on the household as the main unit of consumption and reproduction. The making of Solwezi town makes us appreciate the *collective* and public dimension of reproductive labour, the often unpaid and certainly underpaid production of urban structures. Nina Banks (2020) has recently argued for the recognition of collective unpaid labour among Black women in the United States who engage in activities such as protesting injustice, securing resources and resisting marginalization for their communities. She criticizes mainstream – white – feminists for having ignored that dimension of work disproportionally performed by marginalized communities. Black neighbourhoods in the United States not only often lack sufficient access to public and private sector resources but are also at the receiving end of threats to their safety through environmental hazards and state-sanctioned violence. In the same vein, the household framework alone is insufficient to capturing the collective labour that goes into urban development in Solwezi. Against the absence of state support and the exposure to the externalities of the mining industry, residents' *communal* work absorbs shocks to a global extractive system resulting locally in casualization, unemployment and indebtedness, and offers a cushion for miners and their families to fall back on for housing, goods, services and care.

By exploring both the ordinariness and the specificity of Solwezi's urban development, this chapter is part of a vast scholarship on the urban experience analysed through the lens of post-colonial urban theory, which focuses on the diversity of urban experiences across the globe (De Boeck and Baloji 2016; Pieterse and Simone 2013; Robinson 2006). For the majority of urban residents in Africa, challenges such as limited state capacity and resources, poverty, lack of infrastructure and economic stagnation are a daily reality (e.g. Smith 2019).

From a Northern-normative perspective, African cities have been described as chaotic and breeding grounds for corruption, crime and violence (Davis 2006). What is interpreted as 'unplanned' urban development is seen as a problem and a failure, produced by either economic or political forces (Goodfellow 2013). Scholars working on informality and informal housing in the Global South have however shown that informality neither equates chaos nor that the lack of official planning means the *lack* of people actively shaping their environments and futures (Förster and Ammann 2018; Obrist, Arlt and Macamo 2013). Furthermore, housing can rarely be thought of as simply a plot and a house, but involves, especially in precarious housing contexts, the communities at large, as a relational space of home-creation (Ross 2010).[2] Finally, 'informal housing' in Solwezi must be specified, though, in relation to dominant academic discourses on informality (Förster and Ammann 2018). While Solwezi residents – and Zambians more generally – unequivocally expect service delivery from the state, unlike for instance in South Africa, residents in Solwezi do not look to the state for the provision of housing; there is currently no discourse of *the right to housing* as in post-apartheid South Africa, nor are 'land occupations' sanctioned as draconically as in South Africa (Levenson 2019).

It comes as a surprise that despite the extensive literature on urban growth and urbanity, surprisingly few studies have documented what building actually means to prospective house owners and what steps are involved in it. I do not think we can understand towns without carefully looking at the ways in which they are shaped by concrete building practices, and I hope the chapter has some documentary value in this regard.[3] I therefore describe who actually plans and builds the town by examining practices of house- and property-making – from plot safeguarding to the designing of a house, its construction and eventual occupation. Planning and building are everyday practices which everyone – state and non-state actors – routinely engages in. Owners, tenants, artisans, caretakers; in fact, each and every neighbour continuously makes and remakes the urban order. These practices involve materials I will describe – bricks, planks, soil, cement and the like – but they also involve materialities, that is the qualities objects and 'things-in-the-world' exhibit. Unlike the 'new materialism' scholarship, I do not understand these objects as agents. Rather, agency is the outcome of the dialectic between human and object (Barad 2007; Dant 2004). Accordingly, this chapter only to a certain extent relies on people's predicated reflections and instead prioritizes the description of their actions and skills. It is the result of months of observing, casual conversations, and walking and working along Solwezi's residents.

Analysing their concrete practices of making an urban order also helps us to overcome the dichotomy between 'planned' and 'unplanned' towns and to better understand what planning means when citizens themselves build their own towns. Imagination certainly plays an important role in building – but real people rarely entirely plan before they start building as the ideal of an architect's work suggests. Most work processes are more than just the translation of an abstract plan into material reality. In most human projects, the structure erected in one's imagination beforehand transforms when it meets a concrete reality. Every craftsperson knows this, just as everybody does who has ever built a garden shed or a bookshelf. Building, and working in general, consists of concrete actions that necessarily must engage with the material and social reality they interact with. Even if we know the circumstances well under which we hope to translate our plans into reality, there is still an element of the unexpected which we only learn about when implementing an action. A missing tool, a wrong move or a spontaneous smarter idea force or stimulate one to change one's plans.

Working thus becomes interactive and is never fully controllable beforehand (Spittler 2009, 164–5). Lucy Suchman has called this 'situated action' and saw it in a constant tension with acting according to a plan. Examining human-machine communication (1987) or reconfigurations (2007), she shows that we never just execute plans, we always get involved with objects, adjust to their effects. Working thus always takes into account its context. Plans are but one element in a situation, and while they do not completely determine actions, they influence their outcome (Suchman 2007).

Yet what exactly do we speak about when we say that an action 'follows a plan'? Is the person following a plan who meticulously conforms to the architect's vision in building, or the one who adapts the house's architecture to circumstances she meets on the way, so that she can reach her goal to build a family home that fits to her wishes and economic means? If, for example, the price of concrete rises during construction, two kinds of plans can come into conflict: (1) the plan of the building process as agreed upon between architect, builders, and owner and (2) the owner's plan to pay for the building within the means available to her. In the same vein, seeing a room for the first time in reality when walls have been put up may make one realize that a window conceived of in the plan actually seems too tiny. In that situation, does the person follow a plan who enlarges the window to form reality according to his vision, or the person who follows through with the building plan regardless?

In the view of town planners, following a plan means sticking to a script. Building regulations, zoning plans and the like thus privilege one sort of plan over the other. Their aim is to create a foreseeable exterior uniformity, adherence to common standards and a specific kind of administrative public order. Individual building plans work according to a different logic. They are less interested in foreseeable structures than in achieving aims that change over time; less in *following a plan* than in *carrying out one's plans*.

From different ways of planning follow different visions of what order is. The order and the plans of the town planner's vision finds its expression in clearly structured neighbourhoods, in repetitive and readily understandable patterns of plots and buildings, in conformity to regulations and in easily manageable infrastructure. The order and the plans of those who build may create a different kind of built environment, in which order and plans are carried out on the plot level and on a timeline rather than in the grid and the ahistoric order of town planning. This chapter is about how the interplay between these two sets of plans, when carried into action, forms Solwezi's built environment and, at the same time, structures its urban society.

Securing the land

Where does the process of building a house start? In the eyes of residents, many steps come before the ones I can describe in some detail here. The prospective house owner – usually, although by no means exclusively a man – must gain both independence and the right connections before he can earnestly tackle building a home. He has to emancipate from his parents to gain a seniority and a social status for which building a house makes sense and needs to earn and put aside enough money to buy a plot. At the same time, however, he has to acquire a social network that provides access to information, to mutual help and sometimes to informal credit. Successfully building a house thus is the outward proof of a social status that at the same time is its inner precondition. Acquiring this status lays the symbolic foundations of a house long before its concrete foundations can be built, but it remains outside of the scope of this chapter. In parallel to this status, ideas about houses develop – images of what an ideal house should look like, what type of house would fit one's own position and economic possibilities, and in what village or town and what neighbourhood one should strive to build.

Equally outside of the chapter remains land acquisition. Trying to buy a piece of land is in itself an adventure. In the absence of a land register and given the patchwork of different authorities over land, even identifying the legal owner can be tricky; contract negotiations can be drawn-out and often need trusted brokers; various documents can be drawn up to substantiate ownership in the absence of official registration.

I start when all this is done, and a person feels he or she legally owns a plot on which she or he can now build a house. Even then, tenure security is not an automatic given in Solwezi. If formalization is still pending (or never completed) and the self-understood owner does not hold a title deed, it is necessary to make one's claim to the land visible to others. If the plot's ownership has been formalized through the council and the Ministry of Lands, on the other hand, municipal law requires some kind of development to be visible within eighteen months after its acquisition. Either way, one's claim to the land needs to show if one does not want to risk squatters, opportunistic 'sellers' or investors to encroach on the land or take it over. Marking one's claim to the land becomes important also in the case of a land dispute in the local court. If the court decides in favour of another claimant's right to the land, there is at least the chance to receive some compensation for the already built structures. Some use this fact to make an income. As a civil servant told me: 'There is no land that is not owned by anyone. Because everyone thinks that the council comes and compensates.'

People employ several techniques to substantiate their claim on the land. In this phase, artisans like Mr. Mwanza are already involved, offering their services and expertise. The most straightforward way to make one's claim to the land is to immediately hire builders and start building. This however requires the owner to have the funds necessary to purchase building supplies, hire equipment and pay the workers, which is rarely the case. Many also wait for the building season, which is the rainy season between October and April, to begin with the construction of a house. Starting when the rains wet the construction site daily, also has the advantage that 'the foundation will be strong', as an elderly man explained to me. If the foundation is poured, it should however be done in the dry season for the footing not to sink due to wet soil.

One of the first steps in building a house simultaneously is a clear visual claim to a piece of land: making bricks. Only the most affluent residents can afford to purchase pure cement bricks, so called blocks, from a manufacturer or wholesaler. Most households instead use burned or sun-dried bricks that are typically produced on-site by young men (see Figure 15).[4] The ingredients and thus the quality of these bricks vary considerably. The cheapest and least labour-intensive building blocks are sun-dried bricks made from wet, clay-containing soil, sometimes mixed with

Figure 15. Bricks drying next to an anthill, Saviye, Solwezi, July 2016. Photo by author.

straw. They were and are still widely used in the more rural areas around Solwezi, for traditional houses, a chicken hut or a caretaker's house. On almost every plot, at least one house is still built in this way, even in the more urban areas. It is used as a storage room or for an elderly person preferring to live in the room climate typical for this type of house, less isolated from the elements and the outside air than newer building styles. A few houses still use the older style of plastered clay in between a wooden structure of poles and bars.

Burned, instead of sun-dried, bricks today are the preferred unit for building in Solwezi. To ordinary house owners, especially those living in the peri-urban areas still under customary tenure, using burned bricks means 'making it stronger'. They are still relatively cheap, but more durable than sun-dried bricks. Some builders add cement to the clay to increase the bricks' strength, but unlike the readily available clay, cement has to be bought and is too costly for many. Many instead use bricks entirely made with the fine and hard clay taken from the termite hills dotting the landscape in this part of the country.

Brickwork happens on the plot itself, if possible. To make building bricks, clay is wetted with water. The next morning, the brickmaker oils a steel mould with old engine oil and fills it with clay (see Figure 16). He presses the water out of the clay, pushes the somewhat solid lumps out of the mould from below and puts them on the ground to dry.

To bake the bricks, the brickmakers stack hundreds of raw ones into the structure of a *kibili* (*bibili*, pl.) – kiKaonde for kiln (see Figure 17). In the stack, several tunnels are left open for the fires used to burn the bricks – larger tunnels for wood fires, smaller ones for charcoal. Bibili are several meters wide and

Figure 16. Steel mould for brickmaking, Zangamele, Solwezi, April 2015. Photo by author.

Figure 17. Kibili, Kimasala, Solwezi, November 2015. Photo by author.

usually about two meters both deep and high. When all bricks are laid, the kibili is insulated with earth and mud and the fires are ignited. They burn for about twelve hours; if left burning too long, the bricks will turn dry and crumbling. If the bricks are left unburnt, the rain will dissolve the kiln and make the work futile.

Bibili simultaneously are buildings *in spe* and claims to the land they are built on. After firing, they are often left untouched until construction begins in earnest. If some bricks are missing from the structure, this opens the possibility for thieves to help themselves to ready-made bricks. It is not unusual for a kibili to stand on a plot for months and sometimes for years. The latter is usually an indication that the owner has miscalculated his financial means and postponed or temporarily abandoned his plan to build a house. If a kibili starts to overgrow with grass, this usually wastes the outer layer of bricks only and still leaves most bricks intact for construction.

Brickmaking and kilns are not the only material proof that a plot is taken and construction is underway. Heaps of sand or building stones which builders use for the foundation or the slab of a house can serve that purpose, as well. A ditch marking the contour of a future house or a proper foundation also clearly mark that the plot has been claimed by someone.

Whoever can afford to do so also marks his claim to the land through a barrier running along the boundaries of a plot, such as a hedge, shrubs, pegs, fences or walls. They serve to demarcate the plot and to enforce one's claims to it. AbdouMaliq Simone describes African cities as 'a context for making claims' (2010, 7). In fact, one *must* make claims in order to secure the key resource land. In theory, the municipality uses concrete beacons to demarcate formalized plots, but it does not sink them in a very systematic or timely manner, and people tend not to rely on them. Burning the grass and bushes in the cold and dry season (between June and August) is a first step to clear the land and to mark one's intention to develop it. Chopping down trees and putting them up as poles around the contour of the land is a stronger marker that already involves considerable labour. The poles can later be used for a wired fence, but they can also simply be used as a marker or a deterrent to the neighbour to not encroach onto one's land or, as people say, for people not to 'eat into one's plot'. This is particularly important in areas previously under customary tenure, or in neighbourhoods in the process of being integrated into the urban area and where there is still little municipal presence. Poles are sometimes replaced by pillars made from burned or cement bricks. These often serve as a first step towards a wall fence. Especially in better-off areas (and around planned businesses in the town centre), residents employ walling methods for a future or existing house or a housing complex.

Affluent plot owners sometimes resort to even stronger means to claim and mark boundaries. For instance, an employee of Kansanshi Mine was in the process of building an impressive house close to the mine fence in Mushitala West (a well-off area albeit not connected to municipal services). He planned to move in with his family, offering each of his four children a self-contained bedroom suite. When he started building, two boundary disputes emerged, and he had the council's surveyors come to define the plot's exact boundaries. To prevent further disputes, he decided to mark his western boundary by grading a road. The road now allows for a smooth ride to his house, but it also serves to delimit his property. He was determined to not let 'encroachers' enter his plot again.

One of the most efficient, but also costly ways to secure one's claim to the land is to engage a caretaker who guards the land, the tools and the building materials during day and night. Caretakers often live in a makeshift structure made from sun-dried bricks with a corrugated iron roof and a hole in the wall in lieu of a window. In the case of a well-off owner who grew up in Solwezi, a caretaker would be a relative. Employing the caretaker helps the owner to simultaneously fulfil his duties towards his larger family. In many cases, however, the owner is not from Solwezi and visits the town only intermittently to oversee the construction work. In this case, he employs a 'local' who knows the neighbourhood and depends on a small income or a house to get by. Mistrust is always an issue, and owners prefer to have a relative rather than what they see as a potentially corruptible, poor 'local' on their land.

Caretakers often do some menial work such as slashing grass and clearing the plot if it lies on previously uninhabited land, and they watch over the progress of the construction work. A caretaker and his family are not meant to live on the land permanently but oftentimes the start of the construction phase is postponed for months or years, and the caretaker becomes a long-term resident on the land. If the relationship between the owner and the caretaker proves to be good, the caretaker might remain on the plot with the completion of the house and transform into a guard. Caretakers sometimes also watch completed but vacant houses, but this is rare in a town short of housing.

The result of the described practices of claim-making are an urban landscape of structures at different stages which leave an impression of disorder also for residents. The markers look so different because planning processes drag on for several years during which structural and infrastructural conditions change; they display different logics, individual and time-delayed – and need constant attention, renovation and maintenance, so that structures under construction do not turn into ruins before long.

Planning the house

How do people plan their house, its size and design, the number of rooms and their arrangement? Even if all houses are one-storied and in most cases covered with a corrugated roof, it is easy to identify different types of houses when walking through Solwezi. Traditional forms built from sun-dried bricks are simple structures with an entrance and one or two rooms. This type does not go through an extensive phase of planning, nor the need of a separate layout. Its design is a sketch at most and is mostly generated in the process of construction.

The next, more elaborate type are structures of three to five rooms, with walls made of fired clay bricks and iron-sheeting roof on timber or steel beams. They generally include a porch and an entrance each at the front and the back. They undergo a more structured phase of planning before and during their construction, a process which is partly guided by standards and planning processes prescribed by the council. They involve building plans and therefore specialists.

The third type consists of buildings or complexes planned by private architects for large commercial customers, such as a mining company. Some of them (office buildings, shops, or warehouses, for example) are designed in relation to a particular site, others (mostly housing for workers, as in Kabitaka or the new mining towns further west) build on ready-made blueprints only minimally adapted to local realities.

A family plot often hosts multiple types of buildings: a sun-dried mud-brick house, a brick-lined burnt-brick house and a plastered, spacious cement-brick house all belonging to one family. This variety is witness to the periods of building and to the fact that a family continuously invests over the course of many years. Today, even if new houses of the first variety still exist, most houses are of the second type: mid-sized and based on a layout plan drawn up by an architect.

This is a relatively recent trend in Solwezi. Mr. Mwanza, the artisan and director of Shekina, is a keen observer of building styles and techniques, and he often took me for strolls through the town to show me different types of building. His reflections helped me to acquire an understanding of how societal expectations and individual aspirations relate to one another. Unsurprisingly, perhaps, building practices have changed in Solwezi since the redevelopment of Kansanshi Mine and the resultant rapid increase in urban population.

In Mushitala East, for instance, a compound relatively close to the mine fence and under customary tenure until recently, the majority of plots are occupied by new residents coming from the Copperbelt towns. Newcomers in Solwezi brought their ideas of a good house with them. Mr. Mwanza, originally from Kitwe himself, told me: 'In the Copperbelt towns, people build modern houses because of the mine, they build with cement, already since a hundred years. But here in Solwezi, the building style is changing only slowly.' The building style *has* changed, though, and 'local' residents have started to build bigger. 'Initially, locals were scared to build bigger because of witchcraft. But when they saw that nothing happened to those who moved here and built a bigger house, they also started to build bigger houses.' Mr. Mwanza offered a classic modernization and industrialization argument to explain architectural change in a community: from farmer to urbanite (and maybe employee), from traditional believer to churchgoer, from customary to town land (Fay 2011). Taking Solwezi's urban development over the past 120 years into account (see introduction), his perspective is probably too linear, shaped by his own recent arrival in town, his modernist self-image and his scant knowledge about Solwezi's long history as a regional urban centre. Nevertheless, it points to the fact that Solwezi's urban environment today is socially a relatively free place to build in accordance with one's budget and vision.

During my research, I mostly followed the planning and building of mid-sized houses, the dominant house type in Solwezi. As part of the planning process (future) house owners consult architects, but their ideas of a good house are not fully transformed by the specialists' advice or vision. Architects' inputs are mainly accepted when they fit the owner's idea. Looking at negotiations between owner and architect is thus an opportunity to understand different – often clashing – ideas about a good house.

Fleming Kakoma, with whom the reader is acquainted since the introduction, and his wife Mary, a marketeer, were planning to build a larger house on their plot in Saviye, a compound recently integrated into the urban area. When we studied the floor plans together – dog-eared and damaged by water and use – I realized that, while they clearly embodied a concrete building plan, that plan itself represented an aspiration or an 'anticipatory infrastructure' (Nielsen 2011, 398) which the Kakoma family may have to downscale at some stage. The house in which they currently live with their youngest son and several relatives is much smaller. While the plot's size is considerable and includes access to a small river, it is not yet connected to the electric power grid, and the water tap is outside the house. Like so many, Mr. Kakoma, albeit retired from teaching, continues working for an income. His wife used to work at the market, buying from farmers and selling their produce, but competition grew too fierce and profits too low to sensibly continue the work. The family's savings are stored in houses and land. Combining farming on their field outside Solwezi, some gardening on their urban plot and his casual employment at the mine's CSR Department, they work hard to keep their living standard and their social position. Mr. Kakoma could easily lose his work if copper prices fall. This would directly jeopardize their building plans. Floor plans are therefore provisional and subject to change: a vision for a life one is working towards but may be forced to abandon anytime.

Below are the two floor plans which he had an architect draw (see Figure 18). Mr. Kakoma was not content with the first one and had it redrawn. He complained to me that the architect at first simply drew something without considering his wishes. The second plan took up his ideas, but he was not entirely convinced either. In any case, the family had not started building at the time of writing, and they may well ask for another design or hire a different architect.

Listening to Mr. Kakoma's explanation of what he liked and disliked gave me an insight into the owner's perspective. Both versions are layouts for a generous house with a front entry, which would not be used frequently, and a back entrance, which directly leads into the kitchen and offers some shade during the hot hours of the day. This space is where most of the social activity both inside and outside will take place. The food will be cooked outside on a small charcoal brazier. The first version is much simpler: service pipes are limited to one front, and bedrooms are mostly without en-suite baths. The second floor plan has more and smaller bedrooms, two of which somewhat oddly attached to the building, and the house is larger. One distinct difference is also the shrunk corridor space to move between the rooms. Mr. Kakoma did not like the large open corridor area in the first version which, according to him, was a waste of space. In the second version, this aspect is reduced to a narrow, functional corridor.

Indeed, the first version resembles a standard, council-approved plan which the architect altered little and, in most parts, reproduced, probably hoping to please his client and make some quick money. The Kakoma family clearly deemed it too

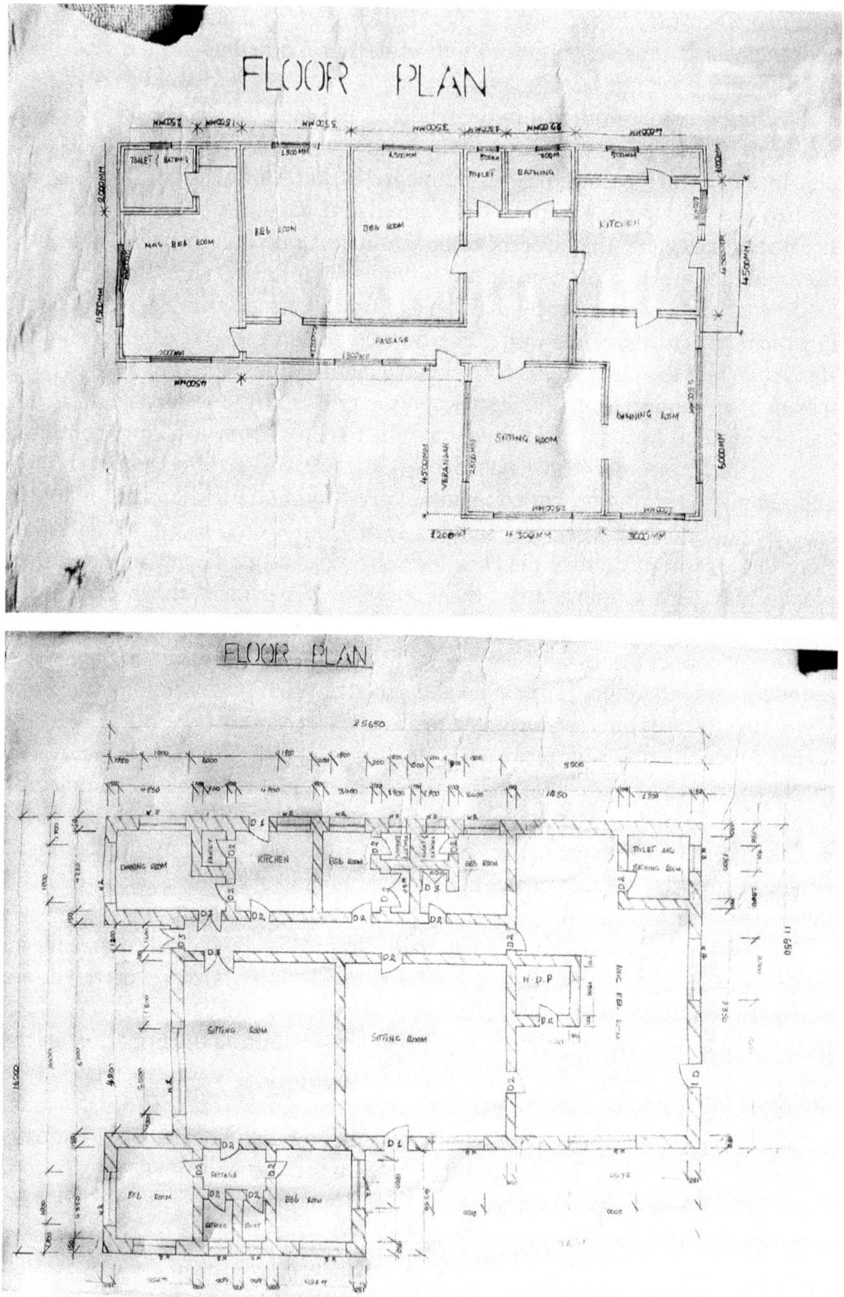

Figure 18. Floor plans made for Fleming Kakoma, (a) first and (b) second version, 2017. Photos by author.

simple and incapable of housing the larger family, hence the increase in size and rooms in the second version. Building the house according to the second version will however be much costlier given the necessary increase in walls, toilets and water pipes.

Mr. Kakoma's architect gives an incomplete impression of the profession's variety of perspective on housing designs. He apparently was a private architect, but his work rather looked like it was penned by a council architect. Council architects' main task is not to understand a client's wishes and fulfil them in an independent house design, but to apply municipal standards. A council architect only gets involved once – to keep with the example – the Kakoma family decides to build. They will have to have all floor plans approved by him, a process that includes extensive documentation and requires a long breath.[5] I got to know the first and at the time only council architect – a certified architect – in Solwezi, Mr. Bwalya (name changed) because we happened to live next door to each other. Before him, clerks with little training in architecture performed the task of scrutinizing and approving building applications.

Mr. Bwalya provides prospective house owners with council-approved standard building plans (including block plan, floor plan, foundation plan, details on elevations and construction, and roof plan), which they can adapt to their needs, wishes and budget and have then certified by him, making sure that the plans conform to the council's standard. He would, for instance, guide someone who budgeted for a so-called low-cost house by ensuring that the rooms necessitating water pipes (kitchen, toilet and bathroom) are situated along one side of the house. He was also in charge of making sure that planned houses correlated with a compound's official classification into low-, middle- or high-cost housing areas.

For some months, Mr Bwalya gave Mr Nkhata (name changed), his subtenant at the time, plans to work on for clients whom he recruited privately while on duty at the council. Mr Nkhata did the background work and passed them on to Mr Bwalya, who then authorized the plans through the official channels.

Mr Bwalya was content with the income his position at the council generated and did not feel undervalued: he saw his task to make sure that the basic municipal standards were followed. By contrast, his colleague Mr Nkhata soon grew bored of what he experienced as uncreative and uninspiring work. Rather, he wanted to experiment with two-story houses or with challenging rectangular forms to get more privacy in rooms. He wanted to draw individual, distinct houses rather than standardize them into the same logic. Often when he caught me on the small veranda at the back of our semi-detached houses, he showed me his extravagant and thoughtful building plans on his laptop. Although he liked the fact that the majority of houses in Solwezi was built sustainably with burned bricks, he was not impressed by what he saw as Solwezi residents' reluctance to diverge from standard plans. He was keen to get a job with a private firm and in the capital Lusaka. Indeed, he soon left Solwezi for a job offer from the cement producer Lafarge's office in Lusaka.

Working for the private sector can be attractive for architects like Mr. Nkhata, but it can also be disappointing and restricting. Ms. Phiri and Mr. Banda (names changed) are two young architects with a bachelor's degree from the University of Pretoria and the University of the Copperbelt, respectively. They worked for a large firm where they executed the planning and building of an entire suburb under the lead of white expatriates. Housing styles varied minimally, and the company was primarily interested in keeping costs low and mass-produce houses in a design that was socially barely acceptable.

In a relaxed moment during one of their tours on building sites, we spoke about their visions and ideas. For Ms. Phiri, thinking 'out of the box' is the prime goal. 'Most houses in Zambia are built as a box; four walls and contained.' While she understands budgetary constraints, if she was in the position to independently design houses, she would speak to the future house owner first, find out what she likes to do in the house, explore her routines and then experiment with the 'permeability' within and out of the house to break open 'the box'. She would also ask her for her colour preferences and discuss the possibility of high ceilings.

Mr. Banda, as well, expressed passionate ideas of possible designs, which for him included the consideration of 'culture'.

> I would build a house very differently. [The way our employer asks us to draw] is not the traditional Zambian way of building houses. Intimacy is a problem in these houses. Sometimes, the married person and the in-laws should not meet. It is awkward. The mother-in-law may not want to leave the kitchen to get to the master bedroom because the son sits in the dining room or lounge. So she will hesitate to go to the toilet or to her room, you see?

He draws me a residential house without a corridor to illustrate his point. 'Instead', he continued, 'I would have a passage where one can move freely without anyone seeing you. I would even have a kitchen in the open: it is just the way people here are used to cooking. It will not replace the inside kitchen.' In terms of a 'cultural corridor', Mr. Banda's ideas reverberate a lot with Mr. Kakoma's wishes as outlined above; they diverge however with Ms. Phiri's in terms of room structure. Mr. Kakoma thinks from the number of family members their house will have to accommodate, visitors or permanent; Ms. Phiri thinks from the daily routines of a household head.

These junior private architects are open to innovations that draw on both so-called traditional and modern ways of building and imagining family life in a house. Instead, they have to deal with large employers restricted in budget and local sensitivities, and individual clients confined by funds, imagination and the pressure to house many relatives.

Both council and private architects base their ideal on an environment that does not exist for (future) house owners: The council architect works on the assumption that there is an existing, organically grown townscape within which to fit a new building plan; private architects would like to plan a project for clients who can draw from the full and finance the project in advance. None of the two relates to owners' reality. Planning (and building) their house over the course of many years, Solwezi's house owners must deal with constantly changing conditions, from their household's finances to larger economic conditions, their neighbours' projects, and municipal regulations, and thereby adjust their plans accordingly. Certainly, even the most planned house like modernist tract houses built in US suburb in the post-war years are never the complete implementation of a pre-made plan, as Lane (2006) describes it: 'The builders of this era responded to the desires and preferences of the buyers, at the same time as they, the builders, helped to shape those preferences' (2006: 3). Nevertheless, adaptations are usually not considered in scholarly ideas of planning, which assume that conditions within which a plan is realized remain the same. In many contexts, it is quite to the contrary: realizing a project means its constant adaptation to changing conditions. The plan is not the implementation of an abstract idea, but the imagination of a *social* house under specific and constantly changing conditions.

We will see that the expansion of a definition of 'situated action' by temporality and sociality will also be necessary to understand the next stage of making a home: building the house.

Building the house

How are houses actually built, which standard and materials are applied, how durable are they and what does the construction of a house tell us about Solwezi town? To answer these questions, I start with a description of one day with five Shekina artisans at work in the compound Mushitala East in April 2015.

The rainy season ended many weeks ago and the nights have become colder, but the days still heated up quickly. The artisans preferred to start working in the early morning hours. When I joined them, they were busy at work mixing concrete for the lintels above the doors and windows. Two artisans hauled building sand and fine white-pinkish gravel from two large piles into the half-finished and still roofless house. On the house floor-to-be, still an area of stamped soil, they mixed it into a small heap with a crater in the middle. They added cement, thoroughly mixed the dry parts with their shovels and finally added water. The water, collected from a communal well by a third worker, was added in the newly established crater, and the mixture of stones, sand and cement was carefully shovelled from the rims to the now wet centre. They worked in sync and without many words spent on the work itself. Once the heap had been thoroughly mixed and has the right texture, the concrete was shovelled into the wheelbarrow.

Earlier, the artisans had built up the brick walls to the upper limit of the lintels, leaving spaces for them above both doors and windows. While three workers were now busy with the concrete, the other two set up the moulds. They used wooden planks to contain the rather fluid concrete. Along either side of an opening, they nailed planks into place which in turn carry a plank adjusted to the width of the opening so that it reached across, the lower side of the mould. As a next step, on each side of the mould, they tied planks to the wall with the help of a fine wire to produce enough tension between the two sides. If necessary, the planks were stabilized with a couple of nails. Since the entire mould risks falling to one side

Figure 19. Late Shekina worker Lewis Mumba pouring the lintel, Mushitala, Solwezi, April 2015. Photo by author.

of the wall, a vertical plank was often added as stabilizer, wired to other planks and fixed to the brick wall with nails. Into this mould, an empty plastic cement or mealie meal bag was laid to later prevent the concrete from dripping through gaps between the planks.

Once the moulds were in place, things ran parallel: two men continued to produce fresh concrete and loaded it into the wheelbarrow, while one of them shovelled concrete from the wheelbarrow into a plastic bucket and handed it over to the person pouring it into the mould with the help of a spattle (see Figure 19). Two others started building a makeshift scaffold from piled bricks and a horizontal plank where the next lintels would be poured. For the scaffold, they used damaged bricks lying around in the rooms. One worker collected them and threw them confidently to his colleague who equally casually caught them and built up two pillars from them (see Figure 20). The pouring of the lintels took quite some time. As the concrete was not completely liquid, the worker used a spattle to poke into the mass, eliminating bubbles or empty corners and spread it evenly. Now and then, the wooden construction shifted under the concrete's weight, and he added a nail or two. He also used the hammer to put the mould back into place when it shifted too far to one side. When a lintel was almost finished, he took a steel beam, let it sink into the concrete and added another layer of concrete on top.

There were always breaks for the workers, except for the person pouring the lintel, who was busy throughout. The others watched him, leaning on the end of their shovel or the walls, making jokes or sharing a story. When all lintels were set, they slowly started to wrap up, cleaned the wheelbarrow and the shovels.

Figure 20. Shekina founder Edward Mwanza at the construction site in Mushitala, Solwezi, April 2015. Photo by author.

They changed from their working clothes and hard shoes back into their neat knockabout clothes and smart shoes. A couple of them kept their blue trousers and hard shoes on, something of a fashion item in urban Zambia even for people who do not do heavy work. On their next day at the construction site in roughly a week, the builders added three further layers of bricks which were then the carrier layer for the roof. In the layer just above the lintels, they added ventilation slots. Until then, they hoped for some rain helping the concrete to dry slowly and not to crack.

Before they left, they had a chat with their customer, the female head of the Lungu household. Her husband worked as a cleaner for one of the mine's subcontractors. The family lived in a modest house built from dried bricks on the same plot. They had their plot subdivided and sold a part of it to a friend in order to afford the building of the house now under construction. Shekina had started building the house for their new neighbour, planned as an interlaced house with a fancy-shaped master bedroom and ensuite bath, but at the time still unfinished. The Lungu family appreciated Shekina's work and asked them to build their new house, too. The house was built in a standard design with floor plans from the council. There are neither water pipes nor a sewerage system in this compound, but the family had installed two water tanks, and the new main house will have an inside toilet.

Mr. Lungu's job was not permanent, and it certainly did not give the family the necessary cash to finance a house in one go.[6] They had it built piece by piece, and they contracted Shekina whenever some funds are available for sand, cement, bricks, window frames or the roof. Shekina brought the tools; the owner organized and paid for the material.

As a result of this piece-by-piece approach and the owners' limited budgets, Shekina and other artisans constantly build below what they see as their standards. They do so because they understand the owner's financial situation, but also because they prefer to have at least a small job than none. On the construction site, the artisans reduced building costs on many fronts. The foundation was not sunk into the ground and secured with large stones, but established directly onto the ground, which jeopardizes the stability of the entire structure. Unlike in the Copperbelt towns where copper is mined underground, blasting in the open-pit Kansanshi Mine does not as heavily affect the substance of the buildings. Nevertheless, many communities, especially those living close to the pits, complain about cracks in the walls and even collapses of entire houses. The floor slab could be much more solid, too. For this house, the builders condensed the existing soil and only used burnt bricks as a foundation to the outer and inner walls. Reducing the number of bricks and stones necessary for the slab in this manner is called 'the Chinese way' since, the story goes, builders in the Copperbelt towns learnt it from Chinese construction companies. It is cheaper because of its spare use of costly material, and it is quicker, too. On top of the pressed soil, Shekina added a thin layer of concrete as a finish. For both the foundation and the concrete, they used second-quality stones. The artisans used burnt mud bricks produced by young men they did not know and cheaply bought by the customers; Mr. Mwanza was not impressed by their quality. Cheaply built walls typically have a lot of mortar between the bricks. Concrete, too, is mixed with as little cement as possible and thus contains a high percentage of sand. The owner also chose to have the roof directly bound onto the walls, thereby avoiding the costs of an additional wooden structure. Mr. Mwanza was rather worried about this decision. The wind can be strong in this area, as there were not many trees left to break it. Finally, for the wooden moulds to pour the lintels, they used unhandy rough planks, crooked, half-round and still covered with bark on one side.

Not only did Shekina adjust to the owner's limited and erratic budget, they also made up for their equipment, which is poor in comparison to the tools they had as subcontractors. Three of the five men wore blue overalls with their previous employer's logo printed on the back. Workers are often allowed to keep the overalls after retrenchment, and some wear them until they fall apart. (Several months later, Shekina proudly presented to me their new overalls with their own logo printed on the back.) Given the lack of piped water in this area, one of them fetched water from the well. Instead of using a concrete mixer, they strenuously mixed it on the ground using shovels only. To prevent the concrete from seeping through the moulds, they sealed them by recycling the cement bags. Their scaffolding was made on the spot with a precarious construction of bricks and a plank. Their only conventional tools were two shovels, one wheelbarrow, two plastic buckets, one hammer and a spattle. Instead of wetting the slowly drying concrete, which would have involved additional labour, they hoped for the rains which in April are not reliable anymore. Finally, they worked for low compensation of their labour, counting that one job would lead to another, better-paid job.

The artisans constantly balance their ideal with the realities of the budget and creatively use things and their own bodies to make up for the gap between the two. Importantly, they can code-switch between different qualities of building, on the one extreme what they consider their own, high standards, on the other end what they feel socially compelled to and financially forced to do due to their customers' low budget. Casualization of work pushed by the mining company, environmental changes due to global climate change (most of all drought), the redevelopment and massive expansion of Kansanshi Mine in the past fifteen years, a small and non-competitive producing sector in Zambia (window frames, for instance, are mostly imported from South Africa), a decentralized but highly hierarchical, bureaucratic, untransparent and selective local state (see Chapter 2) all shape and hamper artisans' everyday work of building the town. As a result, artisans like Mr. Mwanza and his team must cut corners on all fronts. This not only leaves them and many others dissatisfied, but it also has consequences for Solwezi's townscape. The town's structures are less durable than they could be. Many start to crumble soon after their construction and need constant attention, maintenance and investment. Builders cannot adhere to municipal standards; and in some areas, the mine's daily blasts undermine their efforts further.

In Solwezi, a house is rarely ever completed, neither from the builders' perspective nor from the owners' (Nielsen 2011). Some of the incompleteness is obvious to the eye; often, people move in as soon as the roof is installed, filling the windows with bricks while they wait for the money to pay for frames and glass. People start extending the house as soon as it has reached its initial size; they add a chicken house, a room for a tenant, a food stall along the road or, if they can afford it, a water pipe or electric wiring. Inside the house, equally, things are constantly shifted around, displayed and reorganized in different ways: a cupboard, a sofa, a carpet, a ceiling or a lamp are added – whenever one can afford a new acquisition – and new family members require adaptations of the bedrooms.

Conclusion

Having lived in Solwezi town for two years, accompanied residents' building projects and conducted research on the building industry and at the municipality's planning department, I have come to understand that Solwezi residents' lack of official paperwork and resistance to go through formal processes for their building projects do not result in random and anarchical building practices and forms. Certainly, the town's expansion clearly does not happen in a centrally coordinated manner, suburb by suburb, and compounds do not exhibit any single distinct building style (except for the more historical ones that were centrally planned and built).[7] Instead, one can find several built structures in various stages of completion or decay on almost every plot. Different realities are situated next to each other. From a planner's perspective, the town looks thoroughly disorderly. Yet, there is order. This order is not easily recognizable from outside, and it took me quite a while to successfully 'read' the town and its built environment.

To see this order, one needs to leave the bird's eye view of urban development behind and adopt the residents' perspective. They focus on the plot and the house. Unlike in a suburb of a Western city, compounds in Solwezi do not prescribe a specific building style. The owner herself is quite free to choose the shape and size of the structure, and she will adjust it to changing circumstances over the years. Taking up this freedom is the first step of considerable labour that goes into planning and building a house: it needs the owner's imagination to picture a house in a slot encircled either by fields if at the town's fringes or by an already built-up environment with a variety of building styles. A number of steps follow from here: the plot needs to be secured in a context where multiple claimed ownership is the rule rather than the exception. The techniques of marking one's claim to the land which I described above – a kiln, a fence, an access road, a foundation, a ditch or a caretaker's hut – are themselves a material investment in a place, a family home, a future in this town.

Even if plot walls crumble quickly and ditches overgrow sooner than the construction of the house begins, reading such structures as unfinished and ruined would be misleading. Every structure is the result of labour and an investment anchoring a family in a place that is formed and transformed by their actions; recognizing that labour as local knowledge as well as productive practice is important to understand contemporary urban Africa (Simone 2004). Equally, the success of planning the house must not be judged by the dissimilarities between the initial floor plan and the actual house, but rather is a family's skilled and continuous adaptation to a changing environment. A finished house is proof that the owner's family has shown tenacity in sticking to their long-term decision of making a home and has continuously ordered their priorities in relation to it. Because of a general lack of affordable mortgages, building a house needs a lot of long-term planning and of both economic and social investment. A house which looks half-finished to the council architect is not the dream house for the owner either; but the owner knows that this is the best she can do under the prevailing circumstances. She may have had to lower her sight for the time being – because her husband was retrenched from his employment with the mine, or because costs for cement have risen as the Kwacha depreciated in a global economic crisis, but at least she is able to offer a roof to sleep under to her family. In sum, any kind of structure points us to the fact that people are *carrying out* their plan of a social house rather than *sticking to* a plan of a preconceived house.

Such a preconceived house is not only materialized through the availability of cash, materials and labour, but also by a family's tastes and liking borne out of their aspirations. Homeowners are oriented towards the future, the prospect of housing one's family, inheriting solid structures to the children; they are aspirational and creative in the sense that they can deal with the multiple challenges that come with building a house in rapidly changing neighbourhoods. Most are however not breaking out of a general practice of how to build. The material base to do so just does not exist. Residents are not held back by 'culture' or 'tradition', at least not in the urban compounds, but simply must make pragmatic consumption choices. In contrast, junior architects are in their heads in a dialogue with cosmopolitan ideals and they aspire to actively produce the future (their 'orientation' can be compared to actors in the fashion industry, see for instance the work of Balogun (2020) on Nigeria's beauty pageants). In Solwezi and elsewhere in the country, with the exception of some suburbs in Lusaka, they rarely find customers who can afford them.

Every action – laying bricks, grading an access road, negotiating with the architect, sinking a pole – is an action working towards a built order. The built order is the manifestation of thousands of new residents making Solwezi their home by everyday investments in urban life. These investments anchor newcomers not only physically but also socially; the formation of society through the integration of individuals into societal structures (*Vergesellschaftung*) – an aspect I can only hint at here, for instance, with the evolving relationship between the caretaker and the owner. For each stage towards a house – from getting a plot to securing, planning and building a house – one relies on a great number of persons, most of whom do not act in an official role. Relationships are forged between owners, tenants, artisans and neighbours, architects and clients, and many others. In other words, parallel to the steady infrastructural transformation of Solwezi town emerges a social context that is embedded in the physical environment. The making of the urban built environment is a vital part of the town's process of *Vergesellschaftung*.

This brings me back to the view of Solwezi expressed by the mine's expatriate employees – an 'eyesore', a 'mess'; a 'dysfunctional' 'shantytown' in need of proper planning; a 'wasted' space. Seen from the aspirations of the town's inhabitants and the continuous effort they put into building up the town, the combined racism and classism of such statements becomes obvious. More importantly, the view of Solwezi as a dysfunctional mess obscures two important structural points about the making of a town under the unequal conditions of global extractivism.

First, in some instances, the mining company is directly responsible for the messiness of town planning processes. As I have shown in the previous chapter, Kansanshi Mine has the power to substantially change the conditions of residents' practices and frequently does so for its own benefit. Expanding the mining area results in the displacement of communities, building a new access road changes structures of urban growth, and the ability of the mine to set planning priorities (by, for example, achieving a tax waiver in exchange for newly grading a main road deteriorated by its own trucks) limits the local administration's capacity for town planning.

Secondly, and more importantly, Solwezi's urban development and the labour residents put into it are not simply a background to mineral extraction, let alone the nuisance as which the company would like to portray it. Instead, residents' everyday labour put into the construction and running of the town is key to the company's wealth creation or, in more theory-driven words, the result of Solwezi's *articulation* with the extractive industries' northern centres.

Fifty years back, Harold Wolpe (1972) has shown how mining companies in South Africa's apartheid era benefitted – in fact, relied upon – the subsistence economy in South Africa's enforced 'homelands'. To complement men's low wages, homeland households pursued care work and absorbed the externalities of the industrial world, such as illness, early retirement and unemployment (for West Africa, see Meillassoux 1992; for South Africa today, see Benya 2015). This analysis still holds true today. The reproductive work for industrial labour is still borne by families living from subsistence-oriented agriculture or the 'informal sector'. Without these inputs, the mine would have no labour to rely on.

Nor would it have a society to exist in. Complementing the earlier household-based studies, recent feminist scholarship has drawn our attention to the *community* as a site of collective unpaid work (Banks 2020). In her work on women in Marikana, a platinum mining location in the Northwest Province of South Africa, Asanda Benya shows that, first, social reproduction is not external to production and must thus be analysed as 'a symbiotic relationship between the productive and reproductive spheres' (2015, 546), and that, second, households are not entities isolated from the larger urban society (2015, 556–7). In this chapter, I showed how Solwezi residents build the urban and thus a social space for wage labourers to fall back to, for goods, services and care. These structures cushion the effects of ruptures to the globalized mining industry such as casualization, unemployment and indebtedness (Federici 2012; Musonda 2021a). Finally, banks, retail shops and shopping malls would not have opened a branch in Solwezi for miners alone; Solwezi is attractive as a mid-sized town. The mining company relies on these services as much as residents do.

In sum, residents' energy put into urban development must not be viewed as simply 'construction work'. In building homes, Solwezi residents simultaneously build a town and a society on which the mine functionally relies, but from which it simultaneously tries to isolate itself. This will be the theme of the next chapter.

Chapter 4

THE GOLF ESTATE

Chatter at the Golf Estate Club

It is 5.00 pm on a weekday and I am sitting at the Club House on Kansanshi's Golf Estate, the gated area that houses the mine's managers and expatriate employees (about 3 per cent of Kansanshi's direct workforce) and their families.[1] Golf Estate residents make a community of about two hundred persons, including children. With a few exceptions, all of them are white. The Golf Estate is a residential and recreational space for individuals and families and has a preparatory school on-site. Situated between Solwezi *boma* and Kansanshi Mine, it is surrounded by urban residential compounds. Sitting on the terrace of the club house, I see mothers who chat with one another while they watch their children play on the green lawn. The boys have short, sandy hair. A girl wears a pink shirt proclaiming her a 'plaasmeisie' (farm girl in Afrikaans). The main language spoken around me is Afrikaans, and I have the sudden sensation to be back in South Africa, where I lived for two years.[2] As the sun sets, antelopes wake up and walk across the golf course, carefully avoiding golf-playing residents and their guests.

'A new face!', Ms. Maree (name changed) screamed excitedly when she saw me, and immediately started talking to me. She had been here for four years. Transitioning from Johannesburg in South Africa to Solwezi was hard for her. She and her husband have been married for twelve years, but he lived as 'an expat' since their wedding day, working in Rwanda and DRC. Only in Solwezi did they start to permanently live with one another. Co-parenting was a challenge at first, Ms. Maree admitted. However, she smiled happily, coming here had been the best choice she had ever made for their children. 'If people who have been here for one year only complain, I tell them that there is nothing to complain about. You have everything. Here you live on a Golf Estate with animals on it. It is comfortable.'

Ms. Maree's residency was attached to her husband's work permit. She has a degree, but she was not allowed to work. This happened to most spouses, she told me; a dentist, also an accompanying wife, had her application for a work permit declined. 'This is absurd! We could really need a dentist here.'

We were joined by her friends. One of them had been living on the estate for ten years and was happy to leave soon. Her husband was in talks about moving to Panama to help ramp up First Quantum Mineral's new Cobre Mine. The second friend only arrived a year ago. She founded a craft circle where women met weekly to make their own crafts. One had to find things to do, she explained to me, other than support the children in their homework or a little bit of sports. Yet whatever you did, *everyone* knew about it. 'They will say: "Oh, you had a drink at the club house last night…!" It can be claustrophobic.' But she was fine now, she assured me; she had made friends with these ladies.

I felt welcome. Yet, as friendly as this group was, by the way they turned their backs on other persons sitting at the club, I got the sense that there were different groups avoiding one another, and that the place could quickly become very lonely.

While we talked, the sun had set and the carpark that separates the Club House from the tennis court had filled up with large, mostly white four-wheel-drive cars. From each emerged a white man, most of them with bodies in proportion to their SUVs. Some went to the gym next door, but most headed straight to the club to order their first beer. The scene changed from a family area dominated by housewives, their children and nannies to one of male chattering, sundowners and loud laughter. The men were still in their working clothes, their employers' logo – FQM, KMP or a contractor's – stitched onto their shirts. Their clothes were held in khaki, and many wore shorts and heavy mine boots. Some of the men were single or had left their family at home, but most would leave the club after one or two beers and join their wives and children for supper at their house on the Golf Estate.

The reader probably experiences the beginning of this chapter as an unexpected break from the previous chapter. This is intended. The change in reality when leaving the residential compounds and entering the Golf Estate area with its evergreen lawn is as stark (on the specificity of the lawn and its relation to white respectibility in South Africa, see Cane 2019; Sparks 2012). And yet, the estate is part of Solwezi. As I argued at the beginning of this book, the conceptual separation between town and golf estate – 'the other country' – should not distract us from their interdependence. Anthropologists of Southern Africa have long argued that even the strongest conceptual separation does not turn separate spheres of life into separate societies but must be seen as a structural feature of a single society. Isaac Schapera, Max Gluckman or Monica Wilson saw colonial societies of Southern Africa as a specific variant of integrating groups into a common society: 'Blacks' and 'whites' remained conceptually separate but formed functionally integrated parts of one society. In the same vein, I will argue, the golf estate and Solwezi town are conceptually separate, but part of a single social system characterized by mutual yet asymmetrical interdependence. The global division of labour is realized at the workplace in the form of racialized hierarchies, and it shapes daily life on either side of the fence. The infrastructurally exclusive setting and residents' preoccupation with the making of a community inside the fence, I will argue, help to uphold a conceptual divide between those inside and those outside, thereby cementing a global division of labour structured along racial lines and ultimately substantiating conceptual differences between the Global South and the Global North.

By dedicating a separate chapter to life on the Golf Estate, I thus do not intend to reinforce the conceptual divide, but to show its workings in practice. Often, the golf estate's part of society seemed much stranger to me than Solwezi town, but I try not to exoticize its residents. They are as human, as interesting and as partial as the residents of Solwezi, and I hope to be able to do them justice in describing their lives on the Golf Estate. The chapter is based on research in 2015 and 2016 when I lived in Solwezi town but frequented the Club House and the gym, and in 2017 when I lived on the Golf Estate for two months as the guest of a female mine employee to conduct research on its community and the mine's management more purposefully (see also Chapter 6).

Off duty, residents are preoccupied with, firstly, their work and internal company politics, the insecurity of their permits and their job's dependence on the global copper price; secondly, by social divisions and the attempt to create a friendly companionship among people who at first only have their (or their spouse's) employer in common; and thirdly, by the everyday challenges of living in an infrastructurally secluded area. There is little engagement with the world on the other side of the fence, be it Solwezi town or Zambia more generally. Solwezi's urban compounds and Kansanshi's Golf Estate remain conceptually separate, parallel realities. To understand how this situation can be created and maintained, the question of *who* lives on the estate must be looked at. It is at the company's discretion to decide on its residents. I will show that two company policies in particular – Southafricanization and stabilization – bring about a situation that separates the estate from its urban environment.

Company towns

In Zambia, exclusive, gated areas, reserved for white expatriates existed in the Copperbelt towns in the mid-twentieth century (for the 1950s and 1960s, see Phimister 2011), but their time seemed to be gone with independence and the ensuing Zambianization. Since the end of the 1970s, only very few white expatriates worked on the mines, and by the 1990s, their number was virtually zero. Privatization of the mines and the new role of global mining companies has brought back both expat managers and gated areas, and to historians of the Copperbelt, my description of Kansanshi's workforce and organization of life on the Golf Estate will in parts read like a re-enactment of the 1950s and 1960s (for a journalist's description of white life on the Zambian Copperbelt in the 1950s, see Dunn 1959). Then and now, the mines' workforce is structured along a global racial division of labour; expatriate life and company housing are structured by the hierarchy on the mines; the mine organizes sporting events just as it provides schools for the kids; wives hold an uneasy position in the community; male relationships with 'local' women are closely monitored – and dogs are the preferred pets of white residents.

In Kansanshi's Golf Estate, this distinct local history meets with contemporary models of a global mining industry. The revival of the company town model – combining places of production and housing and services for workers (Borges and Torres 2012, 2) – is not unique to Zambia. The mining industry concentrates its sites of extraction in the Global South and builds 'enclaves' for organizing, controlling and attracting its management and expatriate, highly skilled workforce (Ferguson 2006). Descriptions by scholars of expatriate-only residential compounds at oil rigs owned by US-based oil companies at the shores of Equatorial Guinea (Appel 2012a, 2012b; 2019b) or for the expat community at an open-cast coal mine in Indonesia (Lahiri-Dutt 2012) sound very familiar to me. In building the Golf Estate and in building it the way it did, First Quantum Minerals thus followed established global practices.

The set-up of the Golf Estate vis-à-vis Solwezi town is best explained with reference to two recent books on urban enclaves and social boundaries. In her *Global Borderlands* (2019), Victoria Reyes looks at foreign-controlled, semi-autonomous zones of international exchanges. In such sites – embassies, free economic zones, military bases – the regulating norms inside the fence are different from outside, with distinct formal and informal national laws inside. While Kansanshi's management indeed imposes and sanctions its own rules within the fenced location, such as tempo limit, alcohol consumption, animal keeping rules (all documented in its *Resident Information* booklet), and while social norms are very different from those in Solwezi town, the plot does not compare to a zone with special privileges granted by the state. In this regard, the Solwezi town / Golf Estate situation resembles much more what Marco Garrido describes for Manila, Philippines, in *The Patchwork City* (2019) where the city is structured in patches of slums and enclaves in closest vicinity to each other. Unlike, for instance, Johannesburg which is segregated along suburbs and townships, in Manila, we see these spatial segregations along the same road: the upper- and middle class in their estates behind thick walls, the urban poor in makeshift houses in between. This, he argues, has helped for class consciousness to emerge (and to be politicized subsequently). Garrido's work highlights the fact that albeit different in any city in the Global South, spatial boundaries have become sharper since the 1990s and that, as a result, 'class has become more important than ever in the wake of urban structuring' (2019, 5). In Solwezi, the structuring element of the golf estate is – or rather, has again become – racial ascriptions. On the one hand, this is a manifestation of global labour divisions along race; on the other hand, we must understand this racial exclusivity as a regional Southern African expression, which, as a former settler region, privileges not only 'white' above 'African' but also a particular whiteness above others, as I will show. For readers familiar with the United States – or, for that matter, the South African context – the relevance of this insight on Zambia probably needs some explanation: Most Zambians do not seem themselves as 'Black'. Race and identity are not tightly connected like in some historically highly racialized societal contexts. The norm is similar to what an interview partner of Katharina Schramm notes for Ghana: 'When a Ghanaian looks in the mirror, he sees a Ghanaian, not a "Black guy"' (2009, 19). Race can of course become a primary identifier, but usually not for Black Zambians. This is a privilege reserved for 'whites'. In that sense, there is colourism in Zambia.

Beyond the constitution of its residents and next to striking similarities across the world, such enclave-projects necessarily exhibit regional, national and local specificities as well as traits connected to a particular company's history and governance. None of the three oil compounds described by Appel in Equatorial Guinea allows residents to bring their children, so accompanying wives are in their fifties or older. In contrast, Kansanshi's estate is purposefully domestic and family-friendly, which creates a particular social dynamic. As I will show, this is linked to FQM's reason to establish the compound instead of either providing individual housing in Solwezi town or relying on basic structures for fly-in-fly-out (FIFO) arrangements only. Keeping its expatriate workers closely tied to the mine site and anchored by their families is seen as cheaper than the alternatives and thus to the benefit of shareholders, all the more since the expense on expatriate enclaves is just a small fraction of the costs of operating a large-scale mine.

In terms of nationalities represented in such places, a variety of factors are decisive, such as the location of the company town, the type of resource mined and the company's history. Again, in the US oil industry in Equatorial Guinea, the majority of expatriate workers are US Americans and have been involved in the US oil industry in Texas before. My interlocutors at the Golf Estate are mainly South African, Zimbabwean, Australian and British citizens. Almost all residents are white, with the notable exception of the environmental, public relations and human resources managers and, since 2020, the general manager, and their families, and a few African, non-Zambian expatriates mainly from DR Congo.[3] Other Zambian employees (even the few who occupy supervisory or managerial roles or work as teachers in the mine's schools) are expected to find a place in town. Their presence on the estate is limited to leisure activities.

Most mining companies in the current Zambian mining industry – including state-owned Chinese companies – show a similar racial division of labour as Kansanshi Mine, with senior and managerial positions occupied by expatriates. They occupy between 5 and 10 per cent of a company's workforce (Lee 2017, 61).[4] While the 'colour bar' of the colonial period is no longer a legal principle, the same hierarchy has been revived with the re-privatization of Zambia's mining sector in the late 1990s. Today, most positions of power in Zambian mines are filled by expatriates, with a few exceptions: according to Zambian work permit regulations, the senior positions of the human resource management cannot be filled by non-Zambians (Lee 2017, 62; for a similar situation in the Congolese Copperbelt, see Rubbers 2020). There is also a tendency to fill the position of the environmental manager by a Zambian.

These similarities in the industry do not extend into housing arrangements offered to management and senior expatriate employees. At Mopani Copper Mines (MCM) in Kitwe and Mufulira, no housing compound exists for the management and senior expatriate personnel (but there is an exclusive, recreational Golf Estate comparable to Kansanshi's), and Konkola Copper Mines (KCM) in Chingola only introduced it more recently and for its Indian expatriates exclusively (Lee 2017, 102–3). Housing arrangement for the Chinese management and staff in mines run by Non-Ferrous Metal China (NFCA), the top Chinese state investor in Zambia's copper industry, have a 'China House' compound per company or subcontractor where two to three persons share a room and essential facilities (Lee 2017, 99–102).

Indian KCM managers and workers bring their families. Finally, the two other new large-scale mining projects in Solwezi District, Lumwana and Sentinel Mine, share Kansanshi's features with segregated areas for managers and senior white employees and their families.

Ching Kwan Lee, who has had exceptional access to Chinese-owned mining companies as well as to KCM and MCM between 2012 and 2014 (including time at Kansanshi and Lumwana Mines, about which she has not published), concludes that in contrast to Chinese-owned companies 'the managerial ethos in global private companies is much more individualistic, careerist, and entrepreneurial, with a clearer boundary between corporate and personal domains' (2017, 94). For KCM, again as opposed to NFCA, she notes a 'discernibly hierarchical' living arrangement for its senior staff (2017, 103). While it is quite likely that global, private firms generally place more emphasis on hierarchical status and career in contrast to the 'ethos' dominating Chinese-owned companies, even the cursory description above of the variety of living arrangement among global, private companies shows the necessity for more company-specific analysis.[5]

Back on a global level, few scholars have written on contemporary everyday life in compounds of large companies, a fact which can be explained by their exclusivity and inaccessibility (Appel 2019b, 440–1; Lahiri-Dutt 2012, 208). Oftentimes, such descriptions remain at a general level, limited to infrastructural and general social aspects. In her study on managers and workers of large US-based oil companies at the shores of Equatorial Guinea, Appel touches on forms of 'social divisions' within the compounds (albeit limiting her analysis to 'wives'), mentioning nationality, class and social capital just as differences between company policies and the hierarchies within companies (Appel 2019b, 129–31). Appel does not elaborate on how these divisions come into being, nor how people try to overcome them. I agree with Appel that the 'wives', both in the US oil and gas industry in Equatorial Guinea and at Kansanshi Mine in Zambia, are 'the caretakers of white male physical well-being, and the guardians of racialized morality and privilege' (Appel 2019b, 82–3), but at least in the case of Kansanshi, female roles are much more diverse. Just as there are single men on the Golf Estate, there are also single expatriate women, working in the mine or as teachers, and both women and men occupy several different subjectivities within the apparently homogenous group of compound residents.

This differentiation also extends to the higher management itself. In his study on Congolese HR managers in the Congolese mining industry, Rubbers (2020) writes that white expatriates make 'a separate social world', and he explains this separateness by what they have in common: 'The expatriates have a closer relationship with each other as they come alone to the Congo, and share the same language and interests. … they tend to stick together after working hours' (Rubbers 2020, 9). He mentions in passing that companies exhibit different governing styles in accordance with the expatriate directors' nationalities: the 'Anglo-Saxon' – a category including Americans, South Africans and Australians; the 'Belgians'; and the 'French', but he does not dissect these differences, their origins and their making. Writing about daily life on the Golf Estate allows me to both break up and consolidate the category of the expatriate, showing how the very differences between them focus their interest on each other and help constructing a commonality whose opposite pole is everything Zambian. This, I hope, contributes to opening 'the black box of mining companies so as to better understand how mining capitalism is generated out of the work practices, the social networks, and the ethical projects of the mine employees who play a strategic role at the project level' (2020, 12).

The golf estate is indeed both; a place of ordinary everyday life for its residents and a site where systemic power becomes institutional, infrastructural and consequential far beyond its physical boundaries. There is nothing natural about such a place, and this chapter examines frictions, tensions and social divisions that support its presence. I zoom in on the making of a community which lays its claim to living on the estate. Before delving into what people actually do off-duty, I briefly describe the Golf Estate, the hierarchies manifest in the housing structures and an ordinary day on the estate. In the second part of the chapter, I examine two company policies – Southafricanization and stabilization – that inhibit on the possibility of sociality among residents and between estate and town residents. This leads me to a discussion of Kansanshi's racialized corporate structure, with white South African males at the top, as an expression of a global division of labour and of a region-specific history. As such, the mining company's recruitment practices lead to the introduction of spatial segregation in the Solwezi region as never seen before.

Housing and hierarchies

A large part of Solwezi town is planned and built decentrally by the residents themselves (see Chapter 3). Kansanshi's Golf Estate is one of the few areas developed and built entirely as the result of outside planning and in situ implementation.[6] Most Solwezi residents are prohibited from entering the Golf Estate. I was often astounded by the disinterest people showed at life in the estate. They could look at the houses through the electric fence, and children often waved at runners and dog walkers, but most urban residents do not even try to get inside. Even if difficult to enter, the Golf Estate is not hermeneutically sealed off from the outside world. While the provision of electricity neatly differentiates between the inside and the outside, as the Golf Estate's feeder is separate from that of the residential urban compounds surrounding it (see Chapter 5), not every piece of infrastructure does the same. WLAN travels across the fence, and adjacent Solwezi residents – in particular youth hanging around for that purpose – sometimes manage to connect to it. Conversely, loud music played at a bar in an urban compound is heard inside the estate into the early morning hours, and smoke from charcoal cooking hovers over the estate's houses and golf lawn. More than a decade after the mine acquired the land, the golf estate remains an exotic and unknown – yet not necessarily accepted – place to most people in Solwezi town.

The company's purchase of the land was not straightforward. After Solwezi Municipal Council allocated the farmland to Kansanshi Mine in 2006, a lengthy land dispute in the courts followed.[7] The plaintiff, the farmer Rodgers Mwanda, charged the council and Kansanshi Mining Plc for trespassing on his farmland and sued for loss of opportunity to develop the land. He argued that he had acquired the land from the council in 2004 and had been issued a title deed by the Ministry of Lands. The case appeared before the High Court in 2013, but the matter was eventually settled out of court.[8]

While the legal challenge was still pending, the company already developed the area of roughly 150 hectares. It constructed houses, built the golf course and reservoir dams, and established a road network (with a prescribed speed limit of 40 kilometre per hour). The golf course is the green centre of the estate, with residential houses built in relation to the fairways, roughs, greens and sand hazards on the golf course. The construction took several years and happened in nine phases, each of them has formed a cluster shaped by a distinctive building style. Generally, there are three types of accommodation: self-contained, semi-detached and row houses. The latter are single accommodations for the FIFO employees who work for a contractually agreed period of weeks without break and then leave for their homes for several weeks of holiday (more in section Stabilization policy). FIFOs are also frequently housed in the mine village, another residential compound on the mining license area with fewer facilities.

Hierarchies at work decide on the type of housing one is allocated. As important as the house type is the house's *location*, though, and residents have given names to different sections (see also Appel 2012b, 445). The northeastern corner, for instance, the area where managers occupy spacious houses built with sturdy, so-called Kalulushi Clay Bricks, boasting a generous garden and wonderful views due to its elevated status, is called ' (see Figure 21)' after the northern Johannesburg suburb where South Africa's affluent businessmen and politicians prefer to live. In contrast, the southeastern corner on the Golf Estate is called 'Bloemfontein', referencing the Free State town which is known for a cold and rough climate and has the reputation of being a backward Afrikaner place (see Figure 22). In this low-lying area, the houses are not only close to the dam and its mosquitoes but also close to Solwezi's urban residents.

Self-contained and semi-detached houses are fenced entities with a garden and a carport each. At first sight, the fences seem unnecessary when the entire estate is fenced in and tightly controlled, but they offer a sense of privacy and an illusion of ownership to the residents. When walking or jogging on the estate, I, too, was often grateful for them: almost every household has a dog or two. The rules and regulations book for residents advises its residents to keep the gates to their yards closed at all times to keep 'the antelope and zebras from entering your yard and struggling to get out, which could result in them hurting themselves'. Approximately a hundred zoo animals live on the estate, most of them antelopes.[9]

The majority of Kansanshi's managers and senior expatriate employees live on the Golf Estate. There are however additional, exclusive residential areas for specific categories of employees: Visiting FQM board members and directors, contractors

Figure 21. Swimming pool and 'Sandton' at the horizon, Kansanshi Golf Estate, June 2015. Photo by author.

Figure 22. 'Bloemfontein', Kansanshi Golf Estate, June 2015. Photo by author.

and engineers who stay at the mine village, which is the original housing area on the mining license area (see Figure 3), or in one of two fancy hotels in Solwezi town.[10] Expatriate college teachers, the school's headmaster and boarding school supervisors live on the so-called college area which is the boarding school site on the mining license area.

In contrast to their expatriate colleagues, Zambian teachers are offered housing in Kabitaka, a more recent own-as-you-rent housing project for better-paid Zambian employees at the eastern entrance to Solwezi town (Kesselring 2017b). All of the above frequently visit the Golf Estate for its recreational and sports facilities as members of the 'Kansanshi Golf Club'.

An ordinary day on the estate

People live on the estate because they themselves or a family member is employed by Kansanshi Mine or FQM. The estate's raison d'être is the mine. When the mine closes, the company will stop financing the running of the estate, and most residents on the Golf Estate will most likely leave Zambia. Work and work relations therefore constitute the estate. Yet the estate is also the place where people lead their private lives. All daily activities and routines, all face-to-face relationships, all fights and reconciliations within the families take place here, and people strive to make it their temporary home. This often implies trying to escape the all-determining work relations shared by all residents and occupational hierarchies.

Ordinary days on the Golf Estate are not very spectacular. In the mornings, even before sunrise, the boom at the entrance gate to the estate hardly stays down. Managers and expatriate professionals leave their houses, jump into their 4 × 4s mounted with distinctive orange flags that serve as warning signs to the operators of large vehicles in the pit. They open the boom by scanning their access cards and their fingerprints at the electronic reader, waive at the guards and race the 2.5 kilometres north to the mine gate where they do the same, and continue for another 7 kilometres to the mine offices for an early start at work. In turn, cleaners and gardeners (many of whom use the miners' bus to get from their residential compound to the estate) present their credentials at the Golf Estate gate, pass through and gather on the nearest parking lot to then go to their assigned places of work. Meanwhile, children walk or are driven to the school, and the day's social life starts inside the houses or in the back gardens. Spouses supervise their cleaners and gardeners, chat with their neighbours across the fence and meet for coffee or a shared hobby at a friend's place. Generally, there is surprisingly little public and a lot of domestic life. For many, their house is a refuge, and they spend the hours when the children are at school organizing their lives at home, shopping (see below) or communicating with their friends and relatives elsewhere. Keeping front door or windows open does not feel comfortable to many residents. 'It's a bit golfy here,' as someone told me. 'People like to look inside.' The Golf Estate community is very small, and it seemed to me that people tread carefully what to show to this small public.

In this context, the pursuit of leisure activities presents an alternative and for many a way out of potential isolation. It allows residents to assume a subject position more or less independent from their contractual relationship, and to enter new relationships with work mates, other residents and guests. Many are determined to make the estate a liveable and social place, and they invest many hours after (care) work into organizing and exercising the estate's social life.

The largest sporting events are organized by the company itself, such as competitions in rugby, golf, triathlon, cycling and running. FQM encourages employees to engage in a healthy lifestyle. For many, this matches their own ambitions, and they thoroughly enjoy and extensively partake in the company's events. These events accommodate both the fit and the not-so-fit. Rugby games on Friday nights and cricket games on Saturdays are offered along with a braai (Afrikaans for barbecue) and tombola; golf tournaments are followed by a raffle at the Club House. Golf tournaments are often sponsored by mine suppliers, banks and security firms such as Jaid's (a local wholesaler and retailer), Barlows CAT, Pex Hydraulics, Sandvick, Connell Mining, Stanbic, BHL, Toyota Zambia or G4S. The Kansanshi handicaps list showcased at the clubhouse mostly reads as a list of those who live on the estate.

While a large part of residents prefers to watch sports rather than do sports and is often to be found at the Club House, the gym is the most important place at the estate for other residents and some non-residential Zambian club members. It has a workout room with pieces of sport equipment such as bicycles and weight machines and a room with mirrors at one wall open for collective courses like step and body pump. The facilities include two locker rooms with showers and toilets, a squash court, an outside 25-meter swimming pool, and two tennis courts. In 2017, the gym was extended with a generous training room overlooking the tranquil and often empty swimming pool. Most Zambians and the few Congolese expatriates prefer to do spinning and gym work, play tennis or golf and engage in classes such as body pump and step aerobics (offered by the physiotherapist at the mine's Mary Begg clinic); white expats rather do golf, yoga, swimming, running, fishing (in the two dams on site), but also squash and tennis.

The company actively supports employees' and spouses' sports activities. Workout done, one can confirm the previously booked activity on the Fisikal App and collect health points. These health points can be turned into the currency 'LiveLife points' as part of LiveLife, a health incentive scheme and discount rewards programme providing purchasing benefits to members. From a variety of merchants and suppliers in South Africa, these benefits reduce the prize of goods or services. Many Golf Estate residents who collect health points purchase training gear and clothes and have them sent to Solwezi via DHL.

Running or fast walking is probably the most frequently practiced form of exercise on the estate. Few walk on their own; there is a spectrum of either company-loyal or deliberately independent groups. The former involves managers and their spouses, and generally people who do not mind being close to the company's gaze even after work. Often quite competitive, they nevertheless accommodate a variety of skills and physical conditions. People join in for the run which ends when the

Figure 23. Walking on the Kansanshi Golf Estate, July 2016. Photo by author.

sun sets and Solwezi town in the distance glows as if burning, go home to take a shower and have dinner. Unless out of breath, it is easy to make light conversation with one's co-runners. The binding element is the work-out in the open air.

A considerable part of all residents shows a lot of initiative in meeting among themselves, sometimes in a deliberate attempt to be out of their employer's gaze. They see the company-organized events as too managed and deliberately glossing over differences and disagreements. In small and more informally organized groups, they meet for long walks across the greens, often with dogs. Here, residents and some Zambians meet to exercise, but also to chat with one another and enjoy the sunset and the tranquil early evening hours. I participated in many a walk during my residency on the estate (see Figure 23). Very quickly, I learnt to avoid potentially aggressive sables, wet areas and spraying water sprinklers. After some walks, I also routinely avoided the vehicle executing the 'fogging', that is the daily spraying to stop mosquito larva from breeding in the water.

Sporting activities happening outside the estate management's programme are not always welcomed by the estate's management. For instance, the group of people training yoga struggled to get the classes registered on the *Fisikal App* and to receive guaranteed gym space. One of the reasons may be a manager's dislike of this kind of exercise. A fierce attendee of and sometimes-preacher at Afrikaans services on Sunday mornings, he apparently reprimanded one female churchgoer for skipping service for yoga: 'It's of the devil.'

People also meet for non-sport activities and form clubs or groups to pursue their passions. During my time on the estate, I witnessed the attempt to establish a reading group. This club was born in reaction to dominant forms of engaging with one another. A small number of female Golf Estate residents started to meet once per month with the explicit aim to discuss anything of interest *but* work and children. The founders wanted members to listen to each other, to accept different opinions on a topic, and generally to practice openness for one another; something they missed in everyday interactions on the estate. In their view, most groups had a clear ideology attached to them (often linked to religion), and most women only talked about their kids.

All the activities I have mentioned so far take place either on the estate or on the mine. This is not by chance. The estate is designed so as to give residents few reasons to leave it. Buying food and household items is the only regular reason for most residents to venture into Solwezi town. In the first few years, there was little on offer for expatriates used to malls and retail shops, but over the years, some investors set up large retailers (see Chapter 1) such as Shoprite and Pick n Pay. In 2016, a Choppies shop owned by Botswanan nationals opened just around the corner of the entrance to the Golf Estate, complementing Sibo's Café along Kansanshi road. Choppies is slightly more expensive than Shoprite and Pick n Pay and has a smaller supply on offer. Many residents thus still drive to the boma once a week. Once inside the supermarket, shopping is a good experience for estate residents (at least if the shelves are filled up), but the drive to and from the town centre and especially the many children and self-defined carriers who descend on them once they step out of their large four-wheel drives on the supermarket's parking lot are the topic of many unnerved conversations among Golf Estate residents. Some bring their household help with them or even send them to do the grocery shopping for them. Alternatively, residents can order items from Lusaka delivered by minibus twice a week, from UK-based catalogue retailers such as Argos or Amazon, and have them delivered via courier services or take one of the daily charter flights to Lusaka themselves.

Apart from grocery shopping, most residents only drive through town when leaving Solwezi by road or plane, the latter either with the commercial company ProFlight, or with the FQM-owned charter plan (depending on their position in the company's hierarchy, the booking can be cancelled on short notice for a higher-ranked person). Not many residents explore Zambia as a holiday destination. If they do, trips are mostly limited to the high-end Luangwa National Park, the Victoria Falls or Lake Kariba.

The drive from the Golf Estate to the airport which lies at the western end of town is, like shopping, an experience estate residents share and speak about. One drives (or is driven in the company's airport shuttle) along Independence Road, passes through the *boma* and cuts through some densely populated compounds and Kyawama market. At the point where the road to the airport branches off, the market is at its densest and expatriates feel the least at home. Estate residents tell each other stories about Solwezi residents deliberately pushing someone in front of a white person's car so as to get compensation for the caused injury. For those who have access to the mining site, the new access road to the smelter at the western end of the mining site has opened a welcome alternative, a less busy route to the airport.

Estate residents rarely make use of services from local businesses outside the Golf Estate. If a service such as hairdressing is not available on-site, residents prefer to wait until their next trip to Lusaka or Johannesburg. Other needed services – say, of a car mechanic – are mediated by the company, and one does not have to build a relationship with someone in town to get a decent deal.

When the day comes to an end, life happens inside the family house or at the Club House. If couples want a special evening, the Club House offers them a 'romantic dinner' at the dam, being served a 'sundowner' and later food, sitting 10 meters from the shores of the artificial lake, their car parked next to them.

Co-presence: the Golf Estate and Solwezi town

Despite residents' daily rhythms that systematically obfuscate this fact, the Golf Estate needs Solwezi town. The labour creating and reproducing this idyll – and allowing to keep up the separation between the estate and the town – is done by Solwezi residents.

Some residents literally do the work necessary to keep up the estate: cleaning, gardening and security staff. Security personnel employed through the private company Cobra guards the entrance, the fence and particular points within the estate. Cleaning and gardening are outsourced to Mr Clean, a Zambian company owned by a South African holding company, and residents can request these services through the estate management only. To the management of the estate, subcontracting both does away with the hassle and responsibility of direct employment and serves to attenuate local criticism towards the mine for mainly sourcing labour from other regions. To individual estate residents, their cleaners or gardeners sometimes mean a lot, though. Many develop quite a strong, if temporary relationship in which they learn about each other's lifeworld on each side of the fence. The relationship is certainly lopsided as the cleaner or gardener (willingly or not) learns much more about the Golf Estate resident than the other way around. Sometimes, if very rarely, expatriates visit 'the help' at their homes in the compounds and support them financially and in-kind to complement their low pay.[11] This set-up is typical for many segregated societies. Personal relations situationally reach across systematic segregation. They allow the more powerful actors to feel themselves as humane, caring and charitable, but they also distract both sides from the structural dimensions of segregation and prevent structural change.

While cleaners, gardeners and guards come onto the estate daily, a few other groups are let in infrequently and upon invitation only. For the mine's management and the CSR department, mine tours are one of the most efficient means to generate societal and political support for the mining operations. These tours are systematically designed to impress and to show the mine's contribution to the Zambian economy, yet they equally cement the conceptual separation between the town and the mine or the golf estate.

Whenever relationships are strained, management invites politically or economically important individuals and municipal and national state representatives for a tour on the mine. The tour ends with a meal at the Club House where the guests can enjoy the view of the lush green and some substantial food. I participated in a number of these encounters and witnessed Solwezi's mayor and a Kansanshi manager cordially exchanging jokes with one another. But the most moving reactions to the Golf Estate I witnessed were when I joined pupils from a Solwezi secondary school who were given a mine tour (a regular activity by the CSR department). After having nibbled at the massive burger at the Club House (and wrapped the rest of it for their siblings at home), they walked across the green lawn, in awe, turned cartwheels, plucked flowers from a blooming tree, dreaming together of living in a world of serene order away from the bustling urban compounds they live in.

Selectively and sporadically, Golf Estate residents also reach out to the town. Managers necessarily have to engage with political and economic actors at the municipal, provincial and national level, albeit the lobby work with the presidency is mainly done by FQM's country manager General Kingsley Chikuli and the company's government liaison person in Lusaka.[12] Several residents also make a deliberate effort to not limit their lives to work and life on the Golf Estate. I met a passionate market shopper and someone who runs a small charity in an urban compound. There is also a group of residents that decided to explore restaurants in town. When some restaurants offering (non-African) 'world food' opened, such as Indian dishes (for instance, Shamel and Spice Valley), they met there for dinner, testing the food and enjoying an evening out. Such dinners outside the Golf Estate are a deliberate attempt to leave the sometimes choking experience of the estate. I sometimes felt that the physical distance also allowed for a more explicit discussion of one's grievances with the company.

In general, however, the town remains opaque to most estate residents. To them it is, in one word, an 'African' town: busy, informal, dusty, loud and with an impenetrable logic to itself. They do not make the connections between their life and that of Solwezi residents. At worst, the town is a nuisance, at best, it is a different world they are glad to be separated from. The crafts market that allows two marketeers to set up their stalls just outside the estate near the gate one day per month must be seen in this light: it allows estate residents to purchase and consume 'African' art without them having to enter the busy marketplace in town (where little if any craft is sold).

Why do expatriate residents on the estate adopt this perspective of 'Africa', and how does the set-up contribute to its perpetuation? To answer this question, I now turn to the company's labour policies, which decide on who comes to live on the estate in the first place, and housing policies, which shape residents' community-making efforts and their positionality vis-à-vis Solwezi town.

Southafricanization

FQM has been established by two brothers. Philip Pascall, FQM's CEO and Chairman of FQM until 2022, and his brother Matt Pascall, until recently Director of Operations for FQM, were born in Salisbury, Southern Rhodesia (today's Harare) in the 1950s. They studied in England and South Africa and entered the mining business early on as consultants and managers in Southern Africa and Australia. Before his passing in 2023, Philip Pascall resided in Perth, from where most of FQM's business is run. In 2022, his son Tristan Pascall took over as CEO. According to managers I interviewed, during the first decade of FQM's years in the Congolese and Zambian Copperbelts, expatriates recruited for the company held more diverse nationalities than today. Over the past few years, the company has primarily hired white South Africans at the managerial and supervisory level, diminishing the number of employees from Australian and Great Britain. White Zimbabweans are generally looked upon on the Golf Estate as a sub-group of South Africans, as many have work experience in mining management in South Africa. The increased presence of white South Africans in top managerial and white-collar positions at the mine has affected how people see and relate to one another both at work and in leisure time.

From my interviews with several managers (for more on how I gained access to them, see Chapter 6), I could discern at least four reasons for this change towards a more regional recruitment pattern: costs, continuity, technical skills and 'culture'. Putting the latter under its own sub-heading – 'Whitenesses' – allows me to elaborate on my argument that the Golf Estate and by consequence the mine's hiring practice are a driver and manifestation of valuation along racial lines in the global economy and at the same time the result of the particularities of Southern African history.

Cost reduction is probably the most important reason for increasingly prioritizing residential South Africans over FIFOs from Australia and other countries. One manager explained it to me as follows:

> Australians are expensive because you have to fly them from Oz [to Zambia]. So over time, it's changed a bit because there's lot more guys available from South Africa and they are cheaper. Doesn't sound good, but they are a lot cheaper to employ, South Africans than Australians. So over time, there is quite a lot South Africans that are working here, a lot more than in the past. It's a cost thing. And it's easy. In and out. … If you have a FIFO from Australia, it's ten weeks on, three weeks off. So every ten weeks, the guys go out for three weeks. It's disruptive. Whereas a lot of South Africans are residential. They are used to Africa. They like staying here. So it's much easier to work with guys that are residential.

He continued:

> Our expat wages are lower than Lumwana [a mine further west owned by Barrick Gold]. A lot lower than what you get in Congo. But we've got the Golf Estate and that keeps the guys here. So it's a small price to pay that benefit.

In this statement, the second reason – continuity – is hinted at. Unlike other mines in Zambia, such as the Chinese state-owned Chambishi Mine, Kansanshi's plant has grown quickly and was continuously expanded over the years since its redevelopment. As a result, professionals' knowledge and expertise becomes difficult to replace. As the manager explained it to me:

> Every year, we add something new; a new technology. So if you lose a few people of historic knowledge of the plant … it would be very difficult. It's very good for us to have that sort of historic knowledge. They know where things are, how it works, how's been done.

To keep the expertise acquired by its senior employees, the company offers the attraction of the Golf Estate including sports and schooling facilities. The Golf Estate with its set-up as a residential area allows the company to employ a majority of 'residentials' instead of 'mercenary miners' or FIFO. Keeping knowledge of the plant and the mine's history close also necessitates stability which, again, is guaranteed by the fact that employees are at hand at all times. I will elaborate on this below when I explain the 'stabilization' policy in more details. For now, in the words of a manager:

> For us, to have residential guys is much easier. They are here the whole time, they leave 20 or 25 days a year, so the rest of the time you've got them here covered. They don't have to get around because their family are here. We make it as attractive as possible for the families to stay. And then you also keep people longer.

To also attract young fathers (and mothers) and thus a new generation of professionals, the comfortable housing comes with the possibility of schooling: a preparatory school on the estate's ground and a college (boarding) school on the mine license area run by Educore, a company wholly owned by FQM. As the manager confidently said: 'It's a big draw card. A lot of people are still here because of the school.'

Later in the interview, the manager gave a third, more technical reason for the company's preference of white South Africans over expatriates from other countries:

> The South African mining industry is actually … a really difficult environment and the technology is actually quite advanced. – RK: Advanced even in open pit mining? – No, more for underground. Open pits as well. There is actually quite a bit of open pit mining being done, especially in the coal industry and so on. Most of the mining guys go through underground and then surface. So they learn a lot more about mining that way, if you do both sides. You tend to get a more rounded individual that has been through the whole sequence. Whereas if you get guys just doing open pits their whole life [like most Australians], you struggle a bit sometimes.

Whitenesses

The fourth reason for a preference of South African employees over other whites, 'culture', was much more hidden in my interviewees' responses and is not discussed openly; the official line is different. Yet, one manager, a South African, was quite open about it.

> When I was at [another mine in Central Africa], there was a lot of bias towards employing Australian guys. Australians are very good at open pit mining. When you go to Oz, you know – wow! But it's different there because Australians are working with Australians in Australia. So it's easy. You tell a guy to do it, he does it. Africa is different, you know. There's a lot of cultural and language barriers. So you need to understand: okay, you tell somebody to do something, [but then you have to ask him again:] 'what did I ask you to do?'. You know, there is a different interaction.

This quote, in all its racism, starkly reveals a trilateral identity construction by white South Africans. On the one hand, white South Africans and white Australians are equally capable, technically skilled specialists. Their joint competence, in the eyes of the manager, sets them apart from 'the African', someone who continuously needs to be supervised and controlled. 'Whites' are characterized by their capabilities, whereas 'Blacks' are mostly marked by incompetence – a view only thinly clothed in the politer words of 'cultural and language barriers''. Within the 'white' field, South Africans and Australians are set apart by their relation to this construct of the 'African'. White South Africans have (in the eyes of the white South African) more experience with handling 'the African'. In this sense, they see themselves as more African than their Australian colleagues. Here, 'African' is a self-ascribed, positive, and ultimately colonial identity, similar to what Hendriks (2017) calls 'a darker shade of white'. Since much of the workforce is 'African', this skill makes them more valuable on a Zambian mine. While 'white' superiority at the workplace can be shared by Australians and South Africans, only white South Africans have a claim to autochthony: the 'white' South African is on his home turf in Zambia and knows how to deal with 'the natives' (my quote referring to the past). Here, racial hierarchies in a global workplace intersect with claims of belonging and competence expressed in relation to the 'African' other.

This self-image of white South Africans needs the counter image of 'the African'. Solwezi town is one embodiment of this image: colourful, chaotic, undecipherable, the unordered other of the golf estate. The male white South African feels little attraction to this world, even if he is competent in dealing with it should circumstances call upon him to do so.

Another embodiment of 'the African' is wild nature and wildlife. Here, again, the white South African's competence in dealing with African nature (and in protecting it, not least from 'the Africans') sets him apart from other 'whites'. This came home to me during a two-day snake handling course in which I participated in November 2015. The course was offered by Mr. Smith (name changed), an English-speaking South African employee at Kansanshi. He has become the person to call if a snake is in sight on the estate, in the mine village and the workshops at the mine, or even in Solwezi town. To train others in catching snakes, he started to offer these courses to Golf Estate residents and mine employees. In particular, as he told us: 'It is my mission to educate the Zambian people.'

We were eighteen participants, two of whom were Zambians. The latter, 'his Zambian brothers here', were the object of many a comment Mr. Smith made about 'local' beliefs about snakes and their behaviour. 'I know there are many different opinions about snakes that Africans have. And most of them are proven wrong.' According to him, only eight out of approximately eighty-eight species living in Zambia are poisonous to humans. But, he continued, 'Zambians take every snake as a black mamba … Also, the blind worm snake does not have two heads as many of the locals believe.' He encouraged the two Zambians to ask him any kind of question. But 'I can tell you, traditional medicine does not work. There is no medical evidence for it.'

On the first day, he got us going with a theoretical introduction to the various species. Three *forest cobras* cohabit on the Golf Estate, eating fish from the dams. Recently, he was called to catch a snake at the mine village 'in a lady's bedroom' and another one in the bar area outside the general manager's house. Now and then, he is called in by the province's general hospital as an expert. Most recently, a woman from Kabompo, a small town further west, was bitten by a snake. 'In their village, they sleep on the floor.' She survived thanks to the serum provided by the mine's clinic.

On the second day, we learnt how to catch a snake with the respective tools. Three of the eight snakes we practiced with were venomous. Besides from being a little scary, the scene was surreal: running after snakes whizzing away on the green lawn or hiding in trees.

The set-up and discourse at this snake handling course could have come out of a settler's survival guide. The notion that civilization is inside the Golf Estate while something more rough, untamed, underdeveloped and possibly dangerous roams the world outside was omnipresent. In this image, 'Africans' are exposed to that risk daily and fall prey to it, not least due to their beliefs and practices (sleeping on the floor, killing snakes instead of catching them skillfully and gently). The unavoidable fact that different kinds of dangers try to enter the civilized area (the golf estate) necessitates a set of skills which one can acquire. If adventurous and brave enough, nature can be controlled and tamed; and even be protected.

The way in which Southafricanization shapes social constructions of 'whiteness' and 'African ness' in turn has consequences for the workplace. Employees, in particular long-term employees, have noticed the change of policy towards Southafricanization, explicitly describing to me the company's corporate culture and governance style as having shifted from 'Australian' to 'South African'. For these well-travelled expatriates with working experience across the globe, a company described as 'South African' means strong hierarchies at work. For many long-term employees, who remember the early years as adventurous and as run with a shared spirit, the style of managing and governing has changed to the worse – a fact they attribute to the mine's growth but also to the increase in South African employees and executives.[13]

The increased employment of South Africans that went hand in hand with an increased hierarchization extended from governance style at the mine to everyday experience and conversations on the Golf Estate. Australian employees increasingly felt that they were in the minority and that 'their way' of engaging was gradually frowned upon. Their perception, as well, stressed the difference between two variants of whiteness rather than undermining its relevance. They explained their daily confrontations or misunderstandings with their colleagues' 'South African' mindset. According to them, South Africans have 'a race problem'; they could not work as equals with Zambians and continuously had to assert their authority over them; South African men would not treat their wives properly; they were racist, poorly educated and had a 'rural mindset'; and they clung to the luxury offered by the golf estate. Conversely, Australians saw themselves as more egalitarian and more tolerant. Australia, in their opinion, had overcome its race problem and Australians were used to engaging with people from different backgrounds.[14] This self-image, however, was rarely translated into increasing everyday interactions with residents of Solwezi town. One could thus argue that the making of ethnic boundaries (South African vs. Australian whites) and its hierarchization (South African above Australian) serves the economic project of mineral extraction.

The study of whites and whiteness has re-gained some traction since the 1990s.[15] Southern African scholarship in particular has managed to problematize internal white differentiation – 'whitenesses' (Steyn 2001) – with studies on poor whites (Sibanda 2018) and 'nonhegemonic' whites (Money and Zyl-Hermann 2020, 1), answering to Terence Ranger's 1998 call for a historiography that portrays both black and 'ungrounded' white people as 'human' (Ranger 1998, 256). In their writings on whiteness in Southern Africa, Money and Zyl-Hermann (2020) point at class divisions without trivializing racial power.

On Kansanshi's Golf Estate, we see internal divisions between competing 'whitenesses'. With that, life on Kansanshi Golf Estate eerily resonates with Crapanzano's descriptions of a white settlement north of Cape Town, South Africa, in the early 1980s:

> What I found extraordinary about the identity play of the two white groups [Crapanzano refers here to the Afrikaner / English divide] was the insignificance of non-whites. They simply did not enter the self-constituting discourse of the whites … it is my impression … that the Blacks, Coloureds, and Asians were not 'significant others' from whose standpoint the white could look reflectively at himself and discover, so to speak, his identify. They were too different – and too distant. (Crapanzano 1985, 39)

For Golf Estate residents, as well, the 'significant other' are other whites. White South African's and Zimbabwean's aspiration does not lie in Zambia. Zambia is where they live and work; their homes are elsewhere. They are not capital owners, nor are they interested in investing in Zambia. While in Zambia, they send their children to the best school they can afford, either the company-run local ones or the international schools in Ndola. At the same time, South Africa is close enough to keep up strong ties with home, spend the holidays with family and fly to Johannesburg or Cape Town for shopping. The Golf Estate becomes something like an outpost of South Africa. White Southern African expatriate professionals typically have a working- or middle-class background, and they often move to Zambia with a feeling of loss of righteous entitlement and victimization through affirmative action programmes to empower Blacks in South Africa or Zimbabwe (for white blue-collar workers in South Africa before and after the end of apartheid, see Zyl-Hermann 2021; for white workers from the 1920s to Zimbabwean independence in 1980, see Ginsburgh 2020). To them, Zambia has much less to offer in terms of what they value – the quality of education, health provision and infrastructure – and public services in general cannot hold up with South Africa.

For the Copperbelt of the 1950s, Duncan Money describes a white workforce – the labour aristocracy (Phimister 2011, 129) – that is divided along lines of skill and class, sometimes self-defined, but often created by contractual arrangement (such as daily-paid and monthly-paid staff sections) (Money 2017, 708). Besides these divisions, the white workforce 'had a strong sense of collective interests', which regularly provoked industrial unrest (2017, 708). Among Kansanshi's expatriate employees – who are not allowed to join unions – I saw no trace of that sense. Many, it seems to me, were too dependent on their or their husband's employment, particularly against the continuous devaluation of the South African Rand, that they would dare to jeopardize their employment by demanding improved working or living conditions. My research also took place during a global low of commodity prices. Having children in school and not very bright employment prospects at home, the South African labour diaspora did not seem very mobile at the time. In fact, the creation of an almost exclusively white space has an element of cultural preservation along racial lines, of helping 'one's own'. Appel reads the fact that most expatriate workers in the US oil industry in Equatorial Guinea are white as the expression of 'forms of socialized hierarchy – and white supremacy in particular – that unevenly organized life in these countries' (Appel 2019b, 92); 'these countries' being multiracial North American and South Africa. I would agree with her that we should partly understand these spaces as attempts at preserving white supremacy.

While Kansanshi's expatriate residents have the to-be-expected 'bits of knowledge' (Crapanzano 1985, 291) about Solwezi, Zambia and Zambians – primarily fed by interactions with gardeners, housemaids and co-workers – the 'outside' does not hold much importance. Conducting research on white settler descendants in today's Kenya, MacIntosh (2016) found more engagement between them and Black Kenyans – encounters that would sometimes result in a situation of 'unsettling'. For a brief moment, settler descendants in Kenya saw themselves by their critics. These moments pass quickly and generally do not have broader reverberations. They are not at least the result of a larger societal context which shakes 'confident white stances' and where 'colonial-era ideologies of total entitlement will harm them' (McIntosh 2016, 82).

Among Kansanshi's Golf Estate residents, there is little 'unsettling' that I could witness. Indeed, Golf Estate residents have little to no impetus or reason to question their societal position; they can easily ignore power structures and are often oblivious to the fact that they reproduce ideologies and colonial or apartheid structures – something MacIntosh calls 'structural oblivion'.

Stabilization policy

The Golf Estate and its residents are thus the centre of life for residents. This concentration contributes to perpetuation a conceptual divide to the town which, after all, is the estate's raison d'être. Without the image of the town as disorderly and the assumption by the management that it is not liveable for whites, the estate would not be necessary. As one FQM manager explained to me why he would never want to live in Solwezi town: 'Because of the dust. From a health perspective. I can already feel it in my lungs. It's a dysfunctional town.'[16] The management translates this assumption to its white employees as a natural, structural premise on which it bases its housing policy. This directly connects to the previous chapter's argument that Solwezi town may be seen as disorderly but is in fact highly ordered through daily work of its residents. To keep this conceptual separation between disorderly Solwezi and orderly golf estate alive, life on the estate needs to be presented by its management as more orderly than it actually is: the social tensions described above and elaborated below ought not to be talked about.[17]

As elaborated above, the company sees four benefits in expatriate employees moving to Solwezi with their spouses and children: cost reduction, continuity, skills and 'culture'. In this, the company draws on a long history of 'stabilization': the attempt, starting in the post-war Rhodesia, to create a committed (European and) African workforce by providing housing and other welfare infrastructure, and thereby build an urban, modern African society (Heisler 1971; Larmer 2017, 175–7; for a similar development in the Katanga region, see Rubbers 2013). Since then, the societal context has changed dramatically, though. What we see in the golf estate today is the 'stabilization' of the upper managerial and expatriate workforce *with the exception of* the few Black Zambians in similar positions. The golf estate serves this aim; it prioritizes white labour on the basis of a racist construction of the world outside the estate. (To a certain extent, management is also interested in stabilizing its Black workforce, having trained them. But the means to achieve this are different.)

Even among its expatriate residents, the stabilization policy that prefers families and 'residentials' does not include everyone's experience, thus producing further lines of divisions among residents. Indeed, the golf estate was planned for expatriate employees and executives to establish a(n albeit temporary) life in Zambia with their families. In this vision, women are the accompanying spouses and men are employed by the company. Sports activities, schooling and housing infrastructure are all oriented towards family life. Living on the estate as a family nevertheless comes with some challenges. Many female spouses struggle with the fact that their residency is strictly tied to the annual renewal of their husband's work permit and to the company's need of their husband's expertise. They feel their lives are at the company's and the Zambian state's whim. In average, families remain for two years, although many stay for much longer. To get the unpredictability of their situation under control, families share information about the company's economic development and discuss their chances of staying on. To their frustration, the management does not seem to consider people's role in the community. When they hear about the ending of a friend's contract, wives complain about the management's decision: 'They don't consider that our children are in school here and that I have just made friends.' Furthermore, many accompanying wives suffer under the social control they experience. For instance, for young couples, the pressure to bear children is immense. Less dramatic, wives regularly comment on each other's haircut, figure or clothing styles.

Apart from the insecurity and unpredictability of their residency and the tight social control, many spouses also struggle to find something useful to do, and they typically invest much time into their children's schooling. Oftentimes, teachers feel the effects of this.[18] A teacher at the on-site Trident Preparatory School complained to me about the parents: 'They get involved a lot. … Parents compare with South Africa and other schools.' A Golf Estate resident herself, they literally live next door to the children and parents. This can feel claustrophobic, especially when mothers invest so much time in controlling their child's progress and the school's performance.

While life as a female spouse and mother clearly has its challenges, being part of a family represents the norm and conforms to what the company-provided infrastructure supports. In contrast, the company's preference for 'residentials' and 'families' in turn leaves some groups of employees feeling left out, in particular singles and FIFOs.

For male singles, it is easier to hang out by themselves or with others than for female (working) singles. Men drinking together are socially accepted. (Alcohol abuse is a big topic in everyday conversations on the Golf Estate. High-ranking employees who disappear for several weeks are rumoured to have been sent on withdrawal treatment in South Africa by the company.) Yet males also face stigmas. Those who have girlfriends outside the estate, so-called locals, are closely watched by the company. The estate management makes it difficult for them to bring her onto the estate. I heard of one story where the company employee was warned not to get involved too deeply with a Zambian woman; 'moving in with someone means a lot here in Zambia'.

A small number of single expatriate women live on the estate as company employees (including teachers).[19] In comparison to their male colleagues, they face stronger social control and sometimes exclusion, as a result of which many focus on their work. Most of them are not interested in the single men hanging out at the club after work and whom the estate community is quick in labelling as 'disrespectable'. From these working women's perspective, the accompanying wives are preoccupied with themselves, their children and are by far too invested in prettifying themselves for their husbands; they gossip too much and, worse, quarrel with one another. In such situations, the rank of their respective husbands would suddenly become important and place one of the women in a subordinate position. As one working woman told me: 'I am glad I have a job,' a fact which, in her eyes, freed her from quarrels and the pressure to be a perfect wife and mother in a small and watching community.

Just like singles, FIFOs also struggle to have a social life on the estate. Working for several weeks with hardly a day off, followed by three weeks' leave, they have little time to spend on leisure activities and to socialize with individuals beyond their immediate working mates. They are encouraged, as one of them told me in detail, to 'live as if you would not return. We are supposed to not leave anything. And when you are on leave, they might tell you: don't come back.' Many FIFOs struggle with this kind of contractual arrangement: 'It's difficult to know: one day you are important, the next you are gone.' Holidays are also often cancelled without warning or explanation, and three months might pass without the opportunity to spend time with the family. While some choose this way of life and actually cherish it, many struggle to keep up a harmonious family life and live healthily. FIFOs straddle two or more homes, feel little appreciated in terms of housing arrangements on the estate and are under heavy contractual obligations.

The described struggles of 'nonhegemonic' white individuals and groups make up many conversations among themselves and preoccupy the affected persons' thoughts. I have not met anyone who decided to leave the Golf Estate for a place in town due to the difficulties of integrating into the estate's society. The struggle thus remains inside, and the Golf Estate is the centre of attention even for those who feel excluded from the company's hiring and housing policies and its general social conservatism. The assumption that whites deserve something else than 'Africans' is cemented, naturalized by the estate. A young Zambian geologist who grew up in Tanzania and came back to Zambia to work for FQM is a case in point: a great runner, he spends most of his free time training with his colleagues on the estate. He does not have a closer connection to Solwezi or the Northwestern Province than any of his South African workmates. He however is required to live in town. He chose a place that is close to the entrance to the Golf Estate. The fence and the boom gate separating his home from his training grounds (and the homes of his workmates) are both an expression of and a mechanism to reproduce structural, racially conceived, inequalities.

Conclusion

In my ethnography of the golf estate, of its residents and their daily activities and struggles, I have tried to remain close to their everyday lives. I sometimes found it difficult to write with sympathy and nuance about people who are the victims but also integral elements in the reproduction of a racialized, hierarchical environment that in many respects seems to be from a colonial past. The focus of my life in Solwezi was elsewhere: in the town in whose midst the Golf Estate sat like 'another country'. It was this strangeness that brought me to do research in the Golf Estate in an attempt to understand how the conceptual separation of the world between poor and rich, Africa and Europe, Solwezi and Zug extends into Solwezi District and is cemented in people's everyday lives. Here, after all, is the place where the worlds meet and are functionally integrated – interdependent – in everyday interactions. Here, then, if anywhere, could we expect a third space to emerge, a softening of the boundaries and an exchange across them.

What I found happening was the reverse. Where the worlds meet, their interdependence is negated, and their conceptual separation is solidified. In social practices, Solwezi and the golf estate remain neatly separate entities conceptually opposed to each other. Producing and reproducing this negation is work, 'work-intense disentanglement', as Hannah Appel (2012b) has called it. In Solwezi, however, its production seemed to involve surprisingly little work. It can draw on existing discourses and on a claim for autochthony and superiority that many residents know – or even support – from apartheid South Africa.

On the inside, hegemonic masculinities and heteronormativity dominate, which estranges some 'nonhegemonic' whites but does not lead to real attempts for change. Management decisions favour a South African variant of 'whiteness'. This leads to frictions and feelings of exclusion, sometimes even to resignations, but in these frictions, the 'significant other' remains the other white. To live on the Golf Estate, knowledge about what is outside is hardly necessary. There is a 'lack of "real" knowledge of the "other"' (Ntarangwi 2007, 91) with the result that 'The "other" is ... generalizable in a way that the "self" is not; the "other" is an archetype, and the "self" is unique; the "other" is a slave to culture, while the "self" is a rational and choosing individual, outside of any cultural entrapment' (Ntarangwi 2007, 92).[20] Constructing 'Black Africa' as wild, chaotic and impenetrable is key to this negation of complexity and relevance – and of equality. Kansanshi's Golf Estate residents do not fear an upheaval or the raiding of the estate. The 'outside' does not hold any threat to the inside. Venturing into it may be dangerous, but since it can usually be contained, that danger just adds spice when the more adventurous explore the outside. Colonial or settler tropes abound, from residents calling their time in Solwezi their 'African adventure' to practices of snake handling, hunting and outdoor activities.

Looking at life on the estate, we witness attempts to maintain white privilege where political power is now democratically distributed. Scholars have focused on these strategies in South Africa (Steyn and Foster 2008), but it would be a mistake to ignore similar developments in other post-colonial countries. Indeed, since its re-privatization in the early late 1990s, the Zambian mining industry has seen a starkly renewed increase of expatriate managers and employees, bringing the percentage of expatriate workers per company from a virtual zero back to between 5 and 10 per cent of the total workforce. This development has by and large been accepted by both the Zambian public and the scholarly literature; both seem to take it for granted that with re-privatization, the colonial 'colour bar' made its return to a country with 120 years of commercial mining experience and more than 50 years of a policy of Zambianization.[21]

Michael Burawoy (1972) famously wrote about Zambia in the 1960s when the newly independent state had started to implement the policy of Zambianization across all sectors. He saw three elements of dependence of the politically independent Zambia: its economic reliance on the white supremacist regime in South Africa, on the copper industry, and on expatriate workers (1972, 1–3). Burawoy concluded at the time that the continued 'colonial economic base' held back real change in Zambia's social structure (Burawoy 1972, 114).[22] Some fifty years later, his analysis is again strikingly topical, all the way down to South Africa's role in it.

In 1998 Terence Ranger urged us to be attentive to how Afrikaans and English 'postsettler communities' seek to translate their loss of power (relative to colonial and apartheid times) in one field into new areas and geographies such as economic expansion through investment in the agriculture and mining industries into neighbouring countries (Ranger 1998, 266). One example is South African investors in Tanzania, whose mobility is part of post-apartheid South Africa's economy expansion northwards (Schroeder 2012). For former Zimbabwean farmers, Zambia has become a viable alternative for investment in the agricultural sector. Indeed, regional physical mobility has long been a key to 'whiteness' in Southern Africa, in many instances translating into social mobility (Money and Zyl-Hermann 2020, 17–19).

Global mining companies often prefer specific nationalities of their management and expatriate staff. Mopani Copper Mines, for instance, has had people from South Africa, Peru, Britain and the United States (Lee 2017, 103), and Konkola Copper Mines until under Indian ownership (Vedanta) recruited many from India, while senior and managerial labour in Chinese mines primarily hail from China.[23] Rather than sourcing (white) labour globally, Kansanshi Mine – and First Quantum Minerals in Zambia more generally, which includes its Sentinel Mine – sees recruiting from South Africa as the most viable option. South Africans are cheaper, readily available at the mine as residentials and experienced in 'handling the African'.

In ordinary 'Golf Estate chatter', the region's history and its contemporary social formations are non-existent. This ellipsis is a systemic part of what makes 'frontier culture' successful, as Anna Tsing argues, which 'must continually erase old residents' rights to create its wild and empty spaces where *discovering* resources, not stealing them, is possible' (2005, 68). The conceptual separation between the world inside and outside the estate has consequence for how the mining company engages with Solwezi town and Zambians more generally. For the mining company's management, Zambians are stagnant and incapable of action. This, for the mine, justifies its execution of the necessary tasks. These include, as I showed in the previous chapters, resettlements, compensation and generally transgressing into local authorities' work. It is a combination of ignorance and the white privilege ideologies produced inside the estate that also allow the mine's representatives to evade questions of distribution and ignore national planning processes when claiming national resources such as electricity and implementing key measures for its operations such as electrical and road infrastructure, as the next chapter will show.

Chapter 5

POWER AND INFRASTRUCTURE

'The charcoal burners'

In 2007, First Quantum Mineral's Kansanshi Mining Plc wrote a letter to Solwezi's district forest officer, applying for land for a wildlife reserve in an area classified as protected forest land. The application letter is short, but it contains a line symbolic for the theme of this chapter: 'Kansanshi Mining Plc would like to own this piece of land on title after being degazetted but keep it protected from deforestation and deterioration by the surrounding villagers and charcoal burners.'[1]

In the name of environmental protection (but possibly also with the idea of future prospection and exploration in preferably uninhabited land), the company asked for a large piece of land which it transformed into a fenced wildlife reserve strictly guarded against 'poachers'. Kansanshi's management was in good company with its concern to preserve forests: in the very same year, parties to the UN's Framework Conversion on Climate Change agreed at the COP 13 to use forests in the global fight against climate change, recognizing that forest conservation could significantly reduce greenhouse gases. Today, a large part of Kansanshi's CSR funds flow into the wildlife and forest preservation project (O'Callaghan 2019, 87–8).

It is difficult to overstate the hypocrisy. In order to protect fauna and flora in a game reserve open only to largely expatriate mining employees, villagers who had farms in the area were resettled and excluded from land used as commonage (for the production of charcoal, among others, see Mutamba 2007). In the name of conservation, the mine was able to impose its ideas of land use through privatization and enclosure. Read with Olwig et al. (2015), we can see here a 'global moral economy narrative' at work where 'the poor are burdened with the moral responsibility of compensating for the excessive consumption of the more well-to-do in the global South and particularly in the global North' (2015, 2317).

At the same time, the game reserve projects an image of the mine as concerned with nature conservation – as long as the landscape it conserves lies outside of the mining area. The massive environmental changes brought by the mine's open pits, its tailings, the extensive use (and potential pollution) of water and of electricity, its emissions of dust, noise and sulphur dioxide could safely be ignored as long as forest land remained protected from the real enemy to environmental sustainability in the region: from villagers and the 'charcoal burners' (see also Walsh 2019).

Farmers and urbanites indeed use charcoal burnt by young men from forest trees as their main source of energy. For their energy consumption, 78 per cent of Zambian households use on-site sources such as solar panels, wood and charcoal (Central Statistical Office Zambia 2013, 25). Only 22 per cent of households countrywide are connected to the electricity grid. The balance is even more skewed in rural provinces such as Northwestern, where 95 per cent of households rely on wood and charcoal for cooking. Kansanshi Mine, on the other hand, including its smelter, consumes about 9,000 terajoule of energy per year, the equivalent of 2,502 GWh of electricity. Roughly half of that energy comes from electricity from the grid, half from diesel fuel (First Quantum Minerals Ltd. 2019, 5). Kansanshi's energy needs thus amount to between one-fourth and one-fifth of Zambia's total annual electrical energy consumption. All the mines and smelters in the country together consume more than half of the country's total electricity (Energy Regulation Board 2022, 50).

This energy consumption, together with the mining industry's infrastructural power – to negotiate for, plan and implement infrastructure for its own use – affects Zambians far beyond Solwezi town. Due to its place-bound nature and the massive socio-environmental and economic changes at mining sites, the effects of mining often appear in the literature as limited to the site of extraction. The presence of a large-scale mine, however, can have distributive effects on an entire country. I have shown in the last chapter how a hierarchical and segregated order is created and maintained at the site of extraction. In this and the following chapter, I show how that order finds its equivalent on larger scales, within the country and internationally. In both chapters, I follow connections between the mine and the wider world, gradually moving away from Solwezi town. Pointing at the many societal and material consequences of the mine's presence means to write against the extractive industry's casual denial of its impact. To do so, I examine the structures – broadly understood to include roads, electricity, tax and services – which the mining industry needs to ensure a smooth and 'cost-effective' extraction and transportation of minerals to the end producer or consumer. The current chapter adopts a regional perspective and examines the processes around the extension of electric power lines in Northwestern Province and a new transport corridor through Western Zambia; the next chapter follows copper on its journey through the country and the region. It will become clear from both chapters how, at all scales, the specific order that is created by a variety of actors selectively benefits the extractive industry over 'the charcoal burners' and capital owners over workers or the general population.

Zambia's energy sector

Across Zambia, in rural and urban households, the main source used for lighting is the candle (27.7 per cent in 2010), followed by electricity from the public grid (22 per cent), paraffin (20.3 per cent) and solar power (2.9 per cent) (Central Statistical Office Zambia 2013, 25). In rural households, electricity as a source of lighting is used by 3.1 per cent of households only, contrary to 49.8 per cent in urban areas. For cooking, wood is the main source of energy, used by 53.4 per cent of households across Zambia, followed by charcoal (29.1 per cent) and electricity (16.9 per cent). In rural areas, cooking with wood (85 per cent) or charcoal (12.2 per cent) is even more widespread, while only 2.1 per cent of rural households use electricity for preparing meals. In urban areas, electricity is used by 38.6 per cent, after charcoal (53.9 per cent) and before wood (7 per cent).

Given the vast difference in availability of electrical infrastructure across the country and between provinces and even towns, both affordability and availability of electrical power must be considered in an analysis of any given place. For instance, a household may not be able to afford to pay for electricity, even if its compound is connected to the grid. Conversely, a household's classification as poor does not automatically mean it is 'energy-poor' (Tembo, Hatoongo-Masenke and Bowa-Mundia 2020). Despite this, as Aidoo and Biggs show with substantial data on Ghana, it is safe to assume a 'durable relationship between poverty and electricity availability' (2018, 13; see also Bwalya et al. 2022 for Kitwe).

The backbone of Zambia's electricity supply still is provided by one of the largest colonial infrastructure projects in Southern Africa: the Kariba Dam. Damming up the Zambezi which formed the boundary between North and South Rhodesia created an artificial lake stretching over 280 kilometres and resulted in the resettlement of approximately 57,000 people. Two separate generation plants on both riverbanks supply the two countries with the bulk of their energy needs. From the start, the Zambian share was mainly meant to serve the mines in the Copperbelt (Colson 1971; McGregor 2009; Tischler 2013). Today, Zambia relies on hydropower for 80 per cent of its electrical energy. The two main hydroelectric power plants are the Kafue Gorge and the Kariba Dam, followed by the Itezhi-Tehzi plant. Ten per cent of the country's electricity come from a coal-fired thermal power plant (Maamba Collieries) and from smaller diesel, heavy fuel oil or solar generation plants.

Zambia's main electricity provider, Zambia Electricity Supply Corporation Limited (ZESCO), was established in 1970 and the government is the sole shareholder. The energy market was liberalized in 1995 'to attract private sector participation in the generation, transmission and distribution of electricity' (Committee on Economic Affairs, Energy and Labour 2013). This led to the establishment of new utility companies, most of whom cater to large industry customers rather than to private consumers. They operate smaller power plants and buy energy in bulk from ZESCO.[2]

Electricity is the lifeblood of large-scale mining. Mining and mineral processing operations use approximately 6.2 per cent of total global energy consumption (Ernst and Young 2020, 10). The industry has so far largely relied on fossil fuels. Increasingly, companies opt for a mix of energy sources – fossil fuels, hydroelectricity and renewable energy. In this regard, increased use of electrification on mines is the most notable recent global change. From the companies' perspective, access – or the lack thereof – to electrical power is a business risk whose mitigation often requires investments, especially in remote or new mining areas. FQM in Zambia's Northwestern Province is no exception to this.

The mines, consuming more than half of the country's electrical energy, purchase from Copperbelt Energy Corporation (CEC), which has a bulk supply agreement with ZESCO.[3] CEC grew out of ZCCM in 1997 and is an independent company listed on the Lusaka Stock Exchange, which transmits energy purchased from ZESCO and distributes it to the mining industry on the Copperbelt and in the Northwestern Province at high voltage. At the time of privatization, shortly before the turn of the century, Zambia had surplus power. As part of the privatization negotiations, ZESCO offered low tariffs to the potential international investors in the mining sector, which was as a major incentive. These tariffs were cemented in the Development Agreements between the ministries and the mining companies.

Kansanshi Mine Solwezi could soon connect to the national grid that already reached Solwezi town and thereby was able to profit from low tariffs agreed upon in the Development Agreements. FQM's Kalumbila (Sentinel) Mine some 140 kilometres further west had to be powered by diesel engines for many years before it was recently connected to the national grid. It did not connect to the line extending into the Northwestern Province coming from Solwezi, though, but instead had a 330 kV line built all the way from Lusaka (planned to be extended to DRC's mining town of Kolwezi). How this process unfolded and what the impact was on the newly forming urban centre around Kalumbila Mine is what I turn to now.

Kalumbila

In Northwestern Province with its new urban centres around the three mines in Solwezi, Lumwana and Kalumbila, some peri-urban developments and a large rural hinterland, we witness the parallel development of slow and patchy rural electrification on the one hand, massive 'selectively territorialized investment' (Ferguson 2005) in electricity infrastructure through private mining companies trying to secure their energy needs on the other. Until 2017, only Solwezi and Kasempa districts were connected to the national grid through a 66-kV line linked to Luano substation near Chingola. All other districts were, if at all, supplied by local networks. ZESCO operated five diesel stations in the province supplying Mwinilunga, Mufumbwe, Kabompo, Zambezi and Chavuma districts, while the private North-Western Power Company served Lumwana Mine township and Zengamina Power Company supplied Kalene Mission Hospital and the surrounding villages. Since the small diesel plants are expensive to run and maintain while tariffs are regulated on a national level, ZESCO operated with huge losses. In 2017, the line was extended from Solwezi to Lumwana and finally to ten out of the province's eleven districts. The extension was financed by a loan from the Swedish Export Credit Corporation and Standard Bank of South Africa. In 2020, Ikelenge was the province's last district to be connected to the grid, the line now extending up to Jimbe border post on the Angolan border.

Kalumbila/Sentinel Mine, FQM's second mine in the Northwestern Province, may have accelerated the eventual connection of the province's districts to the national grid (via the line-of-rail and through the Copperbelt), but it did not contribute to any of this infrastructure. Instead, it had a 600-kilometre-long, 330-kV line built to its Kalumbila substation that cuts through the Central and Northwestern Province.

Kalumbila has a very different history from Solwezi. The town is a planned company town next to a new mine, the Sentinel Mine, which forms part of the larger 400-km^2 large Trident Project wholly owned by FQM. The mining project is generally known as 'Kalumbila Mine', a description I adopt here, too. The mine is a so-called greenfield project, a new mining site (although Roan Selection Trust, Anglo American and Equinox explored its resources in the late 1950s, the 1980s and the 1990s, respectively). It was constructed into a thinly populated area of small-scale farming. Today, due to the influx of work seekers and employees, its townships form a new urban centre in the region.

Even though the mine's license area had been a pending issue, the mining company started with the construction of a large-scale open pit mine in 2012. Its electricity needs were covered by diesel power plants that supplied roughly 200 MW. Since the company needed at least 30 per cent more electricity to operate at full capacity, and ZESCO did not have the funds to connect the project to the national grid, FQM agreed to provide upfront finance for the construction of a 330-kV, 600-kilometre line from Lusaka West to Kalumbila by ZESCO, with the prospect of receiving favourable rates once ZESCO connected them to its power plants through new substations in Lusaka West and Mumbwa, financed by loans of the African Development Bank and the European Investment Bank. In 2018, ZESCO eventually commissioned the lines and started supplying electricity to Kalumbila substation.

This cooperation could have been an example of positive change: the mine provides finance for much-needed infrastructure to a rural area previously cut off from electrical power. If we look more closely, however, what we see is the selective development of public infrastructure and the exacerbation of inequalities that were already lingering as a result of the mining company's arrival.

The mine's development in the past decade has radically transformed the social composition of the Kalumbila area. Today, people living in the area can be spatially categorized into roughly four types of living conditions, which, among others, are distinguished by unequal access to electricity. Firstly, there is a state-of-the-art golf estate for the (mostly white) expatriate workers and the senior and junior management. I described life on a similar golf estate in Solwezi town in the previous chapter. The Kalumbila golf estate shares its main features where residents live a sheltered and privileged life with unlimited access to electricity, water, garbage collection, cleaning services, high-end private schools, sports and recreation areas and a club house at an artificial lake.

Secondly, the mine, through its Kalumbila Town Development Company (KTDC), started building Kalumbila town, designed by the Danish firm *Gehl Architects* for 10,000 houses, half of which have been built so far. Workers, both contracted and subcontracted and mostly men from the Copperbelt towns, live in houses which they rent from KTDC (see Figure 24). Sometimes their families move in with them; increasingly men are coming on their own, though, with no intention to permanently settle in the town. KDTC's aim is to sell the houses to workers, but there is no bank in Zambia, yet which would offer affordable mortgage. Residents enjoy access to electricity and water, but, unlike residents on the golf estate, they have to pay for these services.

Thirdly, farmers, mostly kiKaonde-, Lunda- or Luvale-speaking, who lived in the mine's license area or in the place transformed into Kalumbila town, were resettled into two small resettlement areas. The more than 500 families could choose whether to be closer to the main road and thus to business opportunities, or further south and thus closer to their original fields. The initial arrangement of the villages – loosely scattered, often shifting and along small pathways – has dramatically changed, especially in the northern resettlement area. The houses are densely arranged within a trapezoid zone. There is, like before, no running water or electricity. But unlike before, the areas are much more densely populated, boreholes to access water cater for many more hundreds of people, and in-flux from often better educated work seekers from the Copperbelt towns limits space and economic opportunities for the original residents in the area.

Finally, Chisasa, initially a small settlement at a junction of the main road and the path to chief Musele's palace, has expanded in the past few years equally due to in-migration from the Copperbelt and other areas in the country. Thousands of work seekers, but also employees at the mine who do not want to spend their salaries on high rents in the company town, share the little infrastructure on land

Figure 24. Monde Sitali and Simon tending to their garden in Kalumbila town, July 2016. Photo by author.

still under customary tenure. Hygiene is a pressing problem as there is neither running water nor electricity.

These four spatial entities are situated across a space of 8-kilometre radius. [4] This stark differentiation between living conditions, access to services and chances for employment was introduced by the mine's arrival and its targeted investment in infrastructure and services such as housing and electricity. In some instances, people were resettled and compensated based on a technocratic logic of loss and repair; in most cases, people moved there by choice. However, the question of where to live and thus which services to access is not really a choice for most people. It depends on income, employment and race.

The more 'local' a person was, the worse off she or he is now, perhaps with the exception of the chiefly family. One could also say that the mine's arrival spatially and socially segregated persons along their place in the production process. The owners of the means of production live outside the country and continent (in Canada and Australia); the managers and white expatriates live on the golf estate and in the capital Lusaka; the workers live in a relatively modern and well serviced town; and the unemployed, the poor and most women and children live in the resettlement areas or in packed informal compounds. The mine has introduced changes beyond the creation of distinct housing areas: inside the license area, forests are cut down for the mine pit, rivers are dammed, and fields flooded for the tailings, while all around Kalumbila town, billboards and small paper boards tacked at trees by representatives of Kalumbila Mine warn villagers to refrain from cutting down trees to produce charcoal.

FQM connected its mine to the electricity grid to run its mine at maximum capacity. The company thereby creates privileges in the Kalumbila area from which only its employees benefit, at the exclusion of original occupants of the land and migrated new residents. I witnessed a situation where a group of resettled farmers complained to the mine's CSR department about the lack of access to electricity to the new homes in the 'resettlement areas'. The CSR staffer was dismissive: 'Look at where you were before the mine came! Did you have electricity? No!' The mining company did not see any reason to compensate them for something they did not have before, he explained. When people living in the overcrowded, informal town of Chisasa complained about lacking electrification of the town, the CSR officer dismissed the claims, too. Expanding the national grid to new urban centres, he said, was the government's and ZESCO's responsibility. The mining company, through its CSR office, refers to the state's role as provider of services – a state whose capacity the mining company regularly undermines through its power to plan and implement the infrastructure it needs (see also Chapter 1).

The mine has the power to forestall the state's planning and actions or push it to implement what the industry needs. The new electricity line from Lusaka West to Kalumbila is an articulation of both sides of this power: it planned the new line and offset the costs with future repayment by the state. As long as the central state is financially incapable of providing a service network in the region, the new line does not benefit the larger area.[5] The mine's exclusive provisioning of electrical power to its workers and the management structures – along a gendered and racialized logic – settlements in the area. Its actions have created even starker fragmentation between groups already segregated by an order created by the mining company: 'skilled' employees versus 'unskilled locals', migrants versus 'original' residents, whites versus Blacks. As a Zambian subcontractor to Kalumbila Mine which provided him with a room in Kalumbila town complained to me, 'People living in the golf estate have many privileges. They get a car, airtime, they get their laundry done and the rooms are cleaned. And if they are off from work, they get on a plane.' (There is an airstrip in Kalumbila.) In turn, a barber with a little shop in Chisasa criticized that people living in Kalumbila town received power for free. He has to load the batteries of the shavers with solar energy and cannot take customers while they are loading. Against the spatial segregation and the attached privileges in some housing areas, access to electricity becomes a stark marker of difference and hinders solidarity between groups.

A new transport corridor

To have guaranteed access to electricity, the mining company took extra measures which have resulted in benefits to a privileged group and in the superimposition of corporate priorities onto the state's. To bring copper not only out of the ground but also out of the country, a functioning road network is as important.[6] Solwezi and Kalumbila Districts constitute the country's contemporary mining hub, yet despite plans that go back more than hundred years, the region is still not connected to the railway. Instead of investing in the central state's explicit aim to move at least 30 per cent of heavy freight by railway, FQM, through a partnership with the haulage company BHL opened a new transport route through the Northwestern and Western Provinces. It thereby also avoids Zambia's flagship one-stop-border-post in Chirundu at the border to Zimbabwe.

To transport copper out of Zambia, several routes are used. Up until recently, all of them led through the Copperbelt province and then – depending on the sites of the contracted haulage companies' infrastructure such as warehouses and customs staff as well as the political and fuel situation in the relevant countries – to Dar es Salaam in Tanzania, Beira in Mozambique, Walvis Way in Namibia or Durban and East London in South Africa (see next chapter for more details). To cut this route to Walvis Bay short, the trucking and logistics firm Buks Haulage Limited (BHL Group) repaired and graded a 220-kilometre section – between Kasempa and Kaoma – to open up a new 2,300-kilometre-long transport route between Solwezi and Kalumbila Districts and Namibia's main and comparatively efficient port Walvis Bay. It runs southwest from Solwezi through Kasempa and proceeds through the Western Province, the small towns of Kaoma and Mongu, from where it cuts south to the border towns of Sesheke (Zambia) and Katima Mulilo (Namibia). From Katima Mulilo, truckers drive along the well-paved road in the Zambezi Region (formerly Caprivi), and pass Rundu, Otavi, Otjiwarongo, Karibib and Swakopmund to reach Walvis Bay. The upgrade of the section between Kasempa and Kaoma was completed in 2018. Some parts of the new route are still unusable now and then during the rainy seasons, with trucks getting stuck in the mud. All in all, however, the new transport corridor cuts two days of a five-day journey and 400 kilometres in comparison to the route via Chingola, Lusaka and Livingstone, which reduces costs considerably. Other trucking firms, like Alistair, also use the road and BHL levies a fee for its use.

Apart from connecting Zambia's Northwestern Province to the Walvis Bay Corridor, the upgraded road shortens the route to South African harbours via Botswana. The 923-metre-long new Kazungula bridge from Zambia to Botswana, which was opened in May 2021, allows truckers to cross the Zambezi River at the four countries' meeting point much quicker than with the slow and unreliable pontoon ferry that was the only means for truckers to cross. The new route through the Western Province also presents the option to expand north from Kalumbila to Kolwezi in the DRC, which would further increase Walvis Bay's market share.

The haulage company BHL has its head office in Solwezi and owns depots in Ndola, Katima Mulilo, Kaoma and Walvis Bay. The company was founded in 2004 by two brothers, the South Africans Buks Jansen and Pieter van Rensburg, specializing in transport and logistics, and operating primarily in the DRC, Angola, Zambia and Namibia.[7] Officially designated as a CSR project, BHL undertook the rehabilitation of the 220-kilometre gravel road at its own costs. For the work, it sub-contracted one of its main business partners, FQM and its in-house roads engineering department Roads. The mining company in turn guaranteed BHL to transport 30 per cent of its copper anodes along the new route to Walvis Bay, thus supporting and committing to the transporter's initiative. For FQM, Walvis Bay is also the preferred port to get the goods in. Trailers built to allow for return loads driving back to Solwezi District are thus never empty but always filled with cargo for the mining operations at Kansanshi and Kalumbila Mines (see Chapter 6).

The upgrade of the new route was a corporate initiative between two big players in Zambia. The haulage contracts are one of FQM's largest procurement contracts, and the haulage company BHL is FQM's largest haulage contractor (for both Kansanshi and Sentinel Mines). In its communication, FQM portrays Buks van Rensburg as a 'naturalized settler' in an attempt to show its willingness to increase local content. Van Rensburg has acquired Zambian citizenship. FQM and BHL not only share a similar history of gradual expansion in Southern and Central Africa, but their founders also get along well. Buks van Rensburg is often seen at Kansanshi's club house. Van Rensburg's and the Pascalls' collaboration on this particular project seems a natural outcome of their high regard for one another and their shared positionality as white businessmen growing up in apartheid South Africa and Rhodesia, respectively. More important for the successful collaboration is the fact that the FQM had bargaining power vis-à-vis the trucking firm, as a manager told me. As I will elaborate in the next chapter, a subsidiary of FQM is one of only two off-takers of Kansanshi's copper products. With such large volumes, FQM can enter a solid collaboration with a trucking firm, and in turn nudge the trucker to investing in a new transport route.

Although BHL entered a 10-year memorandum of understanding with Zambia's National Road Development Agency (RDA), the Zambian state has had little involvement in the project and its planning. Upon completion, the National Road Fund Agency put up three toll stations (one each between Kaoma–Mongu, Mongu–Kalabo and Senanga–Sesheke) in 2018. Residents are also subjected to paying the toll to the National Road Fund Agency (NRFA) albeit at a reduced rate.[8] The new route has transformed the western part of Solwezi town with new petrol stations and repair shops. Residents in Kaoma and Mongu and other small towns and villages along the new route now live along a key transport corridor and in transit towns with hundred trucks per day thundering by, in small caravans, and truckers stopping over in hostels, adhering to the injunction against commercial night driving.

Corporate spatial governance

Electricity links and roads are key elements in public infrastructure. While Zambian citizens vocally demand better connections from government, the state has too little capacity to expand nationwide networks. Like other rural provinces, Northwestern Province is poorly connected both to the national grid and to regional road networks. The central state is, in theory, keen to develop the largely rural province, whose potential for economic growth in the mining, manufacturing, agricultural and even tourism sectors has been foregrounded by government actors for many decades. In practice, government struggles to finance and organize the infrastructure it sees as a precondition for unlocking the region's development potential. In this situation, the presence of large international mining companies offers the possibility to partly outsource infrastructure development to private actors. Consequently, we see a pattern of state-company relation emerging that can be found in many countries with extractive industries (e.g. Welker 2014). The state holds back in putting money into the province arguing that the mines have an economic and social responsibility to take care of the residents where they operate. The companies in turn argue that they pay taxes as part of their duty to help develop the country. In the ensuing negotiations, companies often agree to implement certain infrastructure measures that conform to their own needs, partly offsetting the costs by cuts in rates and taxes (and often discursively framed as 'CSR'; see Hertz 2020). This carries the danger that the private actor primarily 'develops' infrastructure according to its own needs.

The Zambian state does not block these investments because they carry the promise of 'development' and can be pointed at by the ruling party as successful projects. Most importantly, the mining companies' contribution to the national economy is too high for the state to have sufficient leverage to challenge the industry. As a result, infrastructural priorities are guided by a corporate rather than a democratic logic.

As the owner of Zambia's two largest copper mines, FQM, faced with a shortage of energy and poor transport connections, implemented its own priorities through the construction of a completely new electricity line and the upgrade of a road into a transport highway. The deals with state authorities – often described as public-private partnership by the company – pass the cost on to taxpayers through favourable rates and tolls. These investments were not designed by state authorities intent on increasing public access to infrastructure. In the case of the electricity line to Kalumbila, corporate priorities resulted in the exclusion of housing areas surrounding the mine. In the case of the road upgrade, the picture is more complex. An upgraded road may benefit an entire region and facilitate mobility and trade, but with the limited resources available, the development of one road always implies the choice not to develop others. Under these circumstances, privileging copper export routes implies neglecting inter-country connections and road networks able to facilitate inter-regional trade with neighbouring countries. It also comes with direct costs to people living along the roads, such as noise, road deaths and changes in the composition of small towns.

Distributing what is left

A large part of the national infrastructural budget goes into projects that the mining industry needs. This not only sets the wrong priorities but also intensifies the struggle for the remaining resources. The rest of the chapter focuses on the *distributional* effect of corporate power to negotiate and implement their own priorities.

For this, I return to electricity, whose distribution is highly unequal in Zambia. As mentioned, the mining industry consumes more than half of the country's available electricity. Corporate actors are given preference because they are seen as indispensable for development. Households and small businesses are not of the same individual systemic importance and are generally less well organized to voice their collective concerns. Despite the inequality of provision, electricity supply was not considered as a problem in official discourse until recently. The country had always had sufficient rainfall to fill its dams and even sell surplus power to neighbouring countries. Poor rainfalls during the 2014–15 rainy season, however, resulted in low dam water levels and (coupled, it seems, with maintenance problems) in a considerable shortfall in electricity supply. While hydroelectric power is a *renewable* source of energy, it has become clear that it is not a *reliable* source of energy (for a similar situation in Accra, Ghana, see Silver 2015). For the period between September and December 2015, for instance, there was a power deficit of around 560–1,000 MW (peak demand would be 2.616 MW) (Energy Regulation Board 2016, 1).

As a result, ZESCO increased the frequency and duration of cuts, so-called load-shedding. Starting in 2015 until today, most households, but also commercial and industrial consumers across the country, often experience eight or more hours of power cuts per day. In addition, private consumers, small- and medium-sized businesses and even the public administration have had to cope with increased tariffs (see Batidzirai, Moyo and Kapembwa 2017) and highly regressive subsidies (Maboshe, Kabechani and Chelwa 2019).[9] Electricity cuts to domestic customers are so frequent so that today, in Gupta's words, for India, 'being connected to the grid and having electricity are two different issues' (2015, 559). Even households that are not connected to the national grid are indirectly affected by the power crisis, which lets prices for staple foods (such as maize and oil) rise and makes public services even less reliable. In addition to that, the commodity price boom which started in the early 2000s turned into a bust in 2015 again. In combination with low global copper prices, energy shortages have affected both Zambia's exports and the Kwacha's exchange rates.

The expansion of mining activities through massive foreign direct investment in the early 2000s possibly contributed to the power crisis. The mining sector is one of the few sectors that increased its power consumption between 2014 and 2015 – by 6.4 per cent. (Energy Regulation Board 2016, 9).[10] Furthermore, the mines are largely exempt from cuts.

In Zambia, load-shedding has triggered some criticism of the government's distributional priorities, although usually excluding the overall preference for the mining industry. I examine the effects of load-shedding on everyday life and the ensuing political discussions to argue that corporate power to decide on a country's infrastructural priorities affects every corner of the country, be it close to the mine or not. For this, I take the reader back to Solwezi, the place I know the best, and which, if it comes to load-shedding, can stand for any other town in Zambia connected to the national grid.

Load-shedding

Unlike in Kalumbila, most urban compounds are connected to the grid in Solwezi. The exception are the new and densely populated peri-urban areas at the western side of the town where migrants and original residents live. The majority of residents in these areas simply see a power line running high above their heads, leading directly to the mine, and the promise of power has not translated into local feeder lines yet (Harvey and Knox 2015). This is similar to how the Gwembe Tonga people must have felt when Kariba Dam was built in Southern Zambia in the 1950s to feed the mines in the Copperbelt with energy. These resettled farmers saw the power line running across their villages and fields without the prospect of being integrated into 'modernization' (Tischler 2014).

The *general* availability of electricity in the urban neighbourhoods does not mean that every household is connected to the grid, though; connections depend on the house owner's funds and ZESCO's capacities to connect new households. All in all, however, the issue in Solwezi is not so much the connection to the grid but the availability of electricity against the current situation of frequent blackouts.

Load-shedding has several consequences at different levels of urban life: for households, small businesses, public service provision and night life. In households, the lack of electricity is often irritating, but Solwezi's urban residents adapt with relative ease and revert to a number of alternative sources of energy. Cooking with wood or charcoal is extremely widespread (e.g. Mavhunga 2013). In addition, households use solar panels, car batteries and gas stoves. People charge their cell phones at stalls equipped with any of these; they listen to the radio with the help of solar panels mostly bought at one of Solwezi's Chinese shops; and they generally use a combination of energy sources for different needs. This ability to exploit different sources according to the need and availability is certainly witness to inventiveness and resilience, but it should not be romanticized. The work not done by electricity has to be taken over by somebody, and under the prevailing unequal gender relations, load-shedding tends to increase the workload of women. For them and for household aides, load-shedding results in additional work, such as fetching water at a water kiosk when water pressure at the tap has receded due to lack of power. This additional work entrenches the pattern of gender relations where – often young, related – women do the household work. The lack of reliable electricity ties them more tightly to household work and often prevents them from going to school, losing on a key opportunity for emancipation. Almost every household with children is affected by the long and often daily cuts in electricity: pupils and students are forced to do their homework in candlelight. Getting sleepy in the dim light, they struggle to concentrate.

Some urban residents are severely hampered in pursuing their income strategies because they cannot simply revert to other sources of power. Small and midsize businesses which rely on electric power suffer the most from power cuts. Meat or fish stored in electric coolers rots earlier; laptops stop running once the battery is flat; computers need expensive backup systems; water supply becomes patchy when the pumps stop working. All this also increases the prices for basic goods. Individuals who run a business often try to mitigate the consequences by adjusting their working rhythm to the power cuts. A tailor told me that she would get up in the night when the bright light of the bulb she left on woke her, telling her that power was back – and start working on the sewing machine for the rest of the night.

Finally, power cuts have massive effects on the quality of public services. While the civic centre in Solwezi has a generator, it regularly lacks the cash for diesel to run it. When working at the Planning Department, I realized that the council's organization assumes a constant flow of electricity (see Chapter 2). To improve filing and archiving processes, a recently introduced software was meant to help the decentralized units managing data and making it accessible across departments. Power cuts can last an entire morning during which officials are unable to access the system. They thus jeopardize an already ramshackle system of data organization and storage. When power goes off, officers usually sit idle. As a result, residents' dossiers are not worked on, and they are put off for yet another day.

In Solwezi, very few roads have a functioning public streetlight system let alone streetlamps. Cuts which often happen in the evening when electricity would be needed most and when the system is most likely to be overwhelmed nevertheless change the possibilities for social life in the streets after dark. Young women are more hesitant to go out at night. Uneven, washed-out compound paths are pitch-black, and cars with dim front lights endanger pedestrians walking along the roads.

For many, the indirect consequence of power cuts, namely receding water pressure due to idle pumps, is the most serious consequence of load-shedding

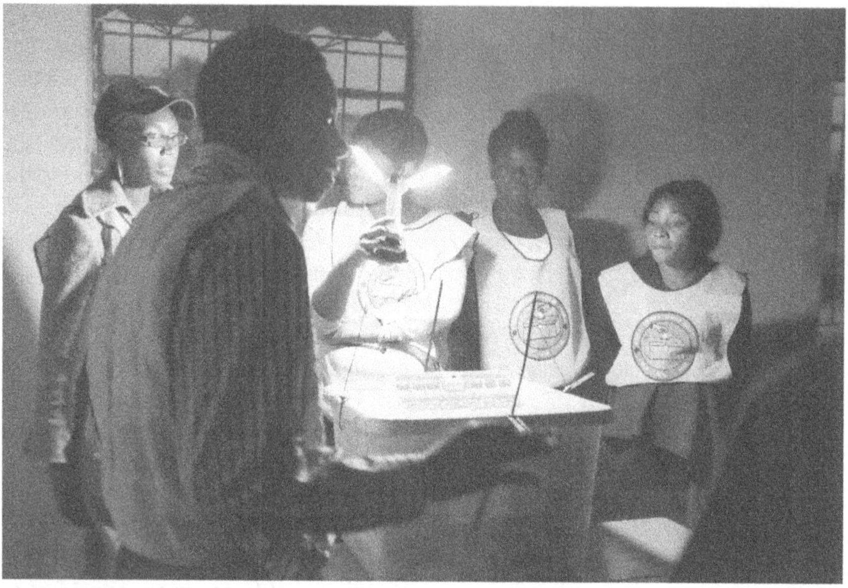

Figure 25. Power cut during vote counting at general elections, Kyawama, Solwezi, 11 August 2016. Photo by author.

(cf. Björkman 2015). It affects people's health and again produces additional work such as fetching water from water kiosks or carrying it from streams, hand-dug wells or community boreholes (see Chapter 2).[11]

A group which is exempt from power cuts are residents on the Golf Estate (see previous chapter). The privilege of the mining companies for almost unlimited access to electricity expands beyond its mining operations to the place where its senior and junior management and expatriate workers and their families live. There are hardly any power cuts on the estate; if there are, they feel like a small hick-up because the generator takes over immediately. Residents on the golf estate heavily rely on electricity for all fields of private life, from imported foodstuff in the freezer to the favourite Netflix series on the computer screen. The golf estate, just like the mine, is an 'energy enclave' constantly lit, even if surrounding compounds are dark.

Faced with this obvious and publicly visible expression of inequality, the estate's management at some stage in 2016 introduced what they called a 'solidarity cut'. Three short, scheduled power cuts across the week were meant to show solidarity with ordinary residents outside of the golf estate. This was a purely artificial exercise not based on any necessity, and it did not bring any additional power to Solwezi residents depending on a different distribution system. Its symbolic effect was mostly lost on Solwezi residents since the solidarity cut was incidentally introduced in a pre-election time when cuts in Solwezi were temporarily suspended (see below). Ironically, however, the solidarity cuts brought more guests into the estate's social venue, the club house, which had a generator and had previously suffered from poor attendance by the estate's residents. Thus, in an unexpected turn, solidarity among a divided golf estate community as described in the previous chapter temporarily increased – everyone was affected by the management-ordered cuts. (I will elaborate on this in the conclusion when reflecting on the limits of joint symmetrical action.) Overall, the fact that the solidarity cuts did not have an effect beyond the fence suggests that in Zambia, only in a few electric enclaves like the golf estate has electricity become 'invisible, indispensable and omnipotent' (Rupp 2016, 111).

The politics of energy distribution

While in theory, load-shedding should hit everybody except for the mining companies and the residents of their housing complexes, reality feels different for many. They see themselves subject to opaque decisions about energy distribution, and blackouts become fodder for rumours and the basis for political moves. At the core here are questions of distribution. So far, the mining industry has managed to escape these political discussions. The industry's discursive claim for its share is so strong that, from the beginning, the public debate only covers the share left to Zambian residents and commercial users.

The energy crisis in Zambia is not a clear-cut issue for many Zambians. While the state has continuously reiterated that load-shedding was due to climate change resulting in low water levels in the reservoirs, people are not entirely sure. Critics attribute it to mismanagement in the ZESCO board, suggesting that the energy company should be taken over by private investors. In ordinary discussions of politics in the opposition stronghold Solwezi, the energy situation is an entry point to criticize the government and the governing party PF. One middle-income suburb of Solwezi, the Stadium Area, is home to many civil servants. Solwezi residents sceptical of the state's willingness to improve the situation would often point at this suburb. 'During the night, Stadium Area has power, you can see it!'. The fact that power is cut off along specific feeders, and cuts are best visible at night, when entire neighbourhoods become dark, is thus used to read the town through the lens of political favouritism.

Many instances feed people's suspicion that the real issue is not the lack of water in the reservoirs. The time between late 2014 – when President Michael Sata passed away, leading to early elections for a temporary successor in January 2015 – and August 2016 – when regular elections were held (both won by PF's Edgar Lungu) – can be described as an uninterrupted phase of campaigning. Both Lungu and his main challenger (also again for the upcoming 2021 presidential elections), Hakainde Hichilema from the United Party for Social Development (UPND), frequently visited Solwezi as it grew into an important power base for either party. Whenever one of them was in town, load-shedding stopped. People wondered how this was possible.

Feeding suspicion even more was the fact that about eight weeks before the regular, general elections on 11 August 2016, the entire country experienced almost uninterrupted power supply. The rainy season 2015–16 was certainly not capable of alleviating power shortages. Where, then, was power coming from? Pre-election rumours circulating among opposition supporters predicted a massive electricity tariff hike in case the PF would win again. This did not happen immediately, a fact which might be related to a tight and contested election outcome (Banda et al. 2020; Fraser 2016). In May 2017, however, the Energy Regulation Board approved ZESCO's application of a 75 per cent tariff adjustment to be effected in two phases. The tariff adjustment applies across all customer categories except for the mines.[12] The state's hesitation to include the mining industry in tariff adjustments ignores some evidence that the influence of energy price in investment decision-making in Zambia's mining sector is actually limited (Tembo 2018).

Faced with criticism of their performance, not surprisingly, the central state and local authorities try to solve the power crisis. While the central state focuses on energy generation, local authorities want to be seen improving access to electricity and expanding the network. Working towards a solution of the energy crisis brings its own problems, though. It is a technical task, but while pursuing it, more than mere technical implementation happens. Local authorities, together with civil servants from ZESCO, have to make decisions as to who should profit first from the extension of the power lines. Rather than a broad rollout of basic services across the peri-urban areas, Solwezi's town council typically focuses on providing access to some key stakeholders in the governance of the region. This process is often driven by elected councillors who are tasked with bringing development to their constituencies. In committee meetings or in informal chats with civil servants, elected councillors campaign for attention of their own ward, and often clash with civil servants' rather exclusive attention on the urban areas. Elected councillors and officers share, however, the interest to have a good working relationship with chiefs and headmen, the main representatives of the traditional authorities in charge of the rural areas. In consequence, both groups can often agree on connecting chiefly palaces even in very remote areas, and large efforts are made to bring electricity and other infrastructure to them.[13]

Access, distribution and availability of electricity is also a political issue for Zambians. Given the visibility of electrical infrastructure (lit compounds, streetlamps, power lines above one's head, etc.), its distribution becomes tangible. Electricity makes differences visible, exacerbates them and offers an entry point for criticism of the elite.

The central state periodically tries to challenge the prevailing key of allocating electricity. Newly elected President Lungu announced that, due to the national power crisis, mines would also see 30 per cent cuts in power supply.[14] At a time when copper prices lingered near their six-year low, mining companies responded by threatening with the retrenchment of 30 per cent of their labour force. This happened several times between 2015 and 2016. Usually, the state backtracked; in one instance, however, there were some cuts of the supply for the mines, and some hundred workers were indeed retrenched by the mines.[15] Like tax, electricity needs could be a lever in Lusaka's negotiations with the mining sector. Regularly, government fails to use it effectively (because if it does, jobs are at risk) and sooner or later has to cave in to demands by the companies.

Conclusion

In the new and vivid political discussions in Zambia on energy distribution, triggered by the country's decreased availability of electricity and ZESCO's measure of load-shedding, the mines rarely play any role. They manage to appear as indispensable actors of development who quite naturally must be privileged. Consequently, the structuring effects of the industry's privilege – that the rest of the country must somehow deal with what is left – become naturalized, as well. The country discusses the distribution of energy under conditions that do not take the entire situation into account. This further exacerbates the state's existing governance challenges. It also jeopardizes political cohesion and solidarity. Political discussions do not focus on the country's overall aims – How do we as a country want to distribute electricity? What kind of development do we want? – but on narrower questions of distribution and access. Under conditions of undersupply, this pits social groups against each other and raises mutual suspicions.

Decisions of how to invest in a country's development and a carbo-neutral future, should, Táíwò (2020) writes, be 'set by community decisions rather than by market forces'. In Zambia, there is not currently any open discussion on the distributive justice of infrastructure. Further, infrastructure investments financed by loans will likely exacerbate rather than ameliorate the general imbalance in infrastructure distribution. Already today, Zambia faces drought and water scarcity, making electrical power supply less stable and sustainable. The agricultural season in the years 2023–4 will be the driest in the past four decades (OCHA 2024).

These extreme weather conditions are outcomes of global warming primarily caused by the Global North's emissions. Currently relying on hydropower, Zambia will have to make investments to mitigate and protect its population and to adapt to climate change in the near future. 'Climate finance', as it is called, usually comes as loans and will add a further burden to ordinary debts (Oxfam 2020). The profiteers will most probably again be foreign-owned mining companies and North-based creditors.

The chapter started with a quote from a letter in which Kansanshi Mine's management points to charcoal burning as the main cause of environmental degradation, offering to save the environment by fencing an area used as commonage by rural communities. I showed that Zambian households revert to the use of charcoal as a source of energy because the mines' infrastructural priorities, such as electric energy, are superimposed onto the development agenda of the state. Once again, a conceptual separation between the mines and the country hides their mutual but asymmetrical interdependence. It enables the mining sector to not only implement its own priorities, but to naturalize them as evident national priorities. This prevents any national debate on the sector's role in the economy and lets its negotiation, planning and implementation power appear as a given. It also enables the mines to shape infrastructure development in the country according to their own needs and hides the wider distribution effects of their presence.

Integrating the mines into an open discussion of Zambia's development aims also needs to include an analysis of its interdependence with economies of the Global North that extract value from it. The next chapter moves from the national to the global dimension of the Zambian extractive sector. It presents the world-spanning network of services for mining that links the mine to the markets and in which a large part of the profit from mineral extraction is made. International companies, many of them headquartered in Switzerland, use these new and more flexible opportunities to capture value in the global production networks.

Chapter 6

TRADING INEQUALITY

Capture of both researcher and value

> I must admit I am a bit surprised. I have not received any request from yourself or any organization to conduct this research at Kansanshi [Mine] nor a request to interview personnel at Kansanshi. Could you please supply me with the remit from the International Project that you are leading. I am going to the [Kansanshi Golf Estate] club for lunch at 1pm if you wanted to drop by.

This email dated 15 August 2017 was signed by the then general manager (GM) of Kansanshi Mine, one of two of Canada-based First Quantum Minerals' (FQM's) Zambian mines. With slightly shaky knees, I went to the club where the general manager often took his lunch. He had ordered his lunch before leaving the mine and found his table already set. Today, he went for a stroll across the golf course to check on the progress of a small dam. I told the waiters that I had an appointment with the GM and was seated at his table where I could watch him approaching. We had not met yet. He seemed nervous and tense to me. I tried to look relaxed and be chatty.

For many weeks now, I had had access to several senior employees and managers of Kansanshi Mine and conducted formal interviews on the mine premises while living in the residential area for the mine's management and expatriate employees, the Golf Estate (see Chapter 4). My access to the mine site had to be authorized by my interviewees on each occasion; the interviews were taped with the interviewees' consent, some of whom requested individual parts of the conversation to be off record. When I finally approached the mine's GM for an interview, he sent me this email, and there we were negotiating my presence. I did not order anything, feeling that he had not invited me for lunch but rather to an interrogation. Other guests looked on curiously as they knew the GM and, by now, they had seen me around, too. Immediately after sitting down, the GM made clear that his fellow managers had violated internal procedures by speaking to me without authorization by the mother company's (FQM) board. They were in breach of an agreement they had to sign annually, in which they vowed to not make public any information about the company without prior consent by him, by the co-founder, president and director at FQM and by the full board of directors. Shareholders, the clearly worried GM repeated multiple times, would otherwise learn things they ought not to know.

I apologized for the inconvenience I caused to him and his team of managers, but I also explained that none of his team of managers had told me about the internal procedure and that I would have expected them to tell me. They should have known better, he agreed. I was quite surprised about the GM sharing with me the extent to which he did not have control over his subordinates. He also seemed to notice this fact himself and quickly found back to what I imagined the GM of the largest copper mine in Africa to be: tough, distanced, and professional. He informed me about the way forward: I should write a letter explaining my interest in conducting research on the mine, which he would forward to the FQM board. It may be that I would have to hand over my notes to the company, he continued. I replied vaguely and cautiously that I could not agree to do that.

That was it. He picked up his fork to dig into his chicken salad. As a marker of my departure, I tried a joke: maybe, pending the board's decision, I was lucky and would be able to interview him at last. He smiled politely and I hastened away, relieved to have survived one of the fraughter situations of my field work. I did not have to go far to reach my temporary home on the Golf Estate. Trying to make sense of it all, I typed my notes, feeling suddenly surveyed and unsure whether I should log into the estate's WLAN. The GM was surprisingly plain in his worry. I had expected him to be over-authoritative, shouting or charming even. He truly was worried, I concluded.

I tried to recall to myself how I ended up in this situation. My research was not an organizational study of the mining company, but on Solwezi town. This means that I treated the mine as one actor among many in the town and I simply tried to see how far I was let in. Early on, in 2013 and more often in 2015 and 2016, I was in contact with the CSR department and accompanied its manager for many days. This is usually where most researchers stop; the CSR department acts as a convincing gatekeeper. In 2015, however, I lived in the mine's housing project for better-off employees, Kabitaka, Solwezi, for several months and in Kalumbila town, run by a subsidiary of FQM, for several weeks. Also in 2015, I became a member of the Kansanshi Golf Estate club, as a researcher, and regularly spent time there. Eventually, in 2017, I moved in with a female mine employee (see Chapter 4). All this needed and implied authorization by company representatives. I consistently made clear that I was there for research, and never tried to do research covertly. Given the smallness of the expatriate community, I am quite sure the GM at least knew about my presence as a researcher. Even when I was able to officially schedule a research interview with FQM's Director of Operations Matt Pascall when he visited the mine two weeks earlier, I was not given to understand that I needed any additional authorization.

When I eventually approached the managers one by one, they all individually granted me access to the mining site where the management's offices are situated, which involves quite a bit of screening. None of the managers told me that there was a formal procedure for research on the mine, but all readily agreed to meet me and allowed me to record the conversations (with breaks when they wanted to go off the record). I took it for granted that members of the mine's higher management controlled access by researchers in the interest of the mine and followed its internal procedures.

Nevertheless, I felt uneasy about the fact that the GM blamed my interviewees and that I, too, could but point out that they did not inform me about the mine-internal process. Immediately after the conversation with the GM, I therefore wrote emails to all managers individually, informed them about the GM's reaction and apologized for the inconvenience I might have caused. All of them replied without showing any concern, saying that it was no problem at all and that I should not worry about them; they had the authority to talk to me and had not said anything they should not have mentioned.

I am not the first person to suddenly find access to a mining company barred, and I was not overly surprised by the decision.[1] What puzzled me was the abruptness of the decision. Why this sudden shutdown now? What was the GM worried about?

During this phase of my research, I focused more purposefully on the mining company, moving away from the topics of urban development and governance. I increasingly realized that, to understand Solwezi, I had to understand the mine's global connections. By then, I knew quite a lot about what went on at the mine fence and the town council, about labour relations within the company, about CSR projects and infrastructure investments. Yet I knew very little about what happened once copper – and profits – left the region. So, when interviewing managers, I asked questions about the off-takers of Kansanshi's copper, about the trucking firms transporting copper from the mine gate to the harbours, about their freight forwarders and clearing agents and so forth. Their answers, along with other research I was doing, slowly made me realize how important a world-spanning network of services is for mining, a network that links the mine to the markets across the globe and in which a large part of the profit from mineral extraction is made. I learnt that servicification creates new and more flexible opportunities for international companies to capture value in the global production networks (GPN); opportunities which rely on business-friendly regulations and tax regimes in Northern countries.

It was even more surprising to me how close these themes brought me to where I had set out to do research on Zambia: to Switzerland, my native country. I had of course been aware of the role Switzerland plays as a global commodity trading hub (see introduction). Switzerland generated 4.8 per cent of its GDP in 2018 from commodity trading (and 8.9 per cent in 2023) – a higher share than banking or tourism. In 2020, the five largest Swiss companies by turnover are commodity traders: Vitol, Glencore, Trafigura, Mercuria Energy Trading and Cargill. Given their growth, large Swiss-based trading firms like Glencore and Trafigura had generated increasing scholarly and public interest (Erklärung von Bern 2011; Interdepartemental Plattform on Commodities 2013; Public Eye and Missbach 2017). In 2023, Trafigura was charged by Swiss prosecutors over allegedly bribing public officials in Angola, and in 2024, it pleaded guilty to bribing Brazilian oil officials and agreed to settle allegations of manipulating a fuel oil benchmark as alleged by the US Commodity Futures Trading Commission. Yet the activities of trading giants remain opaque in general, and I had had little idea about the real scope of the Swiss involvement in the commodity chain of Zambian copper. Swiss companies indeed control key segments of the chain: buying and selling – according to official trade statistics, half of Zambia's copper is exported to Switzerland – finance, insurance, storage, transport, cleaning, weighing, blending, tracking, certification. I will lay out these connections in detail below.[2]

When Kansanshi's GM stopped my access to the mine, I not only had almost set up an interview with a representative of FQM's trading arm in Switzerland (see below) butI also had begun to understand the business model of a global mining company and had started to get access to the inside perspectives of senior mine managers on it. I had also begun to understand that doing research on Solwezi taught me just as much about my native country than about Zambia. This is exactly when my access to inside information was suddenly shut down. The GM followed up on our meeting the day after, writing that 'as indicated yesterday, please refrain from speaking to any KMP employee on this subject matter other than [FQM's country liaison person in the capital Lusaka] John Gladstone. That includes [the person] where you are currently staying.' My follow-ups several weeks later asking for an answer to my formal application to conduct research on the mine site and my letters to the Corporate Community Relations Manager at FQM in Vancouver, Canada, were all politely but firmly declined.

In comparison to other scholars, my access to the mine's management had clearly been extraordinary and, in fact, the fruit of many years of hanging around in the area (see introduction). Large, integrated mining and trading companies rarely allow researchers in (for notable exceptions, see Lee 2017; Rajak 2014; Welker 2014). My access was denied when I moved from the local impacts of the mine, its CSR measures and its role in urban development to where the real bottom line came in: the company's business models and its global profits. Although I cannot be sure, I do not consider it a coincidence that my access was cut off at that very moment. Mining companies draw much scrutiny, and the sites of extraction are difficult to miss. The actual mine sites are the key targets of critiques; they are under general suspicion from transnationally organized civil society. Companies have learnt to live with this publicity and often respond to it on the offense. Sustainability reports, local CSR measures that generate illustrations for these reports and the co-optation of civil society groups are important strategies to counter or even prevent criticism, and so is maintaining good relations to researchers. My being welcomed to conduct research on the company's CSR programmes, partake in tours of the mining area and, most importantly, live on the Golf Estate for several months, must all be seen as part of the critical engagement a company strategically enters to legitimize its operations.

Critical mining scholars' hobbyhorse, CSR research, often inadvertently helps to co-constitute a narrow, contained perspective of what extraction is: the mine and the adjacent communities, discursively reducing extractivism to the narrow confines of the physical mining enclave.[3] The sites of mineral extraction are indeed massive and very visible, and have huge ecological, economic and social impacts. However, as Gavin Bridge (2015) expresses it, 'The hole is an essential feature of the extractive landscape, but the hole is just the start.' In other words, the 'hole's' prominence tends to hide the infrastructure that enables mining companies to work, which are less spectacular, but no less profitable (see also Arboleda 2020, 110; Tsing 2005).

The relative and selective openness serves two aims at once. It concentrates researchers' interest on that to which they can gain access, hiding the fact that information which really matters remains closely guarded; and it builds up a public image of openness and engagement that can be used to portray critical reports as one-sided. This fact came home to us at the final roundtable of a research project I was leading at the time in Geneva, the city where Trafigura is headquartered, and the Swiss Trading and Shipping Association (STSA) has its offices. As a panellist responding to our findings, Trafigura's Head of Corporate Responsibility James Nicholson 'challenged' us to 'engage more actively with the trading sector', saying that he 'would challenge [us] how much voice traders had in this conversation' (UNRISD 2018, 26:45 min). Mining companies' openness and willingness to engage with their critiques must therefore be seen as part of a gatekeeping strategy to hide what really is important: the extent to which a small number of globally operating firms control entire value and production chains, thereby prohibiting local content and a real integration of resource-rich economies into global markets. When he realized that I and my colleagues were about to penetrate this world too deeply, the GM pulled the plug.

What was there to hide? My colleague researcher for this chapter, Gregor Dobler, with whom I partnered for the material contributing to this chapter, and I did not discover any dirty secrets around Kansanshi Mine. What we discovered was much less and much more: the makings of a system that allows one part of the world to profit from the wealth of another part (Appadurai 1986). That system assigns specific value to specific jobs in the making of a commodity; it brings all segments of a commodity chain in which profits can be made under the control of external actors; it shifts profits between countries in a way to minimize taxes paid; and it systematically erects cognitive barriers between those parts of the world which it links in practice.

In *Friction*, anthropologist Anna Tsing invites us to follow commodity chains and the making of a commodity. A lump of coal, as her example goes, 'is transformed as coal-the-diggable, coal-the-sortable, coal-the-transportable, until it eventually becomes coal-the-burnable. In these shifts the lump of coal rubs up against other participants in the chain: unhappy villagers, conveyor belts, contracts. In its shape, its costs, and its composition, coal is made in the friction of the commodity chain' (Tsing 2005, 51). Here, I am less interested in how copper is made in friction, nor in the cultural production of its meaning. What I am concerned with is how profits are made by international companies providing the infrastructure for Southern Africa's mineral extraction: how, by transforming copper from 'diggable' to 'sortable' to 'transportable' and so on, value is defined and appropriated by actors along the chain. With this approach, I draw inspiration from a methodological scholarship that tracks transnational relations through a focus on particular commodity, its production and circulation in the global economy and value extraction and creation – 'follow the thing' (Appadurai 1986; Marcus 1995), and a much smaller scholarship that instead 'follows the money' (Christophers 2011) – both of which are attempts to reveal what Harvey calls 'fingerprints of exploitation' (1990). The result is however closer to an extended-case study (Burawoy 1998) – viewed from Solwezi – than a classic study into the life of a commodity. For, *articulation* may be tracked through a travelling something or someone, but it becomes manifest in a place – on the roadside, in border towns built for storage facilities, at harbours, in towns attractive for traders and service providers and so forth.

Extraction

Copper mines play an outsize role for Zambia's economy. There are currently eight large copper mines operating in the country. The three mines in Northwestern Province are new (or, in the case of Kansanshi, completely re-developed) open pit, the five mines in the Copperbelt Province are decades-old underground with open pit sections at some of them. Until 2019, when the Zambian state temporarily took over Konkola Copper Mines, and January 2021, when it acquired the majority stake of Mopani Mines, all mines were operated by international mining firms with multiple assets in different countries. Each of these firms has its own distinct operational logic shaped by the role an individual mine plays within the larger company structure.

FQM operates eight mines in Australia, Finland, Mauretania, Panama, Spain, Turkey and Zambia and develops one mine in Zambia – most of them focusing on copper. It is the majority owner of Kansanshi Mine near Solwezi and Trident Project including the Sentinel (copper) Mine and the Enterprise (nickel) Mine near Kalumbila. Together, the two copper projects in Zambia make up almost half of FQM's revenue. Its shares are publicly listed on the Toronto Stock Exchange. This makes it a classical mining company for which extraction and the operation of large-scale mines has always been the core business. Glencore, on the other hand, until recently the majority owner of Mufulira Mines and the best-known Swiss company active in Zambia's copper sector, has started out as a commodity trader and only later expanded into production. Its business model is still largely driven by trade, and mines can quickly become an expendable part of the company's business.

These different business logics influence investment decisions and, especially in times of crisis, create diverging dynamics for different mines. While FQM has to rely on mines long-term and recover investment made into them, Glencore treats mining 'as if it was a portfolio' (Müller 2020) and is more closely focused on short-term returns. 'I do not like a mine that does not yield any profit', in the words of the former CEO Ivan Glasenberg (Müller 2020). In times of low commodity prices such as during the ongoing global recession caused by Covid-19, Glencore is more ready to curb production and put mines on care and maintenance – that is, stopping production with the potential of recommencing operations again – since the loss in earnings can be offset by the company's trading arms for whom the higher volatility during crises creates new earning opportunities.

In consequence of their different company structures, Glencore and FQM also have different relations to Switzerland as a regulatory and physical space. In what follows, I briefly detail Glencore's entry in and relationship with Zambia's mining sector, since its mines were the only ones in Zambia directly controlled by a Swiss company. I then proceed to trade and to the many other copper-related activities Swiss-based companies are actively involved in transport, warehousing, fuel supply and distribution, testing, certification and surveillance, and customs.

Glencore's decision to buy mines in Zambia was anticyclical and, in retrospect, came at the best possible moment for the company. During Zambia's privatization process, Glencore acquired a majority stake in Mopani Copper Mines from the state's Zambia Consolidated Copper Mines (ZCCM). Mopani Copper Mines is the largest employer on the Copperbelt – comprising Nkana and Mufulira mines, two concentrators, one smelter, one refinery and two cobalt plants. In 2000, Carlisa Investments Corp, a joint venture between FQM and Glencore International AG incorporated in the British Virgin Islands, acquired a 90 per cent share in Mopani. Very soon, FQM diluted its interest in the company, which reduced its shares in the Mopani Copper Mines from 45.9 per cent to 16.9 per cent and increased Glencore's from 44.1 per cent to 76.3 per cent. The remaining 10 per cent was still owned by ZCCM (First Quantum Minerals Ltd. 2002).[4]

As with all ZCCM assets, conditions for the sale of Mopani were codified in a secret bilateral Development Agreement later leaked to the public. The agreement defined a 'stability period' of fifteen years during which contractual conditions would remain stable. It exempted Glencore and FQM from covering ZCCM's financial liabilities (including pensions for ZCCM workers) and environmental legacies, and from paying most taxes (Adam and Simpasa 2010, 67–8). Although the Development Agreements ceased to be binding following their cancellation in the Mines and Minerals Development Act 2008 (something FQM never accepted, see Chapter 1, footnote 5), many of their provisions remain in place. Global copper prices rose sixfold after Glencore's acquisition of Mopani, from US$1,500 per ton in 2000 to over US$10,000 in February 2011. Due to the privatization of mining assets and an unfavourable tax regime, little of the ensuing profit remained in the country. Government's multiple attempts to increase revenues from mining have largely failed due to companies' bargaining power (Manley 2017; Saunders and Caramento 2018, 5–9). Until early 2021, Glencore was the fourth-largest copper producer by output in Zambia after FQM, Barrick Gold and Vedanta. It also owns Sable Zinc Kabwe Limited, a copper and cobalt processing plant in Kabwe (Glencore 2018, 192), Mutanda mine and 74.4 per cent of Katanga Mining in neighbouring DRC.

Employees of other Zambian mining companies we spoke to felt that Glencore was driven by a different, non-mining logic (see also Lee 2017, 65). Its readiness to put the mines on care and maintenance in times of crisis, for instance, in situations when the Zambian state increased electricity prices or, as mentioned above, during the global Covid-19 pandemic, substantiates this impression. Mopani Mines under Glencore's majority ownership were often in the news, be it for air pollution (sulphur dioxide discharge) or intermittent closure, and other Western, privately owned mines operating in Zambia are anxious to distance themselves from Glencore and its local practices.

FQM, in particular, wants to be seen as a completely different company. Unlike Glencore and the Chinese state-owned mining operators, one Kansanshi manager told me, 'We are an ethical company.'[5] And when I asked another Kansanshi manager about the initially tight and later cooled-off relationship between Glencore and FQM, he said: 'The thing is, they are not the most trustworthy bunch,' adding that they would often breach contracts. The late Andrew Sardanis, Kaunda-appointed chairman and later managing director of the post-independence state's Industrial Development Corporation Indeco, did not mince his words either in our conversation in 2017: 'Glencore is a bunch of crooks.' (He did not speak particularly well of FQM's founding brothers, Philip and Matt Pascall, either. 'Well, if you go by their origins … you know who they are? They are from Rhodesia' – whose white inhabitants, to Sardanis, embodied all things colonial.)

In 2019, the Zambian government seized control of Vedanta's Konkola Copper Mines, but handed it back in 2023.[6] In January 2021, Glencore and FQM sold their shares in Mopani Mines to ZCCM-IH for a $1 and a transaction debt of US1.5 billion. Glencore kept the exclusive right to all copper products until the debt is repaid. Glencore's presence in Zambia thus changed from a miner to an off-taker – and a creditor of the Zambian state. How the 51 per cent-takeover of Mopani Mines by the United Arab Emirates' equity partner International Resource Holding (IRH) in 2024 affects this agreement is still to be seen.

Trade

In Switzerland, as well, Glencore has not the best of reputations. The company goes back to Marc Rich & Co AG, registered in Zug, Switzerland, in 1974. Rich, by then on the F.B.I.'s ten most wanted fugitives list for charges of, among others, tax evasion, racketeering, and evading US sanctions in trading with Iran, sold his trading business to the company's managers in 1993. (He was later famously pardoned by Bill Clinton on his last day in office, after Rich's wife Denise Rich had donated more than US$1 million to the Democratic Party.) The new company, Glencore, went public in 2011 and merged with Swiss mining giant Xstrata in 2012-13. Today, it is the world's largest commodity trading company. Glencore plc is incorporated in Jersey and domiciled in Baar, Switzerland. Shareholders in Glencore plc include institutional investors, such as Qatar Holding (8.27 per cent) and BlackRock Inc. (7.97 per cent), but large shares in the company are owned by managers, for example, former CEO Ivan Glasenberg (9.58 per cent) (Glencore 2023, 138).[7]

Employees of other Swiss trading companies often present Glencore as an opaque and somewhat shady behemoth far too much in the centre of public scrutiny, which has the potential to also harm other members of the umbrella Swiss Trading and Shipping Association (STSA, since recently also known as SUISSENéGOCE), which Glencore later resigned from. If Glencore has become an outsider in the Swiss trading industry, its business model of extending its reach along the value chain since the early 2000s has still been admired and copied by many of the industry's giants. In an age of more readily available pricing information and consequently declining margins from arbitrage, vertical integration came to be seen, for a while, as key to reliable margins (Bloomberg 2017). While Glencore as a trading firm has moved into production, producers have put more emphasis on trade and in-company trading arms.

How does commodity trade work and why has Switzerland become a global centre for it? When copper from Kansanshi Mine in Solwezi – which is mined and smelted and turned into concentrate, cathodes and anodes, and blister (turned into anode on-side) – crosses Kansanshi's 'mine gate', it has already sold to another company (although ownership only changes when the payment is completed). Except for concentrate, which is sold to smelters, if possible, the buyers are not economic actors – producers, who need physical copper for production, or consumers. Rather, they are specialized traders, who then sell it on to other traders or to producers. While FQM is primarily a producer, through its FQM Trading AG, it is thus also a financial investor, a speculator.

Traders – or a producer's trading arm, for that matter – have a double role. On the one hand, they render services to producers and consumers by allocating copper more cost-efficiently than either consumers or producers could do it on their own. Traders have access to many producers and consumers and can save on transport costs by matching supply and demand across different regions of the globe; they finance transport and storage of commodities, allowing producers and consumers to optimize cash flow and save costs; and they can more efficiently hedge against market risks than smaller actors could, keeping costs for other actors stable and predictable. For these services, they receive a share of the production network's overall profits. This share is, at least in textbook economic theory, smaller than the costs the other actors in the production network would have without the traders – otherwise customers would circumvent them and source their copper directly from the mines. Trading firms thus ideally make the production network more efficient. If their business is centred on the allocation element of trade, trading firms typically make relatively small, but predictable profits on each transaction. Their profits add up from high volumes rather than from high margins.

On the other hand, trading firms engage in speculative trade to increase their own profits. They try to anticipate price developments and bet against the markets. In this side of their business, traders are not the agents of either producers or consumers, but act for the interest of capital owners (and their own bonuses). Traders argue that much of speculative trade is in the interest of all market participants since it contributes to fair pricing and overall price stability. Critics however point out that speculative trade creates high risks and contributes to a concentration of profits in the hands of big capital owners while externalizing market risks to less powerful investors.

While mining and, to a lesser degree, industrial production is strictly localized, commodities can be bought and sold independently of their physical location. This has allowed Switzerland, a landlocked country without many natural resources, to become one of the most important hubs of global commodity trade (Haller 2019).

Switzerland has a long history of trade and has often profited from trade commodities – from slaves to cocoa and coffee (Fässler 2005). Partly growing from such earlier roots, Swiss commodity trade has taken off to a surprising degree over the past two decades, surviving the financial crisis unscathed (Beusch et al. 2013). Several factors have combined to turn Switzerland into a commodity trading hub (see also Chapter 1). The country has all the infrastructure traders need. Quick and secure access to finance and insurance, excellent virtual and physical global connections, a vibrant shipping industry, trader-friendly regulations, the proximity to international standard setters (most importantly the different UN organizations and the plethora of international lobby groups in Geneva), a highly skilled workforce, a flexible labour market and a very low corporate tax rate are just the most important factors here. Swiss neutrality and its non-membership of the UN until 2002 was another crucial element, since it allowed companies to engage in trade with countries under UN sanctions, such as apartheid South Africa or Iran.

A great many international commodity traders have their headquarters in Switzerland today. Their variety is huge – from the integrated mining and trading behemoth Glencore to large, specialized trading houses like Gunvor to trading divisions of banks and investment firms to small independent traders. There is no single statistics for the trading sector and the Federal Council can only offer estimations as to its size: an estimated 966 firms are involved in commodity trading as traders; they employ approximately 10,318 persons. Most traders work in firms with less than 250 employees, but the large traders have recently grown quickly. Part of the commodity sector are also firms active in trade-related activities such as finance, certification, auditing, transport, insurance, warehousing with approximately 1,644 employees (Bundesamt für Statistik 2023, 1).

What role do these Swiss trading companies play in the global production network of Zambian copper? Export statistics offer a first approximation. According to UN Comtrade figures, around 40–50 per cent of Zambian copper has been exported to Switzerland every year between 2006 and today. These statistics substantially underreport the percentage of copper traded by Swiss firms, since transit trade is difficult to classify in customs statistics. Zambian customs usually classify copper exports according to destination countries (i.e. the country to which the goods are shipped). Only when no final destination is known at the time of the sale, the buyer's country is recorded instead.

Zambian copper bought by Swiss traders is never shipped to Switzerland. Much of it is sold in transit, often from bonded warehouses. This copper will be recorded as exported to Switzerland; copper bought by Swiss companies and shipped to a known third country will be recorded as exported to this third country. When, for example, a Swiss trading company has an offtake agreement with a Zambian mining company and supplies half of this copper to a firm in China while it sells the other half from a bonded warehouse in Johannesburg, half of the copper bought at the mine will be recorded as exported to China, half as exported to

Switzerland – even though all of it has been traded by a Swiss company. The percentage of Zambian copper traded by Swiss companies is thus probably much higher than the export figures show.

Who a company's off-takers are is not public knowledge even for publicly listed companies. FQM is a case in point. Only with the help of extensive preparatory research and subsequent interviews with managers of FQM's Kansanshi Mine could I find out whom Kansanshi Mine sells its copper to. In its Annual Information Forms, FQM claims that it has 'a limited number of off-takers' (First Quantum Minerals Ltd. 2023a, 130). This is something of an understatement. Since Kansanshi started production in 2005, it has sold its copper to two – albeit changing – off-takers only. Both have always been registered in Switzerland. Since 2010, one of them is a company fully owned by FQM itself.

In the first few years since Kansanshi started production in 2015, the two off-takers were Glencore (for concentrate and cathodes) and Republic House (for cathodes) (First Quantum Minerals Ltd. 2006, 15). Glencore bought between 75 per cent and 85 per cent of cathodes and Republic House bought the rest. At that time, FQM did not have its own smelter in Zambia. The concentrate was thus sold to Zambian smelters; a big part of which was toll-treated at Glencore's Mopani Mines smelter which subsequently bought the cathodes.

Republic House registered as a company in Zug in 2000 and was mostly made up of traders who had worked for MRI, another Swiss trading company. At least since 2005, Republic House was owned by Energem Ressources, an old player in the Southern African mining sector. (Founded as DiamondWorks, it had changed its name in 2004 after allegations of blood diamond dealings.) 'Very competent guys', as one Kansanshi manager told me, 'It was a natural progression to start selling our produce to them.' In 2010, Republic House became a fully owned subsidiary of FQM. In preparation to a takeover of Republic House by FQM in 2010, Energem founded Metal Corp Trading AG in Zug (Metal Bulletin 2010a, 2010b; Wikileaks 2005), a company fully owned by Metal Corp (Sweden) AB, itself a fully owned subsidiary of FQM. From 2010 onwards, FQM's Kansanshi Mine has sold a large part of its copper products to FQM's Swiss trading company Metal Corp Trading AG. In December 2022, Metal Corp Trading AG was renamed into FQM Trading AG.[8]

After ten years, in 2015, Geneva-based Trafigura replaced Glencore as Kansanshi's non-FQM off-taker for cathodes. Trafigura 'aggressively' entered the cathodes market in the region around 2015 and proved, as a manager recalled in an interview, a far more reliable partner for Kansanshi in terms of turnaround of payments than Glencore. Since then, und most likely until today, Trafigura buys 75–80 per cent of the cathodes, and FQM Trading AG buys 15–20 per cent of the cathodes and most of the anodes. (Kansanshi started producing anodes and blister when the new smelter on-site started operating in late 2014.) The concentrate is sold to several smelters, inside (among them the Mopani smelter in Mufulira – 'to keep the relationship' as I was told) and outside Zambia. FQM Trading AG handles all trades for Kansanshi Mine, including the logistics from mine gate. Contracts are long-term, but the terms are negotiated annually.

Beyond Kansanshi Mine, FQM Trading AG most probably handles a large part of FQM's produce from its mines across the world (Mineman 2015).[9] As any trading company, it handles trade finance and LME hedging and supports logistics, trading, operations, and sales contracts for FQM's base metals contracts.

I made one of Kansanshi's manager laugh when I asked for more details of (what was then) Metal Corp Trading's Swiss presence: 'They probably have a brass plaque there!' Indeed, FQM Trading AG/Metal Corp Trading has an acrylic glass plate and a letter box at Chamerstrasse 12A in Zug, close to Lake Zug (see Figure 26). Its main business is carried out through offices in London at the Charlotte Building at 17 Gresse Street, the same building as FQM Ltd.'s UK headquarters, and through a smaller office in Johannesburg, South Africa.

For FQM Trading AG's trading arrangements, Switzerland is not important as a physical place. The copper it buys and sells does not reach the country. Its traders are not working on the shores of Lake Zug; perhaps not even the profits are stored in Swiss banks. 'Switzerland' is a regulatory regime to which FQM Trading AG rents access by paying the minimal fee of Zug's taxes. This virtual Switzerland of course intersects with the physical place. Many other trading companies have a much larger physical footprint in Switzerland, but for all of them, access to the Swiss regulatory regime is a primary asset.[10]

Figure 26. A typical Swiss letterbox along the Bahnhofstrasse and the Baarerstrasse in Zug, Switzerland. The many names are linked to the office of a law firm or a fiduciary representing companies choosing Zug for the Swiss and cantonal tax regimes. Zug, Switzerland, August 2021. Photo by author.

Transport

When living in Solwezi, the aspect of urban life that never failed to fascinate and remind me that Solwezi was a mining town was the trucks thundering along Kansanshi Road and Independence Road. Copper sheets are strapped down to the trucks' beds; and often the trucker tied several charcoal sacks to the side of his vehicle to cook a warm meal at night during his journey to the harbours. It is a long journey out of land-locked Zambia: 2,700 kilometres to Durban, South Africa; 2,000 kilometres to Walvis Way, Namibia; and 2,100 kilometres to Dar es Salaam, Tanzania, the three harbours from where most of Zambia's copper is exported on container ships. On his way – usually by road – from the mines and smelters to warehouses and harbours, the trucker must cross at least one, often several national boundaries. He has to deal with difficult road conditions, frequent congestion and border delays, and sometimes theft (cf. Lamarque 2019; Zeller 2019).

Since copper is costly to transport on land, transport costs to the harbours are a crucial factor for pricing and profits. Today, copper's world market prices are very transparent, and opportunities for arbitrage become scarcer with the omnipresence of electronic media and reporting, so that profits made on the figurative 'first and last mile' become increasingly important for traders' income (Franke, Rechsteiner and Sharp 2017, 5). Here – in Zambian trucking, in warehousing, in cross-border paperwork – presence on the ground, local knowledge and good connections to both local authorities and cross-border actors are indispensable (Dobler 2016), and information about transport costs is much less transparent than information about copper market prices. Consequently, some global commodity traders increasingly invest in the entire transport chain in order to become independent from logistic companies and gain control over profits in these crucial segments (Pirrong 2014, 40). Swiss companies are no exception. While Glencore has mainly invested in trucking companies transporting copper from DRC, Trafigura has moved into warehousing on the one hand, the upstream petrol logistics fuelling all transport on the other (see below).

Glencore uses the trucking company Muzuri Sana to transport copper from its Mutanda mine in DRC to warehouses in Zambia. This company, according to Zambian interview partners, is a joint venture between Mutanda and Hakuna Matata, the trucking business owned by former Katanga governor, mining mogul and opposition presidential candidate Moise Katumbi. (In a very similar arrangement, neighbouring Tenke Fungurume Mine transports its copper to Zambia using Habari Kani trucking, also co-owned by Hakuna Matata.)

These companies transport copper and cobalt from DRC's Katanga Province to Zambia through Kasumbalesa border post. They offload in the Copperbelt and take mining supplies back to the DRC. Subsequent transport from the Copperbelt to the harbours is handled by different companies. The main reason for this arrangement is the difficulty of transporting goods through the DRC. Legally, commodities extracted in the DRC must be transported by companies registered in the DRC using Congolese drivers. More importantly, truck drivers we spoke to indicated they needed a lot of local knowledge and connections to navigate controls on DRC roads – a rather different set of qualifications than that which is needed for the routes to Gauteng or Dar es Salaam.

Swiss firms also invest in transport infrastructure such as railway networks and harbours. For instance, Trafigura through the trading and logistics company DTS, initially a 50/50 joint venture between Trafigura and General Dino's Cochan and since 2021 a company wholly owned by Trafigura, has invested towards the reopening of a crucial train route from Kolwezi in the DRC to Lobito harbour in Angola (Zambia Chamber of Mines 2018). The Lobito Corridor is also one of the economic transportation corridors the United States and Europe intend to invest in with the aim of diversifying supply chains for critical minerals. And in 2012, Geneva-based Vitol acquired a 35 per cent stake in a subsidiary of the South African shipping firm Grindrod, which gives it access to a coal terminal in Mozambique.

Swiss companies' role in transport does not stop at the harbours. Although Switzerland does not have any seaports, the world's second-biggest container shipper, Mediterranean Shipping Company (MSC), is headquartered in Geneva. Just as its competitors Maersk and CMA-CGM, the company is an important player in copper shipments from Southern African harbours. All three companies offer through bill of lading services for Zambia, but since copper transport can usually be planned ahead and are highly routinized, most shippers prefer to organize their own transport, so that vessel owners like MSC only come into play at the harbour terminal.[11]

Warehousing

Looking at the net of transport routes on which to transport copper from Zambian copper mines to the harbours in the region, the town of Ndola is a node point. Ndola, today's capital of the Copperbelt Province and an old inland post in the region's trading routes, is host to the international school where mine managers and expatriate white-collar workers send their children to school but also to much of the country's service industry and its only oil refinery. The town thus serves as an ideal place to store, repack and blend copper products – in short: warehousing, which is another integral part of logistics management.

In earlier years, Zambian copper was usually stored on the mine grounds in wait for being shipped. Today, copper is mostly shipped immediately after production and stored in bonded warehouses in Ndola in the Copperbelt or in neighbouring countries. Many of these warehouses are operated by international logistics companies. To these companies, warehouses are crucial for optimizing truck and rail loads, for storage, repacking and blending and to regulate cash flows by storing and releasing value.

In Zambia, most international logistics companies concentrate their efforts on the route to one specific harbour. J&J, for example, a Mozambican company, is concentrating on transport to Beira, while the French logistics giant Bolloré specializes on the route to Durban. The main Swiss player in the sector is Impala Terminals, Trafigura's logistics arm. Impala has heavily invested in infrastructure along the Kolwezi–Lubumbashi–Ndola-Dar es Salaam corridor. The company operates the largest single-customer terminal in Dar es Salaam harbour and uses its resources to channel copper transports to Dar (and to influence trade policies in Tanzania, including taxation and rail development). The company owns bonded warehouses in Kolwezi, Lubumbashi, Ndola and Dar, all of which have road and rail connections and can handle 20-feet and 40-feet containers as well as break-bulk. Along the road to Dar es Salaam, Impala has constructed dedicated truck stops as safe stopping points for copper transports (Impala Terminals 2016, 35).

In addition to serving Trafigura's own transports, its Ndola warehouse is an important hub for third-party copper transports from DRC and Zambia to Walvis Bay and Durban. The same is true for the second newly constructed copper warehouse, Bolloré's Chingola hub. Its main purpose is to serve as an entrepot for DRC copper and as the meeting point for the southern and northern fleets of trucks. This US$10-million investment opened in May 2014 and today handles around 360,000 tons of copper, cobalt and mining reagents per year. In addition to its warehouses, trucks and terminals, Bolloré is also the biggest clearing agent in Zambia for third-party shipments (Bolloré 2018).

Most haulage, whether by road or rail, is still done by Southern African companies like BHL, J&J or GSM – some registered in Zambia, others in South Africa, Namibia or Mozambique. The strict contract conditions for copper transports can only be met by large transport companies, who usually own and operate a few hundred trucks. Copper cathode is transported to warehouses on either flatbed or container trucks, while transports to the harbours are exclusively done in containers to avoid reloading. (Before being loaded into containers, copper transported on flatbed trucks has to be washed, a service not all warehouses can offer (Smal 2015)). Transport contracts usually insist on convoys, GPS tracking and armed security personnel.

Fuel

'Kansanshi Mine itself uses 8 to 10 million litres of diesel per month,' a manager told me. Getting it to Kansanshi is one of the biggest challenges the mine faces due to poor road maintenance, though. Just like excavators and mine trucks, trucks and diesel trains need fuel. Supplying fuel to Zambia, its mines and transport system, and the neighbouring countries, is an integral part of copper logistics and one in which several Swiss companies play an important role.

Through Puma Energy, Trafigura has become one of the most important distribution companies for petrol products in Southern Africa. Puma Energy, in which it initially held a 49 per cent stake was controversial from the start, especially with respect to its Angolan investment; 28 per cent of the company, which owned most of Angola's downstream petrol business, was in the hands of Sonangol, the Angolan state oil company; another 15 per cent was owned by Chochan Holdings, a company founded and owned by General Leopoldino ('Dino') Fragoso do Nascimento, one of the wealthiest and best-connected Angolan businesspeople-cum-politicians. In 2011, the company bought stakes in the BP stations in Namibia (100 per cent), Botswana (100 per cent), Zambia (75 per cent), Malawi (50 per cent) and Tanzania (50 per cent) and took over a huge storage depot in Walvis Bay.[12] After leadership change in Angola, Trafigura dissociated from its problematic Angolan connections by reducing Puma Energy's shareholding controlled by General Dino in 2020 and purchased Sonangol's shares in Puma and selling its Angolan business and assets to Sonangol in 2021.

Puma is also active in Zimbabwe. In 2014, Puma Energy Africa Holdings acquired a 49 per cent stake in the Zimbabwean company Sakunda Energy, a monopolistic fuel distribution company founded by Kudakwashe Tagwirei, a well-connected businessman with close ties to the Zimbabwean military. Through Sakunda, Puma controlled the Feruka pipeline, through which 90 per cent of Zimbabwe's fuel is imported, between its storage facilities in Beira and Harare. A deal between the Zimbabwean government and Sakunda allows exclusive use of the pipeline from the border between Mozambique and Zimbabwe to the dry ports in Harare which results in Trafigura's de-facto monopoly on fuel supply in Zimbabwe and control over its costs. This has become a major political issue in the conflict between President Mnangagwa and the military (Africa Confidential 2018). Business partner Tagwirei also increasingly became an international liability for Trafigura, which was probably one of the reasons why Trafigura bought out Sakunda in early 2020, renaming it into Trafigura Zimbabwe.

Vitol and Glencore are the two other major firms controlling fuel supply and distribution in Zimbabwe and the region. Geneva-based oil trader and the second-largest Swiss firm by turnover, Vitol recently took over Shell's and Engen's network of service stations in Southern Africa through its major stakes in the fuel retailer Vivo Energy, the company behind the Shell brand in Africa (co-owned by Helios, an investment firm). Another player in Zambia and the region has been AOG, the Addax & Oryx Group, which was founded by Swiss traders in Geneva in 1987 (for more on Swiss fuel traderse, see Public Eye 2016). It quickly expanded from oil trading to oil storage and distribution. Today, its energy subsidiary Oryx Energies owns 26 service stations across the country and fuel storage facilities and lubricants warehouse in Ndola (Energy Regulation Board 2022). These firms increasingly eye the upstream market – exploration and production.

Testing, certification and surveillance

Another very important, but often overlooked element in logistics is the certification and surveillance of goods. Traders often do not themselves have the possibility to assess the quality of the goods they buy and sell. Banks financing trade deals have to know their securities are worth as much as the debtor claims. Insurance companies must make sure the insurance cover corresponds to the goods' value. Buyers want to ensure products match their specification before having them shipped. State agencies evaluate royalties according to metal content. In all these instances, independent inspection and verification services increase trust and enable anonymous transactions.

Perhaps not surprisingly, one of the biggest inspection companies is based in Switzerland: SGS (formerly Société Générale de Surveillance). SGS has a large footprint across the world, certifying everything from hazelnut spreads to nuclear plants, from labour rights to metal content and from fair trade to food safety. Through its involvement in industry bodies and multi-stakeholder initiatives, it is one of the most important private standard setters in the global economy (Bartley 2018; Peters et al. 2009). The company is active in many African countries. It runs Uganda's vehicle inspection; operates weighbridges, electronic cargo tracking services and import verification services for the Kenyan government; and supervises road contractors in Senegal.

In Zambia, SGS owns a laboratory in the small Copperbelt town of Kalulushi that many mines rely on for ore testing; Glencore, for example, used the lab for its samples during the establishment of Mutanda mine (Glencore 2011, 46–7). Similar SGS laboratories operate in South Africa. Even more importantly, SGS supervises container packing in warehouses in South Africa and Tanzania and certifies their content. This service is crucial for trade, insurance and financing; along with its competitors Alfred H. Knight and Alex Stewart, SGS is one of the most important players in Africa and the world. All three companies are also among the listed samplers of the London Metal Exchange.

Customs

A final Swiss input into the Zambian parts of copper's global production network needs at least to be mentioned: every good that is imported into or exported from Zambia – be it machinery, copper, sulfuric acid or oranges – is processed through a Swiss service export. Like most countries in the world, Zambia uses Asycuda (Automated System for Customs Data, currently Asycuda World) to process all customs documents. This integrated customs management software has been developed by UNCTAD in Geneva. It is one of the least known, but most important technical media of trade facilitation and standardization. In a cloud-based service running on servers in Lusaka, transporters, clearing agents and shippers can electronically enter shipments for customs (pre-)clearance. Despite many problems, mostly linked to server downtime, the use of Asycuda has significantly improved workflows and transparency of Zambian customs and greatly accelerated processing times at the borders. It provides the state with the necessary instruments to collect revenue and gather accurate trade data; it eases financing and insurance and allows transporters and owners better control over their shipments. The software is thus a crucial factor in reducing transport costs and increasing efficiency, and neither transport corridors nor one-stop border posts would really work without it (Nugent and Soi 2020).

This might sound universally benign, but it also creates important and understudied distribution effects. Lower transport costs change the distribution of profits within the global production network: benefits for producing and consuming countries are generated by decreasing revenues in mining and transit countries. For resource exporting countries, they might well contribute to a further externalization of profits, which would have to be offset by taxes or royalties to finance the infrastructure on which they rely.

Value capture in global extractivism

Swiss companies are active in different ways in global production networks of copper mined in Zambia. Here, I have only analysed the relatively small segment between mining and Southern African harbours. I have not considered what happens upstream from mining – say, in mining machinery, supplies, patents or engineering education – nor have I analysed subsequent processing after copper leaves the continent (on harbour logistics, see for instance Arboleda 2020, 109–39 for Chile; Paremoer 2015 for South Africa). I have completely ignored finance and insurance, in which Swiss companies play a crucial role globally, and have left aside the role of Swiss capital invested elsewhere.

Despite such limitations, a clear image has started to emerge. Switzerland's role is more important than most people would have assumed. While only one of the five major mining companies in Zambia is headquartered in Switzerland, a substantial part of copper trade, logistics, certification and, to some degree, transport are conducted by Swiss companies. It is very difficult to quantify Swiss involvement; exact figures are hard to come by and the 'Swissness' of multinational firms is often impossible to measure. Yet for a country of just over 8 million inhabitants, Switzerland certainly plays an outsized role. While the country's transit trade has been attracting more scrutiny over the past years, other aspects of Swiss involvement have largely remained unnoticed.

If the data can be generalized, Swiss companies involved in commodity extraction typically invest in services rather than in extraction itself. Services, unlike extraction, require a comparatively low or mobile investment and provide stable profits relatively independent from prices. Techniques and know-how, which of course are very important for these services, are usually much more adaptable to different commodities than is the case for extraction. In short, services are more mobile and less dependent on one single country or one single commodity market than mining.

This tendency towards flexibility explains the avenues in which Swiss services companies usually expand into developing markets. They acquire successful local companies and integrate them into a global brand. Through such acquisitions, they can appropriate local expertise and credibility and combine it with their own global reach and international reputation. This, as well, allows companies to balance different markets against each other, keeping losses local and appropriating gains (see also Parker, Cox and Thompson 2018, 56).[13]

Not all Swiss companies are the same. Some have originated in Switzerland, while others have only recently moved there. Different global companies are attracted by different aspects of the Swiss model; some look for a favourable tax regime and do not need much more than a letterbox in Zug, while others seek access to the trade and finance hub and the qualified personnel working in it. Some Swiss companies – Glencore or Trafigura – are themselves vertically integrated, extending their limbs into many countries, while others – FQM Trading AG – are merely one local part of a global company (First Quantum Minerals).

Despite these differences, many Swiss players in the service economy can profit from global extraction largely without suffering from the downsides of extractivist dynamics. Swiss firms typically build and maintain the infrastructure of global commodity trade instead of committing to the big, localized investment needed in mining. Doing so, they continue a long history of Swiss facilitation of global trade, from slave trade to apartheid gold. 'In the end, the Swiss always win' (Ramge, Schwochow and Garcia-Landa 2018, 92).

Conclusion

In Solwezi, one of the main political issues surrounding the mine is Kansanshi Mine's low employment rate of 'locals', that is, of people who have had little to no experience in the mining industry. They find it hard to compete with experienced miners and established suppliers from the Copperbelt towns (Caramento 2020; Kapesa and McNamara 2020; Negi 2010), generally summarized as 'the Bembas' in reference to the dominance of people originally from the Eastern Province in the Copperbelt towns since the inception of industrialization in the 1940s (e.g. Ferguson 1999; Epstein 1958; Mitchell 1956; Richards 1939). While this is indeed a question of being able to feed one's family and experience respectability, this very localized conflict pits Zambians against Zambians and tends to deflect from a much larger situation of asymmetry: the economic structures of extractivism which benefit foreign investors and leaves very few opportunities for Zambians to profit from the extraction of their minerals.

Social scientists who work on extractivism, as well, often focus on the sites of extraction: on mines, oil fields or plantations. If we however define extractivism as a situation where a country like Zambia relies on the export of raw materials that creates economic and political dependence and redirects profits to other countries (Acosta 2013; Gudynas 2018), we must take the *entire* structure of this political economy into account. When we stand at the roads of Solwezi and are seized by a cough because of the dust raised by trucks laden with copper, we must follow these trucks and take note of the many economic actors involved in bringing the copper to the producer and consumer. We should also try to not only speak with corporate social responsibility staff in town, who often warmly welcome us, sell us, if at all, a narrow perspective of mining's externalities and how their employer allegedly alleviates them, but to get access to managers and other decision-makers.

This is where we can learn about the system of extractivism – but also where we will sooner or later be blocked from asking further questions.

Between their extraction and their use in global industrial production, commodities are financed, insured, moved, stored, cleaned, weighed, blended, bought, sold, certified, tracked – to mention just a few downstream activities. Service providers such as trading firms, transport and shipping companies, financial institutions, certification and software providers are as important agents of commodity extraction as mining companies. These segments of global production networks figure less prominently in the literature. The ensuing imbalance distorts our image of the ways in which commodity-exporting countries are embedded into the global economy.

Scholars of global value chains have long been interested in the different ways value is added to goods along their journey (Gereffi 2014), while theorists of global production networks highlight the functional role of intermediaries such as financial, logistics and standard-setting agents (Yeung and Coe 2015, 42, 50). More recently, a new focus on the 'servicification' of global value chains has made clear that manufacturing firms in advanced economies frequently generate a high percentage of their revenue through service provision (Miroudot 2017). Most studies on servicification, however, have focused on industries in Europe, the United States and Asia, and little is known about the extent to which services contribute to value addition in mineral extraction in African countries.

Servicification affects the distribution of profits as much as the globalization of mining does. Economists have argued that asymmetrical power structures in global value chains lead to an uneven distribution of profits (e.g. Heintz 2006; Milberg 2004), and that domestic value addition can decline with the integration into global value chains due to 'the injection of foreign high-skilled labour content in their exports' (Caraballo and Jiang 2016, 289) – a process as clearly visible in the share of expatriate workers in the higher pay grades of Zambian mines (see Chapter 4) as in the reliance of logistics companies on know-how produced in higher-paying countries. When it comes to mineral extraction in Africa, analyses of these tendencies have rarely taken the service sector into account. The qualitative analysis here shows that higher-skilled service tasks that create stable added value are increasingly taken over by international companies.

These trends change the distribution of profits in global production networks. In such networks, many actors in different countries jointly create value which, when it meets demand on the market, can translate into profits. The production network does not only organize the cooperation between the actors; it also is a mechanism to assign a relative value to each of the actors' contributions, and to remunerate them accordingly. The different actors have different capacities to convince others of the value of their activities and, consequently, to capture value within the network.

Dependence on commodity extraction is problematic for poorer countries for two main reasons. First, it leaves them with only those segments of the production network in which relatively little value is (defined as being) produced. Secondly, a comparatively large percentage of the profit generated even in these sectors is exported to other national economies as dividend on capital investment, so that it cannot be invested to develop economic alternatives to extraction in mining countries.

As the discussion of Switzerland's role in Zambia shows, both arguments hold true for the infrastructure of extraction. Between the mines and the harbours, a great many actors add value to copper – from states building roads and railways to logistics companies to truck drivers, filling-station attendants, security guards or roadside food sellers and charcoal producers. Each of them creates value, but their ability to capture parts of the overall value creation widely differs. Swiss companies are among those who have been most successful in getting a share of the value added to copper between its extraction and its use in industrial production. Their competitive advantages allow them to flexibly invest in the most lucrative segments of copper's production networks. As a consequence, they are able to generate and appropriate an increasing part of the profits generated in the Southern African segments of copper's value chain – profits that then improve lives on the shores of Lake Zug (i.e. in years that companies actually pay tax on earnings (Jey Aratnam 2015, 420)), not in Zambia.

The preconditions for Switzerland's favourable place in global commodity chains are know-how, access to finance, global reputation and not least political stability. These have also turned the country into a centre of international organizations and global regulation – a proximity that again creates an advantage for companies based there. All these advantages allow Swiss companies to control essential parts of copper's global production network, and to generate a great amount of profits on the way.

The unequal distribution of profits should also make governments think twice about the usefulness of infrastructure projects that link the sites of extraction to global markets (Nugent 2018). They might increase economic activity, but without additional changes, the odds are that global companies will earn the windfalls while national taxpayers will face the debts (see Chapters 2 and 5).[14]

In the financialized global economy, capital owners' shares in profits have been increasing for decades. Since the capital invested in extractive industries and related services generally comes from rich Northern countries, this has also shifted the balance of profits between the Global North and the Global South. Attempts to redress this shift and to increase the share of profits remaining in a commodity exporting country can use each of the classic factors of production as a lever: land by increasing mining royalties; labour by negotiating better wages, higher-paying jobs or higher rates of employment; and capital by increasing either taxes or ownership. Zambia has tried, and failed, on all these fronts, and despite the commercial success of its mining sector, the country is confronted with dramatic economic insecurity.[15]

In Chapter 3, I describe the 'disorderly' town of Solwezi and how residents make their own order under given circumstances by putting in their labour power to make a home for themselves and the many other migrants attracted by the large investor. The town's 'disorder' is partly produced by the mine, its blasts and expansion and the general insecurity of planning an industry reliant on the global market generates. It is however even more a product of the entire political economy of extractivism where Swiss companies (and many others) have found lucrative, low-risk investment opportunities in Zambia by targeting mineral logistics and trade. Mining in Zambia creates a steady stream of income for companies registered in Switzerland, while much of the economic, political and environmental costs of mining are borne by Zambians. The ongoing unpaid and unrecognized construction and constant maintenance of Solwezi town by its residents lies in stark contrast with the built environment of the Swiss town of Zug, host to many of the service businesses described above, which exhibits structures going back to the middle ages and has benefitted from capital inflow from global trade at least since the mid-nineteenth century (Haller 2019).

'Decentring the mine', so to say, therefore means that we do not unthinkingly accept economists' perspectives about the production of 'value' in global value chains. Economists typically have a narrow interest in the monetary value of goods and services traded in a market regulated by offer and demand.[16] This perspective normalizes the equation of value and price instead of asking how and why different prices are assigned to activities that create social value. To understand Zambia's place in the global economy of extractivism and to show what implications this place has for everyday life in Zambia, a broad conception of global production networks which explicitly includes reproductive labour at the household and the community level needs to be adopted. As feminist scholars in particular have shown, many significant contributions to value creation become visible in such a perspective that remain hidden if we equate value with market price. Maria Mies (1986) famously challenged a theory of capitalism based on wage labour alone and instead put the household and women's or feminized labour at the centre of a global analysis of capitalism. Along a similar line of argument, Wilma Dunaway (2014) shows that commodity chains routinely incorporate multiple forms of labour, including non-wage, unfree and non-compensated work, much of it done by women. The fact that the returns are distributed highly unequally should not seduce us into ignoring this labour and its value creation. Including the reproductive labour of household members and entire communities (Banks 2020; Benya 2015) is key to any empirical analysis of global production networks, but it is not sufficient. We must also include those who reproduce capital: for example, Swiss voters and residents of Zug, seat of large trading and logistics firms. People paying into pension funds that invest in extractive infrastructure and taxpayers living in tax haven communes cannot be ignored if we truly want to understand global interdependence – and avenues for more equality.

The image of Swiss extractivism would neither be incomplete without including the public climate in which companies operate. CSOs, NGOs and politicians (and sometimes researchers) have the potential to influence what value companies can and cannot capture, and they form a crucial part of the environment in which companies take strategic decisions. Companies are not invulnerable to reputation risks, and the public climate in both Zambia and Switzerland has become increasingly critical towards commodity extraction. The following, final chapter will examine the ways in which people in both Switzerland and Zambia can relate to each other despite a strong discursive separation through capital; it sketches proposals for action and probes the potential for joint symmetrical action across space and lifeworlds.

CONCLUSION: ON BEING CONCERNED

When we look at the world today, we see an abundance of pre-existing connections. When, if not now, does it dawn on us how interconnected we are? The rich world's pollution changes the climate for everybody in this world. Fires, storms, flooding and drought can no longer be seen as isolated events. Wars elsewhere and the human movements they cause can no longer be perceived as happening far away. People on the globe are fatefully interconnected. Yet disasters are still often presented to us in an isolated, eclipsed manner, as episodes rather than epochs, to speak with Frantz Fanon (2005). Societal structures still appear to us as unchangeable conditions of sociality instead of as its contingent outcome. People, all of us, continue to separate the world into us and them, into those who matter and the others. In other words, being interconnected does not yet imply *togetherness*. It does not yet mean people accept and act upon links which exist.

In this book, I showed that life in Kansanshi Mine and Solwezi town in Northwestern Zambia are conceptually and live-worldly separated. They appear as distinct and irreconcilable, at odds with each other. Each side of the fence seems to people living on the other side as remote, opaque and governed by a different set of practical rules. This pattern of conceptual separation coupled with actual interdependence extends to the global level. In relation to Zambia, Switzerland is indeed the 'golf estate of the world'. Not only is its wealth contingent on asymmetrical functional interdependence with other regions, but its character as a place and as a social realm is also defined as fundamentally different from that of the places on which its wealth depends. Asymmetrical interdependence and conceptual separation do not coexist by chance, but they are mutually constitutive elements of each other.

With this book, I refuse to further entrench the conceptual divisions of the world. I tried to write a symmetrical ethnography of a Zambian town, one that does not accept the simultaneity of interdependence and separation and keeps the possibility of change within the horizon. Faced with the choice to either highlight everyday urban life or to analyse the asymmetry of interdependence, to either celebrate people's capacity for agency or to show that the conditions of this agency are shaped elsewhere, I privileged asymmetrical interdependence over urban creativity. The ways in which the Swiss state regulates its trading sector is a part of every Solwezi resident's life, may they – the Swiss and the Zambians – be conscious of the fact or not. For as long as people have as divergent possibilities to decide about their everyday lives, writing a book about the 'real' Solwezi would have contributed to cementing rather than to dismantling global inequalities. My choices in writing this book, however misguided they might be, have been motivated by privileging togetherness over curiosity. I wanted to show what is common to us all in the world we have made, not how different we are.

This last chapter turns to avenues for activist action, an integral part of symmetrical ethnography as I argued in the introduction. It is guided by the possibilities that emerge when people start relating to one another or, in bell hooks's words, 'making community wherever we are' (2001, 143). The late Black feminist, writer and academic was invested in forging alliances among marginalized minority and majority groups and in questions of collective well-being. She was interested in questions of structural inequality, yet to change things, she proposes to start small with the labour of love. Love, for her, includes care, affection, but also responsibility, accountability, respect, commitment and trust (2001, 14). For bell hooks, starting small is collective labour but at first requires little organization. As she writes: 'Unlike larger movements for social change that require joining organizations and attending meetings, we can begin the process of making community wherever we are' (2001, 143).

Taking bell hooks's thoughts as an analytical lens for the remaining pages of this book, I ask how people start to make community wherever they are. How are they trying to overcome the obstacles to community? How, in particular, is it possible to overcome the very powerful conceptual separations between lifeworlds in the global sphere?

I first give an outline of existing activist initiatives in Zambia and in Switzerland, and across the two, that focus on the economic relations between both countries, and I point out the opportunities and limitations of these actions. On an empirical level, I see such an overview as a necessary corollary and a corrective to the critique of global economic connections. Joint activist action is sometimes just as world-spanning as mining companies' activities, and it can sometimes change the conditions under which companies operate. On a theoretical level, this overview will then allow me to reflect on the conditions and possibilities of practical symmetrical action across life-worldly and often physical boundaries. To do so, I take a step back and ask on what basis people begin to understand that they are interconnected with people they have never met. What could lead them to acknowledge their interdependence with other people? Where, in short, is the seed for social change against the grain of structural inequalities? People in the Global South and in the Global North are undeniably differently concerned – 'affected' – by the effects of global extractivism. Instead of lingering on these differences, which tend to result in further hierarchization and constriction, I try to describe conditions for more radical, open-ended avenues for activist action. Such actions, I argue, can be based on two meanings of the gerund *being concerned*. They ground in shared experiences (to relate to; *similarity*) and a shared condition (to have a responsibility for; *interdependence*). In the final pages of the book, I argue that the recognition of our interdependence can lead to practices of *commoning* – 'making community' – a radical practice in response to intense commodification, financialization and alienation.

Activist actions in Zambia

What are some of the activist actions through which ordinary Zambians try to challenge the consequences of their economy's global position? I give examples for nationally organized civil society activities, negotiations at the municipal level and court cases.

Today, workers and subcontractors at the mines are a privileged if precarious elite in Zambia. Both their motivation and their ability to change the general order of things are rather low. While 'skilled', they are not irreplaceable. Today, their leverage seems negligible compared to much of the twentieth century where industrial action was a viable means to put pressure on government and on companies (Larmer 2007). Just as civil society in general, labor unions have been weakened first by liberalization, then by increasing state oppression under the Patriotic Front government since 2011.[1]

NGOs, often (precariously) foreign funded, such as Publish What you Pay (PWYP), ActionAid and Caritas, hold annual national and regional *indabas* to discuss the state of the mining sector and, to a limited extent, alternatives to mining with representatives from industry and government. Testimonies of 'mining-affected communities' are a central part of such meetings. Against an increasingly authoritarian state, only a small number of NGOs or groups are however able to speak out against the exploitation of the country's resources, mismanagement and corruption. Some thus work on a local level and never reach beyond their constituencies. One example is the Mufulira NGO Forum, which demands clean drinking water from Mopani Copper Mines and campaigns both at the municipality and the mine level (see section Across boundaries). Despite their limited reach, such initiatives have presented important challenges to mining companies in Zambia.

In Zambia's difficult economic and – at least under the PF administration (2011–21) – political environment, many activists and community organizers choose conversations with local decision-makers over loud confrontations at the national level. How the Solwezi-based youth organization Youth Alliance for Development (YAD), together with the Solwezi office of Lusaka-based Civil Society for Poverty Reduction (CSPR) lobbied the Solwezi Municipal Council to implement what came to be known as the '10 per cent resolution' is a successful example for this strategy. Taking up YAD's idea after extensive local lobbying, the council in 2015 passed the resolution that 10 per cent of the revenue from the mines (mostly property rates, see Chapter 2) should directly benefit those most affected by the mining operations. What 'most affected' should mean was hotly debated; eventually, the council resolved on the definition that all four wards within the re-drawn Solwezi District boundaries should benefit. Civil society's patient and skilful work with elected councillors over many years resulted in the guaranteed allocation of 10 per cent to communal development projects from 2018 onwards. It is important to note that the increase of the total revenue was never at stake; only a redistribution of the available, limited means among similarly affected groups of actors was negotiated. Despite this limitation, the case shows that local activist action is often successful precisely because it can ground its aims and strategies in a local political space.[2] In a second step, its success can then become agenda-setting beyond that specific place: Solwezi's '10 per cent resolution' has inspired other groups working at the municipal and the national level to demand a similar allocation key.

Zambian courts, although generally weakened by the interference of the PF regime, were able to issue at least two important decisions in recent years. The most successful is probably the legal case filed by the widower of Beatrice Mithi. Mithi, Mufulira's district commissioner, died after inhaling sulphur dioxide released by Glencore's subsidiary Mopani Copper Mines in 2013. In 2016, the Kabwe High Court ruled that sulphur dioxide emissions at the copper plant caused Mithi's death and ordered Glencore's London-listed subsidiary to pay 400,000 Zambian kwacha in damages to the widower. Glencore had rejected the claim, citing an environmental indemnity agreement signed with the Zambian government in 2000. The judge ruled that the agreement did not apply because sulphur dioxide emissions had exceeded legal limits. Glencore has appealed the ruling at Zambia's highest court, which however dismissed it in 2020 and increased the injury sum to 1 million kwacha. Secondly, in May 2020, the Zambian Revenue Authority won a major transfer pricing case against Glencore-owned Mopani Mines in the Supreme Court, in which the company was ordered to pay additional tax of US$130 million. The dispute was about the pricing of copper Mopani sold to its mother company Glencore in Switzerland, and the charges were underpricing to reduce its taxable income in Zambia.

These examples of challenges to extractivism in Zambia show the importance, but also some of the problems and limitations of civil society action within the country. On the one hand, most initiatives focus on the *mining* dimension of the companies, on direct consequences for affected communities and on extraordinary examples of corporate misbehaving – issues around which meaningful campaigns can be organized. Tackling everyday business practices and the consequences of less visible sides of extraction – say, trade and logistics– is much harder.

There are examples of how Zambians challenge the servicing side of extractivism, though. Two hundred and thirty-six former employees of BP, until 2011 a key retailer for fuel in Zambia, have for more than two decades tried to claim their rightful benefits resulting from their retrenchment in the 1990s. While it is a pension claims litigation in Zambia's high and supreme courts, it also targets one of the former key providers to the mining industry (see Chapter 6). Since the case was filed in 2002, 110 of the plaintiffs have died. A very powerful challenge to the mining industry are truckers' strikes in Kolwezi or Kasumbalesa, DRC, and other 'choke points'. Blocking export of copper and cobalt, truckers typically demand higher pay or risk allowances from their employer or the mining companies. In general, however, companies' inner workings remain opaque to outsiders, and the consequences of anonymous market forces are much more difficult to show than the consequences of, say, an acid spill.

On the other hand, civil society groups as well as states struggle with firms' transnational character and their aloofness in a specific locale. Due to the complex legal structure of international companies, often no specific national jurisdiction seems to be the appropriate place to hold them to task. No transnational judicial body has the authority to investigate corporate practices across state sovereignties (Bastin 2014), and due to power imbalances between international mining corporations and governments, chances for supranational action of exporting countries seem slim (for the Zambian Revenue Authority's attempts see Caramento, Hinfelaar and Cheelo 2023).[3]

Since extractivism relies on different national regulatory frameworks and global infrastructure, it cannot be successfully challenged by Zambians alone – especially not under conditions that systematically make it harder for them exercise their agency.

And what are the Swiss doing about it?

Everyday challenges in Zambia are far removed from the lifeworlds of most Swiss citizens. People in Switzerland know, in a general manner, that people in other places of the world are typically worse off than they are themselves. As long as this knowledge remains abstract and unconnected, it is difficult to turn it into a spring for symmetrical action – all the more since the conceptual divide between North and South normalizes the difference and lets it appear as just the way things are.

In this situation, the global role of Swiss companies has become a concrete anchor for attempts in Switzerland to de-normalize the situation and overcome the conceptual separation between functionally connected regions. When people realize that suffering in a different part of the world is not just caused by fate, but by a specific company whose offices lie in their own neighbourhood, this realization can turn abstract suffering into suffering for which *we* are responsible and answerable. The Swiss public thus needs to be included in our analysis of extractivism. They can either tolerate or challenge the legal and economic conditions under which companies operate. CSOs, NGOs, politicians and sometimes researchers have the potential to influence what value companies can and cannot capture, and they form a crucial part of the environment in which companies take strategic decisions.

The regulatory environment in Switzerland is very favourable for international companies. The different cantons in Switzerland compete in the national and international race for the lowest corporate tax rates.[4] This is an important incentive for companies to move to Switzerland and to optimize taxes by shifting profits into the country (Carbonnier et al. 2024; Cobham, Janský and Prats 2014; Public Eye 2017). For international mining companies, intra-firm trade with Swiss branches can be an important avenue to lower the tax burden and increase shareholder profits. This increases the difficulties of commodity exporting countries to effectively tax extractive industries (Moore, Prichard and Fjeldstad 2018). Trafigura Group, for example, gives its effective global tax rate in 2017 as 8.4 per cent (Trafigura Group Pte 2018).

It is notoriously difficult to evaluate whether all tax optimization strategies are legal as they happen 'in a grey zone between tax avoidance and tax evasion by exploiting loopholes in an evolving global tax governance framework' (Carbonnier et al. 2024, §9). In relation to Zambia, the Swiss NGO Berne Declaration (today Public Eye) jointly with other international NGOs filed a formal complaint with the OECD against Glencore and FQM for alleged breaching of OECD Guidelines (OECDWatch 2011) in April 2011. The complaint was based on a 2009 audit report conducted on behalf of the Zambian authorities (GrantThornton 2010). It alleged that Mopani Copper Mines manipulated its financial accounts to reduce its tax bill by overestimation of operating costs, underestimation of production volumes, transfer pricing manipulation and breach of the 'arm's length' principle. The OECD's Swiss National Contact Point (NCP) handled the complaint and facilitated mediation. The result was disappointing to civil society. As described in the NCP's final statement in November 2012, the parties could only 'agree to disagree' – and even this agreement remains confidential.

The example is typical for contemporary challenges to extractivism. The opposition to a company's alleged wrongdoings did not emerge from the states' regulating authorities but from civil society actors. By increasing reputational and regulatory risks, civil society actors can change business strategies and value capture (Wright 2016; Yeung and Coe 2015).

Indeed, public consciousness of the economic and political weight of the commodity trade sector as well as of its problematic aspects has been growing over recent years in Switzerland. A part of Zug's civil society and particularly the political parties the Alternative Green Party and the Young Alternatives, together with activist, historian, author (2020) and politician Josef Lang, have been fighting companies' intransparency and the canton's role in facilitating them for decades (Hobi 2017; Jey Aratnam 2015). More recently, the broader Swiss public also recognizes the potentially harming role Zug, among other hubs, plays for the Swiss economy. Even the *Neue Zürcher Zeitung*, an increasingly right-leaning and traditionally business-friendly national newspaper, felt compelled to the headline 'Whether "Panama" or "Paradise Papers", "Luanda" or "Crypto Leaks": the trail always leads to Zug' (Aschwanden 2020).[5]

Today, the Swiss public receives more information about corporate misconduct by Swiss companies in other countries than ever before. One strategy has been to bring the violations of human rights and environmental standards in connection with Swiss companies' plants to people's attention, an effort for which Swiss public media have played an important role.[6] A focal point was the referendum initiative Responsible Business Initiative, which was led by an alliance of over a hundred NGOs, CSOs and churches, the result of decades of solidarity and campaign work. The initiative came to a vote in November 2020. It demanded that Swiss-based multinational corporations could be held responsible for violations of human rights and for environmental damage caused by one of their subsidiaries or by a company they control. After one of the most aggressive and expensive campaigns in the country's history, both on the supporters' and the opponents' side, the initiative was rejected at the ballot box. To the surprise of many, it carried the popular vote (50.7 per cent), but it failed to reach the prescribed majority in more than half of Switzerland's cantons. Like most cantons in central Switzerland, Zug rejected the proposal by a high 64.8 per cent, following the recommendations by the federal government and by several business lobby groups such as economiesuisse and the Swiss Trading and Shipping Association (STSA).[7] Host of the global trading and mining giant Glencore, Zug had repeatedly been in the headlines in the running up to the popular vote. The company, which vehemently opposed the initiative, had often been singled out by the yes-campaign as an example of the kind of corporate practices the initiative wanted to prevent. Health and environmental disasters in the context of Glencore's oil fields in Chad, its lead mine in Peru and its copper mine in Zambia (Mopani Copper Mines) were in the spotlight. When in May 2024, the Council of the European Union finally approved the 'Corporate Sustainability Due Diligence Directive',[8] which obliges firms and their upstream and downstream partners to prevent, end and mitigate their adverse impact on human rights and the environment, the Swiss initiative committee definitely decided for a second instalment of the vote to prevent Switzerland, not a member of the European Union, from falling behind.

Today, Swiss-based mining companies, trading and logistics companies can no longer rely on remaining unchallenged. The stark difference in living conditions between Switzerland and many countries in which Swiss companies are active draws criticism and, increasingly, calls for regulation and control. The greatest asset of Swiss-based companies, their ability to bridge markets and extract value from all of them, can then become a liability. It is precisely the global connectedness of Swiss companies that might also create conditions under which civil society pressure in Switzerland can bring about material changes for people living in other countries.

Across boundaries

Because the extractive industry operates globally, challenges to it also need to be organized across national borders. This comes with its own challenges. Linking activist action across national boundaries is difficult and time-consuming, and only stable and long-lasting relations can help to avoid that existing hierarchies seep into civil society relations. I give two very different examples of how Zambia is connected to activist action abroad.

Firstly, court cases are a promising avenue not only to institute change but also to draw international attention to the violation of environmental and human rights standards by corporate actors. *Lungowe and Others* vs. *Vedanta Resources and Konkola Copper Mines* was filed extraterritorially in a UK court in 2015. With the help of the attorneys' firm Leigh Day, 1,826 Zambians allege that because of toxic effluent discharge from the Nchanga Mine in Chingola (Copperbelt), they suffered loss of income since land and waterways their livelihood depended on were damaged. They further allege that many suffer personal injuries as a result of the use of polluted water. The defendants, Vedanta and its subsidiary Konkola Copper Mines, challenged the jurisdiction of English Courts. In 2016, after a three-day hearing, the judge found an English Court the most appropriate forum for the resolution of the claims and allowed the claims to proceed. The companies' appeal was dismissed by the Court of Appeal on 13 October 2017, which allows the parties to proceed to a full trial of the raised issues. Despite an eventual settlement between the parties in January 2021 – 'without admission of liability' from the company – the case remains significant because it confirms that UK-based parent companies can be held liable for activities of foreign liabilities; something the Swiss responsible business initiative had tried and failed to write into Swiss law.

Another example is a much less spectacular collaboration. The Clean Water Campaign in Mufulira, Copperbelt Province, already mentioned above, was project-financed by Solifonds, a Swiss NGO founded by the Swiss Federation of Trade Unions and a number of other institutions and very active when it comes to the global role of Swiss companies (Solifonds 2018). Community members involved in the campaign are organized around the Mufulira NGO Forum. The forum was founded in August 2017 in the presence of members of the Swiss Apartheid Debt and Reparations Campaign (KEESA), including myself. Mufulira and KEESA activists came together for a day, which included visits to community members' homes, an inspection of their pipe water samples and the experience of the choking feeling after the routine emission of sulphur dioxide from Glencore's Mopani plant. Back in the office, we jointly brainstormed about possible campaigns, based on which Solifonds later received a funding proposal by Mufulira NGO Forum to kick-start the campaign. Mufulira activists work for a variety of environmental and community organizations, mostly voluntarily. Similarly, KEESA consists of six executive members, who work voluntarily, drawing on decade-long experience of low-level solidarity work with Southern Africa's liberation and post-liberation struggles. Both organizations struggle to raise the necessary funds for their activities, since both are too small to compete in a funding environment which prefers to support established, larger organizations on a project-by-project basis with 'measurable' impact. Their size and non-monetary alliance are their strength, allowing for flexibility, unbureaucratic processes and communication at a level playing field.

The difficulties of the work done by Mufulira's residents and the limitations of the alliance with KEESA to change anything are also obvious: Both the local state, the parastatal water company and the mining company are powerful actors. Mufulira's residents tried to challenge them by collecting technically challenging data on water quality and thereby assign responsibilities for water pollution. All of this happens against a weak environmental regulatory framework. The group is loosely connected and its members live in vulnerable – environmentally, economically and politically – conditions themselves. Here, the small group in Switzerland can lend an ear and try to advise from a distance and amplify their voices if some tangible evidence emerges by reaching out to Swiss media or inviting Mufulira activists to Switzerland for a public event. We have written letters to Glencore in

Zug and to the Swiss Federal Council and communicated Mufulira's situation to our supporters and the interested public via regular newsletters and podcasts.[9] Yet the main support are probably frequent WhatsApp calls and the knowledge that *we are concerned*. Knowing that their work is appreciated and needed for informed activist action abroad motivates Mufulira's activists to continue their work against all odds.

In Switzerland, only a small minority of people, often limited to professionalized circles, is active in this field, with some larger-scale mobilization centred on particular issues at specific moments. Such mobilizing issues are typically narrowly framed and focus on visible corporate excesses. The Responsible Business Initiative has shown the potential for a larger part of Swiss society to be concerned about such issues. People debated their own positionality in a globalized world in church and neighbourhood groups, in street actions and as part of public discussions, film screenings and theatre plays. This campaign has however also shown the limits of mobilization focused on narrowly defined issues and the dangers – as my students pointed out in relation to the campaign poster, see below – of moralizing the self and essentializing the other. What can the basis of *concern* be for an activism to develop that avoids these pitfalls and has lasting impact?

Joint action

At the time of the vote on the Responsible Business Initiative in 2020, I was teaching a seminar on the anthropology of mining. We started the course by discussing the role of Switzerland as a commodity trading hub and as host to major logistics firms operating in global production networks. The week after the results of the vote were in, I asked the students what they thought had enabled the initiative to carry the popular vote.[10] Many of their responses were based on a critical reading of the yes-campaign, whose committee was formed by a coalition of churches and Swiss civil society organizations working in human rights, development and environmental protection. Its main campaign poster depicted a girl from Cerro da Pasco, Peru, where Glencore is accused of neglecting its responsibility to protect inhabitants from systemic lead poisoning. She looks straight into the camera, sad, yet also a little defiant. For my students, the campaign and the imagery it used directly appealed to people's *morality* and to a sense of charity honed through decades of donation campaigns for good causes. Students felt that the appeal to morality had probably helped increase the vote share, but they were still critical of what they saw as de-politicization. Responsibility, they felt, should not be framed as charity. Yet students also believed that voters, exposed to the arguments of the campaign, became more conscious of their responsibility for others as part of a globalized world and started to consider the values Switzerland should stand for in the world. Things became more relatable and closer to home; 'it could be me', as one student expressed it.

After the vote, the initiative committee, which was disappointed by the initiative's failure to get the cantonal vote but invigorated by the popular support it had received, evaluated voting patterns at the municipality and commune level. They found that active campaigning by innumerable local groups correlated with support for their concerns. In other words, the greater the voluntary participation in the mobilization of family, friends, neighbours and the general public had been, the higher the chance that a particular county supported the initiative.[11]

Taken together, these two points – students' critique of the campaign's appeal to charity and the analysis that active engagement of people in their everyday lifeworlds increased awareness for asymmetrical interdependence – are at the core of my concern here. What practices can help to make participation in global production networks more just and equal, what are the conditions for their emergence, and how can they avoid cementing the very separation of the world they want to overcome?

What needs to happen for a resident of the canton of Zug to demand that a Swiss-based logistics firm share profits generated through its Zambian subsidiary more equally with the Zambian citizenry? What could induce her to demand that commodity traders in Switzerland make agreements with Zambian clients public and transparent? What would bring her to demand higher company taxes? A teacher in Zug lives far away, geographically as well as in their everyday experiences, from an elderly woman in Zambia, routinely exposed to poor-quality water and mine dust and under threat of resettlement. A Zambian truck driver, who fears to be killed in an incident which would be interpreted as xenophobia while sleeping in his truck carrying copper sheets through South Africa, is very far away from the owner of a Tesla powered by 70–90 kilograms of copper. What can joint action be based on in the absence of actually meeting another person? What and how much needs to be shared *at a physical distance* to work as a basis for joint symmetrical action?

To illustrate what I mean and how difficult it is to engage in joint action against the backdrop of persisting inequalities, I come back to my description of Kansanshi's Golf Estate instituting so-called solidarity cuts on the estate to create some kind of connection with residents in Solwezi proper (see Chapter 4). To reiterate, it was the Golf Estate's management that called for – ordered, by switching off power for some hours – solidarity to be extended by Golf Estate residents to Solwezi town residents. Here, the more resourceful and powerful actor decides on a solidarity action with the less powerful, deciding unilaterally on the focus of the action. I will argue below that this approach cements power structures rather than opening possibilities of engagement across boundaries. The less powerful ought to have the prerogative to formulate the rules of how to achieve symmetry. Secondly, not unexpectedly so, the solidarity cuts did not reach the less powerful materially for technical reasons. Electricity in Solwezi is not structured as a zero-sum game where abstinence of one leads to its enjoyment by the other person (precisely because the conceptual divide is also manifest in a division by way of feeders). And finally, the solidarity cuts had the unexpected consequence of furthering solidarity among Golf Estate residents in that they were drawn to the one public place that offered electricity and thus cool drinks and warm meals. This strengthened internal cohesion and, at the minimum, redrew boundaries to the 'other' outsiders. All these three pitfalls can be extrapolated to a more global and abstract level: the Northerners engaged in an action decided on by themselves that had them feel good *and* strengthened their position in the overall asymmetry. Furthermore, the action was not only centred on a source that cannot simply be more equally shared by temporarily do without it, but the action was also not intended to achieve any structural changes towards more symmetry.

The question how people can relate to each other across conceptual and material boundaries is fundamental to any social theory, and it can be framed in a variety of ways. We can ask what keeps society together (Durkheim 1967), what makes us recognize some persons as relevant to our social field, while denying this recognition to others (Honneth 1992, 2003); we can inquire into the roots of social obligations towards each other (Graeber 2011; Mauss 2012); we can ask what morality is and how a sense of ethical action emerges (Lambek et al. 2015). Many individual studies have provided empirical insight into transnational movements – be it in humanitarianism (Redfield and Bornstein 2010), in women's transnational liberation (Dufour, Masson, and Caouette 2010), and anti-apartheid movements (Thörn 2009) or other advocacy networks (Keck and Sikkink 1998), in anti-slavery (Araujo 2020) and de/colonization groups (Mignolo 2000) and in (new) social movements in general (Eyerman and Jamison 1991; Porta and Tarrow 2004). Some commonalities emerge from all these studies. Togetherness emerges when particular historical processes and structural contexts become relevant in face-to-face encounters, direct experience and participation in particular social formations (cf. Cabot 2016). In such processes, media and other mediators are crucial if they contribute to a sustained practice of transgressing discursive boundaries (cf. Thörn 2009). The danger of creating new boundaries between 'them' and 'us' and other exclusionary practices is also consistently mentioned. Rarely do scholars ask how we can expand who belongs to 'us' and how new connections can be created, as Richard Rorty (1989) demands. The question how lines of solidarity can emerge without direct encounters and across differences is and remains a difficult question (see also Glick Schiller 2020). Often, solidarity is seen to be extended to the 'suffering other' and not to an equal (Debele 2021). Indeed, literature on solidarity is pre-occupied with situations where hierarchies are (analysed as) the conditions for its emergence such as in migration and refugee studies (for instance, Fleischmann 2020).[12]

I build and expand on this scholarship to examine how divergent positionalities along the global value chain can serve as a heuristic lens to make visible that people in different places of the world are *concerned with* and in a relation with each other.

On being concerned

To be concerned has three pointed meanings: 'to be affected by', 'to relate to' and 'to have a responsibility for'. Residents in Mufulira, to stay with the example, are affected in their everyday life by drinking polluted water, inhaling polluted air and eating, if anything grows at all, contaminated vegetables (Peša 2020b, 2020a,

2020c). There is evidence that residents in Solwezi, too, are increasingly affected by similar environmental damage (Chansa 2020; Southern Africa Resource Watch 2020). Zambia's mining communities are also affected by the fluctuations of global copper prices, retrenchment threats, racial and gendered hierarchies in the labour force, poor health services and a state incapacitated by financial reforms, among others. For residents – waged, unwaged, women and men and children – being affected becomes the basis for analysing the situation, jointly developing a critique of its wrongness, and acting upon it.

Why Swiss residents *are concerned* is much more difficult to establish. For the early phase of new international division of labour, when large-scale industries were relocated to the Global South, Maria Mies (1986) examined the increasing structural similarity between the production relations of the Western housewife and those of female agricultural and industrial workers in the Global South. They were, she argues, materially connected via commodity production, but oblivious to the existence of other people. For her, this gap of knowledge about 'the other' precluded a transnational, anti-capitalist political project that could challenge patriarchy and its locally specific manifestations.

In his book *Planetary Mine* (2020), Martin Arboleda also presses for the 'need to overcome the fragmentation of human productive subjectivity imparted by the international division of labour, and to envision a trans-Pacific horizon of linked labour histories and geographies' (2020, 210). He sees promising avenues of global social resistance in connecting the ends of the mining supply chain, in his example in Chile and China, coming together in the realization that 'late capitalism tends to homogenize the conditions of workers in primary, secondary, and tertiary sectors across the international division of labour' (2020, 241). Yet, Arboleda argues, continued ideologies of difference and cultural essentialism hamper the success of global resistance (2020, 242).

Jake Alimahomed-Wilson and Immanuel Ness (2018) also take into view the entire value chain in their search for 'choke points'. The fact that commodities need to be transported with the help of pipelines, railroads, ships and trucks, among others, automatically produces 'the openings for labour and social movement organizations to resist, disrupt, perhaps even reshape firms' supply chain strategies' (2018, 21). Focusing on workers exclusively, they also readily identify the main challenges: fragmentation (disparate groups of workers in spatially distinct locations), uneven organization (unionized or not; subcontractors), but also different priorities (jobs versus environment) (2018, 29–30).

This scholarship lays out possible avenues for transnational resistance based on similar class and work experience. Once we know about the other person, we can solidarize with her, because we can relate to one another's conditions. The obstacles primarily are of a practical, geographical nature. True to their Marxist orientation, the scholars seek resistance from those affected and from their joint organization once they realize that they belong to a common class. They do not ask for the possibility of solidarity across classes.

This, I think, describes an important avenue for change, but it still falls short of an effective answer. What differentiates most residents of Zug and residents of Solwezi are precisely their starkly different working and living conditions. If the term makes sense across these two very differently grown and organized societies: they do not belong to the same class and cannot be expected to share the same class standpoint.

In the absence of similar experiences of everyday deprivation, do we need to resort to 'altruism' or 'empathy for the other' as the link between producing and service economies, falling back on colonial hierarchies and the imagery of the other as pitiable? I do not think we do. If we acknowledge the functional links between the different contexts, we can develop different grounds for joint action: similarity ('to relate to') and interdependence ('to have a responsibility for'). I will explore these in the remaining pages of this book.

Similarity (to relate to)

A focus on similarity could be one way of coming together for activist action between Zambia – an exporter of copper – and Switzerland – 'a sizable exporter of services' (Tille 2017, 4). It is based on the realization that extractivism structures lifeworlds in the Global South and in the Global North in similar ways. Some experiences are indeed shared by inhabitants of Solwezi District and of the canon of Zug, two urban centres with a long history of extractivism: rising costs and rents due to the expansion of the extractive industry, the slow financial and social expulsion of some milieus (middle-class exodus to the town's fringes in Zug, continuous resettlement of poorer communities in Solwezi), increased scarcity of land and high real estate prices, a high percentage of short-term expatriate residents and the presence of services catering for them exclusively (i.e. international schools), a rapidly changing urban landscape, corporate social responsibility programmes as the main means of corporate engagement with the general public, a critical but also entangled civil society – and tax income dependent on the success of the industry and global commodity prices (DNS Transport Zug, Kleeb, and Lötscher 2017; Hobi 2017; Jey Aratnam 2015; Schmid 2020). In 2022, the canton of Zug had 131,164 permanent residents. The canton consists of three municipalities (Zug, Baar, Cham) and eight (rural) communes. With roughly 30,000 residents, the municipality of Zug is the most populated municipality (see Figure 27). Together with Baar and Cham, it roughly makes up the canton's urbanized area. Like the municipality of Zug, the municipality of Baar is attractive for expatriates and business and is, together with Zug, the municipality with the highest increase of international migrants most recently (Statistik Kanton Zug 2023). While the population grows continuously, between 2011 and 2021, approximately 30,000 people (out of today 131,164 residents) left the canton of Zug, a third of which settled in a neighbouring canton, many of them just across the cantonal border (Fagetti 2023). In June 2023, Swiss voters decided to adopt the new OECD minimum rate of 15 per cent for corporations. Initially, 25 per cent was suggested as the minimum rate, but it was negotiated down by, among others, Switzerland. Initially, too, the countries where multinational companies produce their profits

Figure 27. Shoreline at lake Zug, Zug, Switzerland, August 2021. Photo by author.

were to benefit from the difference to the global minimum tax rate. This, too, was quickly changed into beneficiation for countries which host the companies, such as Switzerland. With that, from a global perspective, the global minimum tax rate was completely rid of all its ambitious intentions. When Swiss voters agreed to these conditions, it was clear that tax income will increase for the canton of Zug. In a second vote, the canton's residents entitled to vote thus agreed with a 72 per cent yes rate to a further reduction of the wealth tax in a poll in November 2023. This will further attract the affluent, as Luzian Franzini, co-president of the Alternative Green Party, commented (Fagetti 2023), and it also increases the canton's reliance on corporate taxes. All attempts by the left in Switzerland to at least share some of the benefits of the new minimum tax rate, the so-called top-up tax, with countries of the Global South failed. In fact, Zug and other cantons hosting a large number of multinationals such as Basel have developed ways to funnel back the funds 'lost' (because of the difference between the initial tax rate and the new 15 per cent) by companies to companies and the canon to guarantee 'location attractiveness' (Kanton Zug 2024). This, Dominik Gross, tax policy expert at the Swiss NGO Alliance Sud, states factually turns the minimum corporate tax rate into 'a tax haven rewards programme' (Gross 2023).

As political entities, both Solwezi and Zug witness global processes of differentiation that turn them into small rent-seeking polities with local specificities. If Solwezi suffers from the 'resource curse', Zug suffers from 'Zugisierung' (*Zugization*) (Eichenberger and Stadelmann 2012). Zugisierung is increasingly used as a critical, popular term to describe how the combination of low-tax policies, increased land prices and rents and (often short-term) in-migration of international migrants and expatriates leads to the exclusion of ordinary residents. Despite the vast differences, Solwezi and Zug are both subject to developments residents feel exposed to and from which they cannot escape.

In both cases, such developments are linked to global extractivism. Being affected by such developments, people start to question the role of global companies and the ways they are politically regulated. Zug and Solwezi residents thus face similar challenges in terms of the inequalities global extractivism produces. How can they remain/become democratic arenas if the logic of governance and participation is considerably shaped by a country's position in the global economy? How can political participation and equality be guaranteed under conditions of social inequality and global markets? Against these questions, my focus on house-making practices and safeguarding the home in Solwezi in Chapter 2 suddenly opens for comparison with the practices in Zug. Indeed, many Zug residents critically view the dominance and simultaneous urban enclavement of financial service providers, transnational companies and corporate-oriented service providers like legal and business advisors (W.I.R.E. et al. 2015, 8).

While negative consequences might lead people in Zug and in Solwezi alike to question the order of things, this experience of similarity only goes so far. Solwezi residents usually feel such consequences much more quickly and much more radically. It takes a while until a middle-class native of Zug is forced financially to shift residency to a neighbouring canton, but a Solwezi resident may very quickly be pushed from her land by the expansion of urban compounds or the mining area. As shown in the introduction and Chapter 2, public services in Solwezi have never been adequate since at least the 1970s. Those who can afford to reside in Zug benefit from highly efficient public services. We thus speak of very different scales of *being concerned*. This limits the similarities' potential for acknowledgement of a joint positionality and for joint mobilization.

From interdependence (to have a responsibility for) to …

I have used the concept of *interdependence* (to have a responsibility for) as a thread in the book, a critical lens that allows us to describe orders created by global extractivism. While people in Switzerland and Zambia are dependent upon one another, the conceptual separation between their worlds masks this fact and allows us to ignore it. Interdependence can remain asymmetrical, with very different consequences for both sides.

If we manage to break through the conceptual divides, our interdependence can also become a basis for joint action between citizens in export and service economies. Zambians and the Swiss may not share a class standpoint, but they share their embeddedness in a global economic order that creates practical connections between both. Recognizing the extent of these connections would also make it much more difficult for people in Switzerland to deny to Zambians the recognition as equals. If the other person is part of the same world as I am, functionally connected to me and a full participant in the order that defines my own place in society, she should also be granted the same rights as I.

The asymmetrical order of extractivism *concerns* us all. We might not know about it, but we are implicated in it and remain, through it, connected to other regions of the world. Really acknowledging these connections can only lead to the recognition of unknown others as endowed with rights, whether they live in the same world region or not. This would be the starting point for symmetrical, collective action to bring about change.

Commoning

Clearly, acts of 'making community' across the so-called value chain remain rare and difficult to practice, precisely because strong forces keep people separated from one another, making it difficult to find entry points for joint action. How such action could look like, where it would take its participants and how it would change the status qua – these questions are outside of the scope of this and in fact outside of the scope of any book. Answers can only emerge in practice. Such practices need to have a firm commitment to reflexivity and an awareness for power differentials (Gill 2009; see the example of Sobizana Mngqikana in Thörn 2009, 428). Research – and art (Acosta 2018; Gómez-Barris 2017) – has a role to play in this much larger process of recognition and joint action (see also Cann and DeMeulenaere 2020). Research has the resources to show how corporate actors dis-embed and dis-entangle themselves in order to produce and keep up the normalcy of capitalism (Appel 2019b), and to *re-embed* companies in order to push for accountability and repair (Wylie 2018).[13] Out of this can grow forms of engagement that 'lead us out of the deadening impasse that is extractive capitalism' (Gómez-Barris 2017).

Practices of 'making community' offer the affordance for social change if we understand the world not as a chain but as a shared – common – space. Research on the commons has traditionally focused on rural areas and on small groups where questions of the maintenance of the commons over time dominated. A newer strand of research focuses on the commons at a global scale and how commons can be *reclaimed* from a capitalist landscape. Typically, it refers to the process of a community independently self-managing its own resources, or reclaiming it from the state, on behalf of the community at large (Leap, Stalp and Kelly 2022). Just like others, notably feminists (Clement et al. 2019), have done before me, I would like to free the notion of the commons from its material connotation and from its focus on self-managed property regimes, and rather look at commons as open and constituted by social relationships, everyday practices and care (Federici and Linebaugh 2018; Huron 2015).

For the purpose of bringing this book to a close, we can loosely understand commoning as a practice that is a response to intense commodification, financialization and alienation, that attempts to overcome separations created by these very processes and that proposes political alternatives. In that sense, all the activist actions described above engage in commoning – in making the world a place of community and shared experience. They also show that commoning is hard labour and carries risks, especially in situations of deep global and local inequalities. As bell hooks knew, 'making community' is a revolutionary practice because it goes up against all odds. There is lots to do, also on the academic front. Where are these social spaces, these places of commoning? What are the conditions for their emergence – and maintenance?[14] What role do scholars have to play in and in relation to them?

In the end, I believe it is ultimately in the interest of the Global North to acknowledge its interdependence with the South. We are utterly ill-prepared for the massive changes that are coming our way – think of climate change – when we do not ask ourselves the inward-looking question: Can I have a true relationship with myself without acknowledging my interconnection to other people?

NOTES

Introduction

1 To the ordinary reader, FQM has probably come to their attention in October 2023 when country-wide protests against its subsidiary Minera Panama – and later the Panamanian government itself – broke out in Panama after the government prolonged its Cobre Panama Mine contract to operate for another twenty years. The contract was seen as too favourable to the company and its operations to be harmful to the environment by protesters. The Supreme Court confirmed the concession contract unconstitutional in November 2023 and FQM was ordered to shut down the mine, upon which the miner initiated international arbitration.

2 For a detailed analysis of these and other population growth figures, refer to the next chapter and for more details Kesselring (2021a).

3 Not completely incidentally so, this is also how critical civil society approaches the topic of mining's externalities in Zambia and elsewhere. Often, 'mining communities' are the focus of attempts to unearth the negative effects of mining on communities. Hardly is there any research on the mining company per se; a fact which is largely determined by the company's unwillingness to allow critical investigations on the mining site and into its operations.

4 The terms 'Global South' and 'Global North' are of course also part of these artificial separations. One could argue that they are simply a duplication of what used to be called 'First World'/ 'Third World' or 'developing'/'developed country'. Many scholars however see at least some emancipatory potential in the use of the term 'Global South', not least the possibility of solidarities across the South. In general, the term 'Global South' is seen as less hierarchical and evolutionary than earlier ascriptions. For some reflections on the potential and limitations of the term 'Global South', see Hollington et al. (2015).

5 This is a nod to Samir Amin who described development and underdevelopment as 'two sides of the same coin' (2019, 9).

6 To use another example, if necessary: Migrants in the camp known as 'the jungle' in Calais, France, do not chose to live 'disorderly'. It is the order of states that puts them there under these existing living conditions. If we ignore this connection, we externalize and subjectivize 'disorder' (*That's how they are.*) and we ignore the question of who created the order which allows the disorder to exist.

7 Much of their analysis had already been formulated by Rosa Luxemburg (1913).

8 To explain the difficulties faced by commodity export-oriented countries to accrue and re-invest rents from the extractive sector in a more locally sensitive manner, scholars have developed a variety of explanatory approaches, emphasizing national factors more explicitly. These explanations have emerged from particular regional scholarships and hardly engage each other. The lens of 'Resource Nationalism' as a strategy is primarily applied to Central Asia and East Africa, foregrounding the states' attempts to raise tax, nationalize or increase the state's ownership in the extractive

sector to generally achieve greater control and value out of it (Caramento 2020; Kragelund 2020; Saunders and Caramento 2018). Scholars adopting the concept of 'Neo-Patrimonialism' focus on the political regime in African countries and observe a concentration of power (Mkandawire 2015), while scholars framing the development-through-resources debate as 'Neo-Extractivism' point to Latin American state's intensification of commodity exploitation, paralleled with social spending (Burchardt and Dietz 2014). The framework of the 'Developmental State' debate is chiefly used for East Asian countries to explain economic growth, productivity and technological advantage at the aegis of a strong, technocratic state. Finally, the 'Rentier-State' debate is reserved for the Middle East and North Africa as oil-producing countries, their political regimes with the domination of the public sector over the private.

9 Even Roland Robertson's concept of *glocalization* (2012) with which he describes the co-presence of both universalizing and particularizing tendencies remained trapped in this dichotomy.

10 I owe this point to Tolga Demiryol.

11 My answer is very different from hers. She resists the coloniality by unearthing that which is submerged, thereby turning to arts and the perspectives of artists and activists to understand the potentiality of other worlds.

12 I lived in Solwezi for two months in 2013, ten months in 2015, three months in 2016, three months in 2017 and two months in 2018.

13 Unintentionally – but of course not coincidentally – I thereby copied Claude Meillassoux's method of structuring his book:

> Colonialism has brought capitalism and the domestic economies into direct contact; the in-between modes of exploitation and their related classes of masters and lords vanished amidst this encounter. The abrupt transition between the first part of the book, which deals with anthroponomic societies, and the second, which jumps to modern conditions of labor, was forced down upon me as it is forced down on African peasants by the callousness of the colonial relationship. (Meillassoux 1981, x).

14 Under the notion of 'resource curse', scholars have debated the relationship between resource dependence and performance of the national economy since the early 1990s. More recently, to open a rather chicken-or-the-egg argument, a group of scholars have highlighted not only the nature of institutions but also the balance of political power as key ingredients to theorize the relationship between resources and development more productively (Bebbington et al. 2018, 4–6). This book does not explicitly engage with this literature although a reader may find arguments that substantiate the theorization with the data on local, municipal governance and an urban areas' interdependence with other global centres.

1 Copper's promise from Solwezi to Zug

1 Elsewhere I document Kansanshi Mine's and Solwezi town's histories in much more detail (2021a).

2 Both Konkola and Mopani Mines are however old, underground, investment-intensive mines with little opportunity for automation and with many safety gaps for workers and communities. Zambian journalists judged Lungu's dependency

on the Copperbelt constituencies for his re-election in August 2021 as a key component to the selection of the mines. Increasing the state's stake in the three new and most profitable mines in the Northwestern Province would be much more viable, though.

3 The 2015 SUBS study produced reliable data for the area covered by the planned extension of the urban Solwezi area. The numbers from the 2022 census (332,623 for Solwezi District) are the best estimation of how the town grew since 2015 (Central Statistical Office Zambia 2022, 20). The census only offers data down to the district level. The district boundaries of Solwezi District are more or less identical to the boundaries used by the SUBS study. Both reflect the actual urban built-up area.

4 In 1999, Cyprus Amax was taken over by Phelps Dodge Corporations.

5 Like other foreign investors, the Canadian company entered a so-called Development Agreement (DA) with the Zambian government that provided for a corporate tax rate of 25 per cent and a royalty rate of 0.6 per cent (Lungu 2008). The Zambian government unilaterally terminated the DA in 2008, and ever since, the mineral royalty and tax regime in Zambia has been changing regularly (see Bebbington et al. 2018, 143 and Chapter 6). In the company's view, it has the right to be compensated for taxes and royalties paid in excess of those agreed upon in the DA (First Quantum Minerals Ltd. 2020, 125). In May 2020, KMP filed a request for arbitration against the government of Zambia with the International Centre for Settlement of International Disputes (First Quantum Minerals Ltd. 2023b, 160).

6 For the construction of the smelter, Filipinos and Indonesians were brought in on short-term contracts in 2013/2014 (O'Callaghan 2019, 45).

7 Stressed is defined as a situation where households 'have minimally adequate food consumption but are unable to afford some essential non-food expenditures without engaging in stress-coping strategies' (IPC 2020, 7).

8 https://repository.jctr.org.zm/handle/20.500.14274/366, 8 November 2023.

9 The goods are not captured by the official trade statistics, yet the proceeds show up as 'merchanting trade' in the balance of payments – defined as the good sales by a resident to a non-resident minus the good purchase by a resident from a non-resident.

10 'JCTR Basic Needs and Nutrition Basket for Solwezi, June 2020', https://data.snb.ch/en/topics/aube/cube/bopmercoua, last accessed 8 November 2023.

2 The council

1 The resource curse is certainly a reality, but we gain little new understanding from statements that the state is corrupted, 'hollowed out' or 'weakened' by the extractive industry (Schubert, Engel and Macamo 2018), a 'crude resource curse analysis' that overlooks variations in historically context-specific situations (Bebbington et al. 2018, 119). See also footnote 14 in introduction. If local authorities cannot live up to the expectations of a town's residents, we should not just take that fact for granted, but use it as the entry point for empirical scrutiny.

2 With the exception of a few pages in Negi (2014, 1007–9), contemporary scholarship on Solwezi, which is small, does not address the council's role but instead focuses on chiefs (Negi 2010), resistance to the mining company (Hobi 2019) and the mining expansion's impact on rural communities, their displacement and resettlement (Chansa 2020; Cheelo 2008; Kapesa 2019; Van Alstine and Afionis 2013).

3 The pre-feasibility study report for North Western Water Supply and Sanitation Company (Draft) from May 2015 shows how important SUBS's findings could be if integrated into planning processes. The water company's report makes its calculations and plans for the future based on the estimate of 152,155 inhabitants in its license area, and thereby assumes at least 100,000 fewer residents than what the SUBS revealed. This undercounting contributes to even poorer service provision and the municipality's incapacity to plan ahead.
4 Part of this conclusion is my observation of the ability of a local elite – Kaonde, Lunda and Luvale speakers from the Solwezi region – to benefit from possibilities produced by the mining boom more than 'non-locals' as described here. The conclusion is also based on what I describe in the previous chapter: that the labor force in the mines is primarily Bemba-speaking and from the Copperbelt towns. Here, ethnic or tribal group membership intersects with gender (it is mainly men in both instances) and, in the case of business opportunities in mining-related sectors, clearly intersects with a certain standing in the traditional and political structures of the Solwezi region.
5 Before the amendment of the constitution in 2016, the mayor was elected by the councillors. However, under the terms of the new constitution, he or she is elected directly by the electorate and the position is full-time.
6 SMC has four standing committees: Finance, Human Resources and General Purposes; Plans, Works, Development and Real Estate; Audit; and Health, Environment and Social Services.
7 'Update on 2015 Budget Estimates', FHRGP/15/06/15.
8 Minutes of the FHRGP Committee Meeting, 17 August 2015; Report of the Director of Finance to the FHRGP Committee, FHRGP/02/08/15. The estimated total revenue for 2015 (in kwacha) included local taxes (30 million), fees and charges (10 million), licenses (600,000), levies (3.8 million), permits (1 million), service charges (19 million), other income (500,000), national support (8.8 million) and constituency development funds (4.2 million).
9 SMC's property rates for the two mines in 2015 were five times higher than, for instance, those of Kitwe City Council, which hosts seven mining operations, among them Mopani Copper Mines and NFC Africa Mining (copper), Kagem and Grizzly Mining (gemstones). It represents 29 per cent of the total revenue from the mining sector going to all host councils in Zambia (Zambia EITI 2017) – Report of the Director of Finance to the FHRGP Committee meeting, 12 March 2015, FHRGP/09/03/15. The collected revenue represented only 52 per cent of the budget estimate.
10 'Utilisation Report on Funds Received from Extractive Companies in Solwezi District for January to June 2015' in minutes of the FHRGP Committee meeting, 17 August 2015.
11 Although, in 2015, the Kalumbila/Sentinel Mine was already producing, it was not yet on the district's valuation roll.
12 Report of the Director of Finance in the minutes of the FHRGP Committee meeting held on Monday, 12 December 2016, FHRGP/13/12/16.
13 Report of the Director of Finance in the minutes of the FHRGP Committee meeting held on Monday, 12 December 2016, FHRGP/13/12/16. The Council's revenue from Kansanshi Mine increased from ZWM 16,714,804 per annum to ZMW 25,324,000 per annum, added to which SMC will receive ZMW 6,518,000 from Lumwana Mine as part of the three councils' agreement to share Lumwana's revenue.

14 As reported in the Director of Finance's report to the FHRGP Committee, 12 December 2016, FHRGP/15/12/16.

15 The entire volume delivers poorly on taking into consideration non-Western contexts. The chapter by Kiser and Sacks (2009), for instance, suggests to compare contemporary African states' capacities with pre-modern states' low capacities to centralize tax administration. The volume also adopts normative framework to tax collection by assuming the state's monopoly in these matters, something that scholars of Africa have clearly rebutted (for instance, Förster 2009).

16 For a detailed analysis of manipulation and violence in both urban and rural areas before, during and after the 2016 elections, see Wahman (2020).

17 It is possible that the Municipal Council's composition now begins to follow the general population patterns more closely. Since the general elections in 2016, however, many UPND councillors either defected to the PF or gave up their posts, thus triggering by-elections. Many of these by-elections were won by the much more resourceful and aggressive PF.

18 For instance, the Solwezi District Development Plan for 2006–2010, a forty-seven-page document, addresses mining-related changes with just one word in the preface. Given that the largest copper mine in Africa was establishing itself in the district during those years, the council's indifference seems remarkable.

3 *The house*

1 While conditions for credits and loans are not favourable, many workers are nevertheless forced to buy into loan services offered by their employer's subsidiaries or banks (Musonda 2021b).

2 The idea of a home as a physically fixed place has a long colonial and missionary history in Southern Africa (Comaroff and Comaroff 1997, 275).

3 It thereby contributes to a diverse scholarship on building, which ranges from a deterministic view informed by archeology (Buchli 2013) and buildings as manifestations and carriers of cultural meaning (Bourdieu 1979) to building – 'making' – as artisanal skills (Ingold 2013). Although influenced by that literature (with a clear preference to the making-as-skilling approach), my main concern here is not so much the meaning or constitutive character of a built structure nor how skills are acquired and practiced, but rather how an economic, political and environmental context shapes planning and building practices and, as a result, the 'look' of a town.

4 Solwezi is a favorable region for the manufacture of building bricks (Milisavljevic 1978, 2).

5 To receive official permission to develop a plot, owners have to go to the council with a filled-out permission-to-develop form, a copy of the title deed or a copy of the letter of offer from the ministry of lands, a signed site plan, the extract from the full council minutes and building plans. The drawings have to be A3 or larger and contain the block plan (showing position of septic tank, boundary and building line), floor plan, foundation plan, section elevations (side, front and back) with construction details and descriptions, door and window schedule, and a roof plan. Once the application is scrutinized against a fee, the landowner will receive signed and stamped drawings and an approval letter. A structure can be retrospectively approved by the council with service charges double as high as before the actual construction.

6 At the time of building (April 2015), a bag of cement cost ZMW75 and a ton of sand ZMW100.
7 There are some differences between compounds and areas. For instance, for the lack of land close to the town centre and the knowledge that state scrutiny is less likely, most mid-scale investors apply for land in chiefs' land and then formalize it through the council. 'Elite capture' is thus much more visible and impactful in these areas. This results in a segregation of the town between more regulated areas with clear compound characteristics and less regulated and poorly planned areas at the urban fringes. Peri-urban areas are not unattractive to residents either, though, and many better-off families move to the urban fringes and build their home more or less independently from state regulations, combining what they see as the country side's tranquility and the vicinity to town's attractions.

4 *The golf estate*

1 On the history of the term 'expatriate' in Northern Rhodesia/Zambia, see Money (2022).
2 After a presentation where I read out this passage, Duncan Money told me that I unintentionally quoted journalist Cyril Dunn writing for *The Observer* between 1954 and 1958 from his book *Central African Witness* (1959), when he discusses his time on the Zambian Copperbelt: 'To hear them [white miners] gossiping about the peculiarities of their 'Kaffirs' down the mine gives one, momentarily, a sense of being back south of the Limpopo' (1959, 136).
3 In July 2020, FQM appointed Anthony Mukutuma as its first Black and Zambian general manager of Kansanshi Mine. He started at KCM under ZCCM and later Anglo American and was with FQM in Finland, Australia and Mauretania (general manager at the Guelb Moghrein Mine) before, transitioning from engineering to management, to the position of its general manager. A first at Kansanshi Mine, it remains to be seen to what extent this appointment brings real change of perspective into the management of the mine or whether it is, as Burawoy wrote in relation to the appointment of Zambian's into supervisory positions in the 1960s, merely 'window-dressing Zambianization' (1972, 5). John Gladstone, formerly FQM's contact person in Lusaka, became its assistant general manager for a brief period. Gladstone did not have a background in mining before joining FQM in 2012 but had been a military officer and pilot in the Royal Air Force, with an aeronautics degree and an MA in Defense Studies. Overall, the positions of general and assistant general manager have had quite a turn-around in recent years, mainly but not only because of their shifting between FQM's Kalumbila/Sentinel and Kansanshi Mines. At the time of writing, Colin Du Plessis, a South African with work experience with Anglo, Xstrata, Glencore, BHP in South Africa and Australia and with FQM's operations in Zambia, held the position of the assistant general manager at Kansanshi Mine.
At Kansanshi Mining Plc, the following manager positions exist: general; assistant general; project managers for housing, plant, finance, commercial, engineering, public relations, FQMO, safety, environmental, mine, resource optimization, acid plant, human resources, CSR and clinic. FQM had its own mining division called FQMO in Zambia, which recently merged with Kansanshi Mining Plc (KMP). The departments of former FQMO Mining Division, now KMP, are also headed by

managers: administration, engineering, safety, training, maintenance/workshop, maintenance/electrical, maintenance/auto electrical, maintenance/new workshop, purchasing, stores, roads, load & haul, and drills.

4 It is difficult to access statistical data on this, not only as a question of access but as a question of their existence. As Lee notes, 'The paucity of official reports and data on the copper mines since independence and especially privatization was shocking, especially when compared with the colonial period' (2017, 170–1). I thus heavily rely on ethnographic, qualitative data in this chapter.

5 For instance, the preference of FIFO commute arrangements is an ongoing trend in some areas and for some types of resouces, in particular in Australia, relieving the companies from the provision of long-term settlement options for its workers and their families in regions away from urban centres (Cheshire 2010).

6 See also Rubbers' (2019, 93–4) typification of 'camps' in relation to the location of mining sites.

7 *Rodgers Mwanda* vs. *Kansanshi Mining PLC & SMC*. Minutes of the Council Meeting held in the Council Chamber, Independence Avenue, Solwezi on 31 March 2014, item C/136/03/14 *Rodgers Mwanda* vs. *Kansanshi Mining PLC & SMC* Cause No: 2011/HK/224 (plot number 15573/m) (certificate of title number 33651). According to the Solwezi Baseline Study (SUBS), the estate is on plot number L/19870/M. Rogers Mwanda owns a plot in Magrade (compound adjacent to Mushitala and the Golf Estate) according to the SUBS database.

8 The claimant accepted cash and an alternative plot in Kabitaka, a new residential area built by the mine for rent-out to better-off Zambian employees and their families, as compensation.

9 Sometimes, an entire kind becomes too aggressive to live with humans, in which case they are resettled to the game reserve on the mine site or killed. The game reserve hosts over 500 animals. Some species must be culled routinely because of their age or an imbalance in sex. Especially impalas are used as gifts to other golf estates in the Copperbelt or to chiefs at the occasion of annual traditional ceremonies, to which the CSR manager and his staff are invited. Residential families sometimes bring their cats along but tend to not take them with them when they leave again. The management reminds residents now and then that cats will be killed if not chipped.

10 Board members do not live in Solwezi and only intermittently come for site visits.

11 The following formulation in the booklet adumbrates the companies' idea of a 'local': 'Please do not allow Mr Clean employees to cook lunch in the garden shed or bushes surrounding the house' (page 15).

12 Chikuli received the title 'General' as Commander of the Zambia National Defence Force and Deputy Minister of Defence.

13 Not only expatriates but also some Zambians have been with the company for many years and have witnessed the hardening of hierarchies which became noticeable as increased distrust. A person working in the procurement department was reminiscent of the time when they were allowed and even encouraged to leave the office and the warehouse and learn on-site about the production processes. Their favorite was to be at the gold plant. This has changed; access to the plant was very restricted now. When their told me about this change, I had the sense that they felt estranged from their work more than before. Earlier, they knew better what they worked for and for what purpose they procured the items they was asked to.

14 A similar discursive differentiation between South Africans and Australians was expressed by my Zambian interlocutors. They often struggled with a South African superior's abrasiveness and explained it by him being from South Africa.

15 On whites in South Africa before and after the end of apartheid, Crapanzano (1985), Goodwin and Schiff (1995) and Steyn (2001) stand out (for both an overview and an insight into the disagreement with regard to studies on white(ness), see Nyamnjoh 2012; Niehaus 2013). Literature on whites in Zimbabwe includes work by Fisher (2011), Kalaora (2011), Pilossof (2012) and Rutherford (2001).

16 The impossibility of management and senior-level, expatriate employees to live in Solwezi town also extends to Kabitaka (where I also lived for several months), the pay-as-you-rent housing project designed for better-off Zambian employees. When driving through it, one manager revealed to me in what I felt were offensive words that he and his Golf Estate colleagues 'would not want to live in these shithouses'.

17 I want to thank one of the anonymous reviewers for suggesting the point of looking for 'disorder' on the Golf Estate.

18 Expatriate teachers work under contract with Educore Services, a company wholly owned by FQM, which runs the three company-owned schools in Solwezi: Trident Preparatory School Solwezi (on the Golf Estate; with children aged between three and eleven years), Sentinel School Kabitaka (east of Solwezi town on the Kabitaka housing project), Trident College Solwezi (on the mine area). The schools offer the Cambridge curricula in English. Some parents prefer to school their children in Afrikaans and home-school them.

19 There are a small number of highly qualified Zambian women employed by the company, but they do not live on the estate.

20 According to Sally Engle Merry (1981), the same holds true also among urban residents where residents' perception of danger roots in their inability to differentiate among people and places. People are most afraid of strangers as their 'behavior' is unpredictable.

21 Zambia is no exception here; see for instance Christine Williams's (2021) work on the gendered and racialized US oil and gas industry and Vanesa Ribas's (2015) ethnography on African American and Latina/o workers under white dominance in the south of the United States.

22 Upon the publication of Burawoy's *The Colour of Class*, a heated debate between Burawoy and Bernard Magubane started, particularly on the notion of succession (Burawoy 1975; Magubane 1975, 1974).

23 To understand race relations at Chinese state-owned mines in Zambia and Africa more generally, one needs a whole different set of analytical tools, given both the long China-Africa history and contemporary strong political discourses on the Chinese in Africa. Chinese state-owned construction firms are increasingly present in Zambia's Northwestern Province. Research access to Chinese investments in Zambia has been notoriously difficult, yet there is a small collection of ethnographic works available, see Chapter 5, footnote 7.

5 Power and infrastructure

1 This letter was followed by several others to the traditional chief and the ministry of land, showing the company's confusion about whom to turn to with their request.

Also, unsurprisingly, in its response, the council first requested more details regarding the precise use of the land. The company ended by receiving the land, although slightly reduced in size.

2 ZESCO engages in cross-border trading of electricity through the Southern African Power Pool and bilateral markets. Typically, Zambia exports five times more electricity than it imports, but in 2014–15, its power imports increased by more than 6,000 per cent (Energy Regulation Board 2016, 8). Amidst complaints about bad performance and inefficiency of state-run ZESCO, calls for privatization are on the rise. The Zambian government attempts to invest in new electrical infrastructure. Due to lack of funds, it tries to engage in public–private partnerships or looks for donor funding. The state tries to attract investors to set up solar projects for affordable electricity in rural areas (BMWi 2016). At the 2016 Annual Meeting of the African Development Bank in Lusaka (23–27 May 2016) under the theme of Energy and Climate Change, the delegate for Zambia, ZESCO's managing director, argued that 'Lighting up and Powering Africa' – one of the ADB's five priority areas – could only become reality through public–private partnerships. Most recently, the Ministry of Energy started negotiations with China and Russia in relation to plans to set up nuclear energy infrastructure. Also, the European Union signed a €65 million grant – co-financed with the European Investment Bank – to rehabilitate the low-voltage distribution network and install new connections in the Lusaka City area. Up to today, however, these partnerships have only produced declarations of intent and could not revert the ongoing power crisis.

3 Overview of the Copperbelt Energy Corporation (CEC) Business, 9th Germany – Africa Energy Forum, 26 May 2015.

4 Ibid.

5 In Kalumbila, the local state is hardly present (even though a master plan for a new municipal area close to Kalumbila town exists). The mine has much leeway as a governance actor in the region, and conflicts with the chief, for instance, are dealt with the mine management's direct line to various ministries in the capital Lusaka. Since 2016, the Solwezi Municipal Council (SMC) has some staff in Lumwana – the Lumwana Management Board – initially organized as a satellite office of SMC to serve what was then still the western part of Solwezi District.

6 Contrary to electrical power, roads have received much more scholarly attention in relation to spatial governance and its effects on livelihood (Beck, Klaeger and Stasik 2017; Dalakoglou and Harvey 2014; Harvey and Knox 2015; Peša 2019).

7 On his LinkedIn profile, Buks Jansen van Rensburg summarizes BHL business growth as follows:

> At BHL we have an innovative spirit. In 1996 we started with 2 subcontractor trucks. In 1999 we bought our 5 own trucks, and 30 subbies. In 2003 we sold our SA operation to BEE. In 2004 we relocated to Zambia. In 2011 we invented the Bucksta trailer. In 2012 we changed to Chinese brand trucks. In 2017 we build a 221 km road to cut out 400 km. In 2018 we have 270 own trucks and 100 subbies. In 2020 we have 300 own trucks and 350 subcontractors. In 2022 we have 400 own trucks and 100 subcontractors. In 2023 we have 500 own trucks and 150 subcontractors. In 2024 we have 700 own trucks and 150 subcontractors; Jiayou International Logistics (Shanghai Listed company) bought shares in BHL. https://www.linkedin.com/in/buks-jansen-van-rensburg-433358b0.

8 I thank Rebecca Peters for sharing this information in a conversation in March 2021.
9 The Energy Regulation Board approved ZESCO's application to increase electricity tariffs for domestic consumers. This decision was first reversed by President Lungu in January 2016 when his election campaign for re-election in August 2016 started to gain momentum but was again approved by the Energy Regulation Board and re-implemented in May 2017.
10 The mining sector consumed 54.5 per cent of the country's total electricity in 2015, followed by the domestic sector with 30.4 per cent. In 2022, the distribution remained the same with 53.4 per cent for the mining sector and 33 per cent for the domestic sector (Energy Regulation Board 2022, 49).
11 Lusaka has a cholera outbreak almost every year.
12 Zambian Energy Regulation Board, press statement on tariff decision, 10 May 2017. http://www.erb.org.zm/press/statements/tariffDecisionSpeech10.05.2017.pdf.
13 This of course reflects a long history of relation between administration and traditional authorities (Negi 2010).
14 'Zambia to Cut Copper Mines' Power Supply by 30% on Shortage' by Matthew Hill, 11 August 2015.http://www.bloomberg.com/news/articles/2015-08-11/zambia-to-cut-copper-mines-power-supply-by-30-amid-shortage.
15 'Starved of electricity, First Quantum to cut 730 jobs at Zambia copper mine', 7 July 2016, Mail&Guardian. http://mgafrica.com/article/2016-01-07-starved-of-electricity-first-quantum-to-cut-730-jobs-at-zambia-copper-mine.

6 *Trading inequality*

1 With my experience of a sudden end of research access to mining premises and personnel, I however join a number of scholars working on the Zambian Copperbelt (see also Straube 2020), most prominent of which is A. L. Epstein's remark in the introduction to his book *Politics in an African Urban Community*: 'Initially, I was able to secure the full support of the Mine Management at the Roan Antelope for the study. Shortly afterwards, as a result of a series of unfortunate misunderstandings, this support was withdrawn, and for the greater part of my stay in the town I was denied personal access to the mine compound' (Epstein 1958, xvii–xviii).
2 The material contributing to this chapter was published as 'Swiss Extractivism: Switzerland's Role in Zambia's Copper Sector' (Dobler and Kesselring 2019), co-published by my colleague researcher Gregor Dobler and myself. Because of the hardened relationship with the company, I have decided to use the material obtained through freely given interviews, without however giving the names of interviewees or assigning quotes.
3 It is by now part of scholarly consensus that mines or large infrastructure projects are not 'enclaves' as James Ferguson (2005, 2006) suggested, but entangled in several ways with local communities and the state (see also Chapter 2). Considerable research has gone into showing how companies try to disentangle themselves from their environment to precisely operate like an enclave (Appel 2012b; Côte and Korf 2018; Hönke 2010; Kirshner and Power 2015; Rubbers 2019).
4 For a detailed account of the privatization process of Luanshya Copper Mines (LCM) – comprising Luanshya and Baluba mines – with particular attention to the role of international financial institutions and private investors and their strategies to

avoid responsibility for the economic and social consequences of their activities, see Gewald and Soeters (2010).

5 This differentiation partly relies on the geographical and historical distinction between the 'Old Copperbelt' where Glencore's mines and the Chinese state-owned mines are located, and the 'New Copperbelt' where FQM owns two out of three large-scale mines (see also introduction). In her work, Lee (2014, 2017) compares private 'Western' and state-owned Chinese investments in Zambia, particularly in the mining and construction sector. In their comparison of private 'Western' und state-owned Chinese oil-related investments in Chad and Niger, Behrends and Schritt (2018) criticize scholars' over-emphasis of differences between 'Western' and 'Chinese' investments while recognizing divergent spatial effects depending on the respective corporate strategy. Besides Lee's scholarship, there is little work published on Chinese investments in Zambia, mainly due to the failure to gain access (see Straube 2020). Li and Shi (2020) and Wu (2020) have conducted ethnographic work on Chinese associations and migrants in Zambia.

6 All the legal cases against Vedanta were dropped 'because you cannot mine in court', as the Minister of Mines Kabusuwe explained at the press conference in the Mulungushi Center, Lusaka, on 5 September 2023.

7 Aristotelis Mistakidis who used to hold more than 3 per cent of the shares (Glencore 2020, 121) resigned as Glencore's head of global copper trading by the end of 2018 amid inquiries of Ontario's Security Commission and the US Department of Justice about Glencore's Katanga mines.

8 The renaming into what it is – a subsidiary of FQM – and a note on its website that FQM Trading indeed is associated with FQML, may very well be the result of an article which I co-published with Gregor Dobler where we revealed some of this information to the larger public (Dobler and Kesselring 2019).

9 Most of FQM's mines only produce copper in concentrate form. For instance, the large Cobre Panama mine in Panama only produces concentrate and sells it to Franca-Nevada, a Canadian trader (First Quantum Minerals Ltd. 2023a, 38). Besides Kansanshi which produces concentrate, anode, cathode and blister, only the Cobre Las Cruces Mine in Southern Spain produces copper in cathode form. FQM Trading AG markets and trades copper in concentrate, anode and cathode forms.

10 Swiss traders are of course also involved in Zambia's agricultural sector. For instance, the Geneva-based grain merchant Louis Dreyfus acquired a 40 per cent stake in South Africa-based NWK Agri-Services in 2012 (formerly Dunavant), which started as a state-owned company under the name of Lint in 1976 to develop Zambia's cotton industry. The cotton trader and ginner works with smallholder farmers and outgrowers. Its products are traded via its Geneva trading desk.

11 The bill of lading service has two main advantages for Zambian customers: It guarantees access to empty containers for loading (since Zambia does not have an empty container depot, containers used by independent shippers have to be pre-ordered from South Africa, often at several weeks' notice); and it shifts the risk of demurrage (fines paid for late arrival of goods loaded on vessels) to the transporters hired by the carrier. None of these advantages is usually worth its cost for high volume copper transport through warehouses. – On MSC's role in shipbreaking, one of the endpoints of copper's value chain, see Daems and Goris (2019).

12 Sonangol and the entourage of José Eduardo dos Santos are linked to Switzerland in different ways, allegedly using its banks as conduits for money gained in corrupt

deals. In spite of several charges, no Swiss court has so far found anyone guilty in this regard; e.g. OSISA (2014).

13 Glencore's (and FQM's) sale of Mopani Copper Mines to the Zambian parastatal ZCCM-IC must be seen in this context. Compared to the relatively 'clean' service sector, mines, especially old mines, are complicated to handle because of their social and ecological entanglements which is visible and thus prone to criticism.

14 Zambia's government has periodically (ten times over the past sixteen years) tried to increase revenue from mining, typically when copper prices slumped, and revenues decreased. In 2014, the government increased mining royalty rates to 30 per cent, offsetting the increase by removing the 30 per cent corporate income tax for mining companies. The aim was to link revenue to production, not to income. Mining companies argued that the new regimes increased their production costs, made Zambian mining less competitive and revenue collection more complex for the authorities. Subsequently, the government lowered the royalty tax to 9 per cent and reintroduced the corporate income tax of 30 per cent. In 2016, under renewed pressure from the mining industry, it replaced the 9 per cent royalty with a price-based royalty and removed the variable profit tax. As a result of these changes, the tax burden for companies dropped considerably, relieving high-cost mines in times of low copper prices. Even when prices rose again, taxes did not attain their former level, since the tax rate no longer progresses with the taxable amount. This has motivated the most recent attempt at reform. From January 2019, government planned to increase royalty rates at all levels by 1.5 per cent and to introduce a fourth royalty tier at 10 per cent, which applies when the copper price rises above US$7,500/ton. In addition, a non-refundable sales tax was planned to replace the value-added tax. It remains an open question whether the Zambian government would have managed to implement these changes (since mining companies were able to fend off almost all earlier reform attempts with threats of mine closure or retrenchments) because the new administration under UPND's Hakainde Hichilema who came into power in 2022 changed the mining tax regime yet again in favor of the industry in late 2022.

15 This is not to say that there are no attempts to create more local content. Recently, the Parliamentary Committee on Transports, Works and Supply in Zambia suggested to create the legal framework to allocate a percentage of import and export contracts to Zambian truck drivers, and the Zambian Presidency suggested that the country should start trading a portion of its own copper, by receiving physical copper rather than royalties from the mines. As the president's economic advisor is quoted saying, 'It gives us transparency. We will see "Ah! That's what happened in Switzerland"' (Hill 2024). And finally, Zambia and the DRC signed a cooperation agreement to develop a cross-border integrated value chain to produce EV batteries in 2022, although the United States tagged along the cooperation with an MoU later in the year.

16 Economic theorists of global value and supply chains adopt a firm-centered, policy-oriented perspective of the global that allows them to understand how value is added to goods along their journey (Gereffi 2014). Unsatisfied with an all too linear theorization, theorists of global production networks (GPN) have recently highlighted the functional role of intermediaries such as financial, logistics and standard-setting agents (Yeung and Coe 2015, 42, 50). All in all, GPN theory reads like a 'sanitized' version of earlier attempts to understand the production of global inequalities through the chain heuristics (Alimahomed-Wilson and Ness 2018; Bair and Werner 2011), such as world system approaches or dependency theories with their key interest in uneven development as an outcome of the organization of global networks.

Conclusion: On being concerned

1 It does not mean that unions have become unimportant for workers and their families. They still play an important role, which can include the labour of care (Lochery, McNamara and Musonda 2024).

2 This is a success in terms of strategy, but for it to change people's lives to the better (which is not clear; it may also produce further inequalities), it first needs to be translated into reality. To do so, it does of course not help that the council seems to have spent funds unaccounted for every couple of years as reported in the media. For its challenges to build its revenue base, see Chapter 2.

3 Carbonnier at al. (2024) also open their article with this conundrum, illustrating it with the statement of a centre-right Swiss parliamentarian to a Ghanaian journalist: 'We don't know the situation in your country. It's you: You have to make regulations for your country. Not we in Switzerland' (2024, §1). In their article, they outline detailed recommendations for both host and home countries to curb illicit financial flows.

4 The global average for taxes on earnings, capital tax and property tax combined is 26.4 per cent; the Swiss average has been 14.4 per cent, while many cantons stay below 11 per cent (BAK Economics 2020). The July 2021 decision by over 140 OECD countries to introduce a global minimum corporate tax for large multinational companies with a minimum rate of at least 15 per cent forced Switzerland to put the question as whether to implement the minimum taxation to a popular vote (see section Similarity (to relate to)).

5 The Crypto AG was a Swiss company secretly owned by the American Central Intelligence Agency and the West German Federal Intelligence Service, manufacturing encryption machines and decipher devices. In 2020, journalists revealed that the Swiss Intelligence Service and members of the Swiss Federal Council were aware of the United States's access and use of encrypted messages. Prominent members of Zug's conservative parties were involved in the Crypto AG, presiding its board of directors, among others (Fagetti 2020).

6 An important example is Res Gehriger's (2014, 2016) television contributions, which helped to expose excessive pollution by Glencore's smelter in Mufulira.

7 The secretary general of the then Swiss Trading and Shipping Association (STSA, now Suissenégoce), an umbrella organization of the majority of the large trading companies, described the responsible business initiative as going 'way too far' (Hoffman and Bosley 2020). In late 2023, the audit commission of the Swiss Parliament ruled Karin Keller-Sutter, member of the Swiss Federal Council and then justice minister, to have overstepped her competencies by too openly lobby for the rejection of the initiative.

8 'Corporate Sustainability Due Diligence', https://commission.europa.eu/business-economy-euro/doing-business-eu/corporate-sustainability-due-diligence_en (30 June 2024).

9 See http://www.keesa.ch.

10 Most analyses focus on the impact of the ethically questionable campaign *against* the adoption of the initiative into law. For instance, fög (Forschungszentrum Öffentlichkeit und Gesellschaft at the University of Zürich) concludes that most major media houses in Switzerland sided with businesses and conservative

politicians: http://www.foeg.uzh.ch/de/news/Abstimmungsmonitor-November-2020.html (last accessed 26 December 2020).

11 Email from the campaign office dated 21 December 2020, offering a preliminary evaluation.

12 I found that students and scholars reacted very strongly to my use of the term 'solidarity', seeing it as a notion that is inherently hierarchical, one-sided and extended to 'the other'. Together with its use in scholarly literature, this is the reason why I do not use the notion of solidarity extensively here but rather speak of joint symmetrical action and commoning.

13 Matthan (2020) made this point of putting Wylie's *Fractivism* and Appel's *The Licit Life of Capitalism* in conversation with each other in her review essay.

14 We also need to keep in mind, as feminist Silvia Federici reminds us, that looking at reclaiming only does not answer the questions of *maintenance* yet; that is, we also need to ask how commons can support everyday existence.

REFERENCES

Abu-Lughod, Janet L. 1999. *New York, Chicago, Los Angeles: America's Global Cities*. Minneapolis: University of Minnesota Press.

Acosta, A. 2013. 'Extractivism and Neoextractivism: Two Sides of the Same Curse'. In *Beyond Development. Alternative Visions from Latin America*, edited by M. Lang and D. Mokrani, 61–86. Quito: Fundación Rosa Luxemburg.

Acosta, Ignacio. 2018. *Copper Geographies*. Barcelona: RM Verlag.

Adam, Christopher, and Anthony Simpasa. 2010. 'The Economics of the Copper Price Boom in Zambia'. In *Zambia, Mining, and Neoliberalism: Boom and Bust on the Globalized Copperbelt*, edited by Alastair Fraser and Miles Larmer, 59–90. Africa Connects. New York: Palgrave Macmillan.

Adams, Zeno, and Thorsten Glück. 2015. 'Financialization in Commodity Markets: A Passing Trend or the New Normal?' *Journal of Banking & Finance* 60 (C): 93–111.

Africa Confidential. 2018. 'Trafigura in a Tug-of-War' 59 (22). https://www.africa-confidential.com/article/id/12473/Trafigura_in_a_tug-of-war. Accessed 29 August 2024.

AFRODAD, and JCTR. 2020. 'Zambia, Debt and Covid-19'. *Eurodad* (blog). 25 September 2020. https://www.eurodad.org/zambia_debt_and_covid_19.

Aidoo, Kobina, and Ryan C. Briggs. 2018. 'Underpowered: Rolling Blackouts in Africa Disproportionately Hurt the Poor'. *African Studies Review*, 1–20. https://doi.org/10.1017/asr.2018.78.

Alimahomed-Wilson, Jake, and Immanuel Ness, eds. 2018. *Choke Points: Logistics Workers Disrupting the Global Supply Chain*. London: Pluto Press.

Amin, Samir. 2010. *Eurocentrism*. 2nd edition. New York: Monthly Review.

Amin, Samir. 2019. 'Keynote Address at the Second World Congress on Marxism: Beijing, PRC, 5–6 May 2018'. *Critical Sociology* 45 (1): 7–11. https://doi.org/10.1177/0896920518795003.

Appadurai, Arjun, ed. 1986. 'Commodities and the Politics of Value'. In *The Social Life of Things: Commodities in Cultural Perspective*, 3–63. Cambridge: Cambridge University Press.

Appadurai, Arjun. 1990. 'Disjuncture and Difference in the Global Cultural Economy'. In *Global Culture: Nationalism, Globalization and Modernity*, edited by Mike Featherstone, 295–310. London: Sage.

Appel, Hannah. 2012a. 'Offshore Work: Oil, Modularity, and the How of Capitalism in Equatorial Guinea'. *American Ethnologist* 39 (4): 692–709.

Appel, Hannah. 2012b. 'Walls and White Elephants: Oil Extraction, Responsibility, and Infrastructural Violence in Equatorial Guinea'. *Ethnography* 13 (4): 439–65.

Appel, Hannah. 2019a. 'To Critique or Not to Critique? That Is (Perhaps Not) the Question…'. *Journal of Business Anthropology* 8 (1): 29–34. https://doi.org/10.22439/jba.v8i1.5713.

Appel, Hannah. 2019b. *The Licit Life of Capitalism: US Oil in Equatorial Guinea*. Durham, NC: Duke University Press.

Araujo, Anna Lucia. 2020. *Slavery in the Age of Memory: Engaging the Past*. New York: Bloomsbury Academic.

Arboleda, Martin. 2020. *Planetary Mine: Territories of Extraction under Late Capitalism*. London: Verso.

Arrighi, Giovanni, and Jessica Drangel. 1986. 'The Stratification of the World-Economy: An Exploration of the Semiperipheral Zone'. *Review (Fernand Braudel Center)* 10 (1): 9–74.

Aschwanden, Erich. 2020. 'Egal ob "Panama» oder" "Paradise Papers", "Luanda" oder "Crypto-Leaks": Die Spur führt immer nach Zug'. *Neue Zürcher Zeitung*, 18 February 2020. https://www.nzz.ch/schweiz/warum-immer-zug-die-skandaltraechtigsten-239-quadratkilometer-der-schweiz-ld.1540263. Accessed 29 August 2024.

Bair, Jennifer, and Marion Werner. 2011. 'Commodity Chains and the Uneven Geographies of Global Capitalism: A Disarticulations Perspective'. *Environment and Planning A: Economy and Space* 43 (5): 988–97. https://doi.org/10.1068/a43505.

BAK Economics. 2020. 'Steuern für Unternehmen – Taxation Index'. 2020. https://baktaxation.bak-economics.com/besteuerung-von-unternehmen. Accessed 29 August 2024.

Ballard, Chris, and Glenn Banks. 2003. 'Resource Wars: The Anthropology of Mining'. *Annual Review of Anthropology* 32 (1): 287–313.

Balogun, Oluwakemi. 2020. *Beauty Diplomacy: Embodying an Emerging Nation*. Stanford, CA: Stanford University Press.

Banda, Tinenenji, Kaaba O'Brian, Marja Hinfelaar and Muna Ndulo, eds. 2020. *Democracy and Electoral Politics in Zambia*. Leiden: Brill. https://brill.com/view/title/57421.

Banks, Nina. 2020. 'Black Women in the United States and Unpaid Collective Work: Theorizing the Community as a Site of Production'. *Review of Black Political Economy* 47 (4): 343–62. https://doi.org/10.1177/0034644620962811.

Barad, Karen. 2007. *Meeting the Universe Halfway: Quantum Physics and the Entanglement of Matter and Meaning*. Durham, NC: Duke University Press. http://catdir.loc.gov/catdir/toc/ecip0619/2006027826.html.

Bartley, Tim. 2018. *Rules without Rights: Land, Labor, and Private Authority in the Global Economy*. Oxford: Oxford University Press.

Bastin, Lucas. 2014. 'Transfer Pricing and the WTO'. *Journal of World Trade* 48 (1): 59–80.

Batidzirai, Bothwell, Alfred Moyo and Michael Kapembwa. 2017. *Willingness to Pay for Improved Electricity Supply Reliability in Zambia: A Survey of Urban Enterprises in Lusaka and Kitwe*. Cape Town: Energy Research Centre, University of Cape Town.

Bebbington, Anthony, Abdul-Gafaru Abdulai, Denise Humphreys Bebbington, Marja Hinfelaar and Cynthia Sanborn (eds). 2018. 'The Politics of Natural Resource Extraction in Zambia'. In *Governing Extractive Industries: Politics, Histories, Ideas*, 116–51. Oxford: Oxford University Press.

Beck, Kurt, Gabriel Klaeger and Michael Stasik, eds. 2017. *The Making of the African Road*. Vol. 18. Africa-Europe Group for Interdisciplinary Studies. Leiden: Brill.

Behrends, Andrea, and Jannik Schritt. 2018. '"Western" and "Chinese" Oil Zones: Petro-Infrastructures and the Emergence of New Trans-Territorial Spaces of Order in Niger and Chad'. In *Spatial Practices: Territory, Border and Infrastructure in Africa*, edited by Ulf Engel, Marc Boeckler and Detelv Müller-Mahn, 211–30. Leiden: Brill. https://doi.org/10.1163/9789004367012_013.

Behrends, Andrea, and Remadji Hoinathy. 2017. 'The Devil's Money: A Multi-Level Approach to Acceleration and Turbulence in Oil-Producing Southern Chad'. *Social Analysis* 61 (3): 56–72. https://doi.org/10.3167/sa.2017.610304.

Behrends, Andrea, Sung-Joon Park and Richard Rottenburg. 2014. 'Travelling Models: Introducing an Analytical Concept to Globalisation Studies'. In *Travelling Models in African Conflict Management: Translating Technologies of Social Ordering*, edited by Andrea Behrends, Sung-Joon Park and Richard Rottenburg, 1–40. Africa-Europe Group for Interdisciplinary Studies 13. Leiden: Brill.

Bell, David, and Mark Jayne, eds. 2006. *Small Cities: Urban Experience beyond the Metropolis*. London: Routledge. https://doi.org/10.4324/9780203019269.

Benya, Asanda. 2015. 'The Invisible Hands: Women in Marikana'. *Review of African Political Economy* 42 (146): 545–60. https://doi.org/10.1080/03056244.2015.1087394.

Berman, Bruce J. 1984. 'The Concept of "Articulation" and the Political Economy of Colonialism'. *Canadian Journal of African Studies / Revue Canadienne Des Études Africaines* 18 (2): 407–14. https://doi.org/10.2307/484338.

Beusch, Elisabeth, Barbara Döbeli, Andreas M. Fischer and Pinar Yesin. 2013. *Merchanting and Current Account Balances*. Basel: Swiss National Bank.

Bisson, Michael. 1980. 'Pre-Historic Archeology of North-Western Province, Zambia'. In *Handbook to the North-Western Province 1980*, edited by David S. Johnson, 53–66. Zambia Geographical Association Regional Handbook Series 8. Lusaka: Zambia Geographical Association.

Björkman, Lisa. 2015. *Pipe Politics, Contested Waters: Embedded Infrastructures of Millennial Mumbai*. Durham, NC: Duke University Press Books.

Bloomberg. 2017. 'Commodity Traders Have a Really Big Problem'. *Bloomberg.Com*, 21 May 2017. https://www.bloomberg.com/news/articles/2017-05-21/commodity-traders-lament-world-where-everybody-knows-everything. Accessed 29 August 2024.

BMWi. 2016. *Subsector Analysis: Zambia. The Power Crisis and Its Consequences for Solar Energy in the Zambian Mining Sector*. Berlin: Federal Ministry of Economic Affairs and Energy BMWi.

Bolloré. 2018. 'Transport and Logistics in Zambia, Market Focus by Bolloré Logistics'. 2018. https://www.bollore-logistics.com/en/Pages/FOCUS/Zambia.aspx. Accessed 29 August 2024.

Boltanski, Luc. 2011. *On Critique: A Sociology of Emancipation*. Cambridge: Polity.

Borges, M., and S. Torres. 2012. 'Company Towns: Concepts, Historiography, and Approaches'. In *Company Towns: Labor, Space, and Power Relations across Time and Continents*, edited by M. Borges and S. Torres, 2012th edition, 1–40. New York: Palgrave Macmillan.

Bourdieu, Pierre. 1979. 'The Kabyle House or the World Reversed'. In *Algeria 1960*, 133–53. Cambridge: Cambridge University Press.

Bridge, Gavin. 2015. 'The Hole World: Scales and Spaces of Extraction'. *Scenario Journal* (blog). 8 October 2015. https://scenariojournal.com/article/the-hole-world/.Accessed 29 August 2024

Buchli, Victor. 2013. *An Anthropology of Architecture*. London: Bloomsbury Academic.

Bundesamt für Statistik. 2023. 'Medienmitteilung: Rohstoffhandel: Die Zahl der Unternehmen wächst weiter, bei der Beschäftigung zeigt sich ein differenzierteres Bild'. Bern.

Burawoy, Michael. 1972. *The Colour of Class on the Copper Mines: From African Advancement to Zambianization*. Zambian Papers 7. Lusaka: University of Zambia, Institute for African Studies. http://burawoy.berkeley.edu/books.htm#Color.

Burawoy, Michael. 1975. 'Race, Class, and Succession: Reply to Magubane'. *American Journal of Sociology* 81 (1): 163–7.

Burawoy, Michael. 1998. 'The Extended Case Method'. *Sociological Theory* 16 (1): 4–33. https://doi.org/10.1111/0735-2751.00040.

Burawoy, Michael. 2001. 'Manufacturing the Global'. *Ethnography* 2 (2): 147–59. https://doi.org/10.1177/14661381010002002001.

Burchardt, Hans-Jürgen, and Kristina Dietz. 2014. '(Neo-)Extractivism – a New Challenge for Development Theory from Latin America'. *Third World Quarterly* 35 (3): 468–86. https://doi.org/10.1080/01436597.2014.893488.

Bwalya, Bridget Umar, Moses N. Chisola, Beverly M. Mushili, Chibuye Florence Kunda-Wamuwi, David Kafwamba, Garikai Membele and Eunice N. S. Imasiku. 2022. 'Load-Shedding in Kitwe, Zambia: Effects and Implications on Household and Local Economies'. *Development Southern Africa* 39 (3): 354–71. https://doi.org/10.1080/0376835X.2020.1870934.

Cabot, Heath. 2016. '"Contagious" Solidarity: Reconfiguring Care and Citizenship in Greece's Social Clinics'. *Social Anthropology* 24 (2): 152–66. https://doi.org/10.1111/1469-8676.12297.

Çağlar, Ayse, and Nina Glick Schiller. 2015. 'A Multiscalar Perspective on Cities and Migration. A Comment on the Symposium'. *Sociologica*, no. 2/2015. https://doi.org/10.2383/81432.

Cane, Jonathan. 2019. *Civilising Grass: The Art of the Lawn on the South African Highveld*. Johannesburg: Wits University Press.

Cann, Colette, and Eric DeMeulenaere. 2020. *The Activist Academic: Engaged Scholarship for Resistance, Hope and Social Change*. Gorham, ME: Myers Education Press.

Caraballo, José G., and Xiao Jiang. 2016. 'Value-Added Erosion in Global Value Chains: An Empirical Assessment'. *Journal of Economic Issues* 50 (1): 288–96. https://doi.org/10.1080/00213624.2016.1148991.

Caramento, Alexander. 2020. 'Cultivating Backward Linkages to Zambia's Copper Mines: Debating the Design of, and Obstacles to, Local Content'. *Extractive Industries and Society* 7 (2): 310–20. https://doi.org/10.1016/j.exis.2019.10.013.

Caramento, Alexander. 2023. 'Resource Nationalism and Indigenous Capital Accumulation: Interrogating the Motivations Behind the Zambia Industrial and Mining Corporation (ZIMCO) Bond Redemptions, 1969–1975'. *Journal of Southern African Studies* 49 (3): 455–75. https://doi.org/10.1080/03057070.2023.2271599.

Caramento, Alexander, Marja Hinfelaar and Caesar Cheelo. 2023. 'Asymmetries of Power and Capacity: The Zambia Revenue Authority (ZRA) as an Instrument of Resource Nationalism, 1994–2021'. *Journal of Southern African Studies* 49 (3): 415–38. https://doi.org/10.1080/03057070.2023.2270645.

Carbonnier, Gilles, Fritz Brugger, Elisabeth Bürgi Bonanomi, Fred M. Dzanku and Stabandith Insisienmay. 2024. 'Curbing Illicit Financial Flows in Commodity Trade and Beyond'. *International Development Policy | Revue Internationale de Politique de Développement*, no. 17 (March). https://doi.org/10.4000/11q96. Accessed 29 August 2024.

Castel-Branco, Carlos Nuno. 2014. 'Growth, Capital Accumulation and Economic Porosity in Mozambique: Social Losses, Private Gains'. *Review of African Political Economy* 41 (sup1): S26–48. https://doi.org/10.1080/03056244.2014.976363.

Central Statistical Office Zambia. 2013. *Zambia 2010 Census of Population and Housing. Report on Characteristics of Households and Housing*. Lusaka: Central Statistical Office.

Central Statistical Office Zambia. 2022. *Zambia 2022 Census of Population and Housing. Preliminary Report*. Lusaka: Zambia Statistical Agency.

Central Statistical Office Zambia. 2023. 'The Monthly: September 2023'. 246. Lusaka: Zambia Statistical Agency.

Chansa, Jennifer Chibamba. 2020. 'Regulating Copper Mining: A History of Environmental Management in Zambia (1964–2018)'. Unpublished PhD thesis, Bloemfontein: International Studies Group, University of the Free State..

Charles, Thierry. 2024. 'Request of Investigation to ACC Concerning Ridiculous Penalties for FQM Tax Dispute Amounting US$7.6 Billion'. *Lusaka Times*, 13 June 2024, sec. Feature Politics. https://www.lusakatimes.com/2024/06/13/request-of-investigation-to-acc-concerning-ridiculous-penalties-for-fqm-tax-dispute-amounting-us7-6-billion/. Accessed 29 August 2024.

Cheelo, Kingsley Haanyembe. 2008. 'Behind the Economic Figures: Large-Scale Mining and Rural Poverty Reduction in Zambia. The Case of Kansanshi Copper Mine in Solwezi'. Master thesis, Palmerston North, New Zealand: Massey University.

Cheshire, Lynda. 2010. 'A Corporate Responsibility? The Constitution of Fly-in, Fly-out Mining Companies as Governance Partners in Remote, Mine-Affected Localities'. *Journal of Rural Studies* 26 (1): 12–20. https://doi.org/10.1016/j.jrurstud.2009.06.005.

Christophers, Brett. 2011. 'Follow the Thing: Money'. *Environment and Planning D: Society and Space* 29 (6): 1068–84. https://doi.org/10.1068/d8410.

Clement, Floriane, Wendy Jane Harcourt, Deepa Joshi and Chizu Sato. 2019. 'Feminist Political Ecologies of the Commons and Commoning'. *International Journal of the Commons* 13 (1): 1–15.

Cobham, Alex, Petr Janský and Alex Prats. 2014. 'Estimating Illicit Flows of Capital via Trade Mispricing: A Forensic Analysis of Data on Switzerland'. Working Paper 350. Center for Global Development.

Colson, Elizabeth. 1971. *The Social Consequences of Resettlement: The Impact of the Kariba Resettlement Upon the Gwembe Tonga*. Manchester: Manchester University Press.

Comaroff, Jean, and John L. Comaroff. 1997. *Of Revelation and Revolution, Volume 1: Christianity, Colonialism, and Consciousness in South Africa*. Chicago: University of Chicago Press.

Committee on Economic Affairs, Energy and Labour. 2013. 'Report National Assembly'. Third Session. Eleventh National Assembly. Lusaka. http://www.parliament.gov.zm/sites/default/files/documents/committee_reports/REPORT%20OF%20THE%20COMMITTEE%20ON%20ECONOMIC%20AFFAIRS%202014_0.pdf.

Côte, Muriel, and Benedikt Korf. 2018. 'Making Concessions: Extractive Enclaves, Entangled Capitalism and Regulative Pluralism at the Gold Mining Frontier in Burkina Faso'. *World Development* 101 (Supplement C): 466–76. https://doi.org/10.1016/j.worlddev.2016.11.002.

Craig, John. 2001. 'Putting Privatisation into Practice: The Case of Zambia Consolidated Copper Mines Limited'. *Journal of Modern African Studies* 39 (3): 389–410.

Crapanzano, Vincent. 1985. *Waiting: The Whites of South Africa*. New York: Random House.

Crehan, Kate. 1997. *The Fractured Community: Landscapes of Power and Gender in Rural Zambia*. Berkeley: University of California Press.

Daems, Ebe, and Gie Goris. 2019. *Behind the Hypocrisy of Better Beaches. Shipbreaking in India, Ship Owners in Switzerland, Lobbying in Belgium*. Brussels: Shipbreaking Platform.

Dalakoglou, Dimitris, and Penny Harvey. 2012. 'Roads and Anthropology: Ethnographic Perspectives on Space, Time and (Im)Mobility'. *Mobilities* 7 (4): 459–65.

Dalakoglou, Dimitris, and Penny Harvey, eds. 2014. *Roads and Anthropology: Ethnography, Infrastructures, (Im)Mobility*. London: Routledge.

Dant, Tim. 2004. 'The Driver-Car'. *Theory, Culture & Society* 21 (4–5): 61–79.

Davis, Mike. 2006. *Planet of Slums*. London: Verso.

Debele, Serawit. 2021. 'A Requiem to Allyship'. *University of Bayreuth, News* (blog). 17 May 2021. https://www.africamultiple.uni-bayreuth.de/en/news/2021/2021-05-11_Allyship/index.html. Accessed 29 August 2024.

De Boeck, Filip, and Sammy Baloji. 2016. *Suturing the City: Living Together in Congo's Urban Worlds*. London: Autograph.

DNS-Transport Zug, Ueli, Ueli Kleeb and Caroline Lötscher, eds. 2017. *ZEITBILD Zug, 1873–2016*. Zug: DNS-Transport GmbH.

Dobler, Gregor. 2015. 'Fatal Words: Restudying Jeanne Favret-Saada'. *Anthropology of This Century*, issue 13. http://aotcpress.com/articles/fatal-words-restudying-jeanne-favretsaada/. Accessed 29 August 2024.

Dobler, Gregor. 2016. 'The Green, the Grey and the Blue: A Typology of Cross-Border Trade in Africa'. *Journal of Modern African Studies* 54(1): 145–69. https://doi.org/10.1017/S0022278X15000993.

Dobler, Gregor, and Rita Kesselring. 2019. 'Swiss Extractivism: Switzerland's Role in Zambia's Copper Sector'. *Journal of Modern African Studies* 57 (2): 223–45. https://doi.org/10.1017/S0022278X19000089.

Dufour, Pascale, Dominique Masson and Dominique Caouette, eds. 2010. *Solidarities Beyond Borders*. Chicago: University of Chicago Press. https://press.uchicago.edu/ucp/books/book/distributed/S/bo70089364.html.

Dunaway, Wilma A., ed. 2014. *Gendered Commodity Chains: Seeing Women's Work and Households in Global Production*. Stanford: Stanford University Press.

Dunn, Cyril. 1959. *Central African Witness*. London: Victor Gollancz.

Durkheim, Emile. 1967. *De la division du travail social*. 8th edition. Paris: Les Presses universitaires de France.

Eichenberger, Reiner, and David Stadelmann. 2012. 'Die "Zugisierung" der Schweiz'. *Der Sonntag*, 27 May 2012.

Eggert, Nina, Giovanni Ferro-Luzzi and Difei Ouyang. 2017. 'Commodity Trading Monitoring Report'. *SRIC and IREG, Geneva*. https://archive-ouverte.unige.ch/unige:94096. Accessed 29 August 2024.

Elsby, Angus. 2020. 'Creaming off Commodity Profits: Europe's Re-Export Boom and Africa's Earnings Crisis in the Coffee and Cocoa Sectors'. *Review of African Political Economy* 0 (0): 1–13. https://doi.org/10.1080/03056244.2020.1842186.

Energy Regulation Board. 2016. *Energy Sector Report 2015*. Lusaka: Energy Regulation Board.

Energy Regulation Board. 2022. *Energy Sector Report 2022*. Lusaka: Energy Regulation Board.

Epstein, A. L. 1958. *Politics in an African Urban Community*. Manchester: Manchester University Press.

Erklärung von Bern, ed. 2011. *Rohstoff: Das Gefährliche Geschäft Der Schweiz*. Zürich: Salis Verlag.

Ernst & Young. 2020. *Top 10 Business Risks Facing Mining and Metals in 2019–20*. London: Ernst & Young.

Escobar, Arturo. 2020. *Pluriversal Politics: The Real and the Possible*. Durham, NC: Duke University Press.

Eyerman, Ron, and Andrew Jamison. 1991. *Social Movements: A Cognitive Approach*. Pennsylvania, PA: Pennsylvania State University Press.

Fagetti, Andreas. 2020. 'Stacheldraht und Polizeischutz'. *Die Wochenzeitung*, 20 February 2020. https://www.woz.ch/2008/agentenplatz-zug/stacheldraht-und-polizeischutz. Accessed 29 August 2024.

Fagetti, Andreas. 2023. 'Unruhe im Steuerparadies'. *WOZ*, 16 November 2023. https://www.woz.ch/2346/rundgang-in-zug/unruhe-im-steuerparadies/!GVXR8N368VBA. Accessed 29 August 2024.

Fanon, Frantz. 1967. *Black Skin, White Masks*. London: Pluto Press.

Fanon, Frantz. 2005. *The Wretched of the Earth*. Translated by Richard Philcox. Reprint edition. New York: Grove Press.

Fässler, Hans. 2005. *Reise in Schwarz-Weiss. Schweizer Ortstermine Zur Sklaverei*. Zürich: Rotpunktverlag.

Fay, Derick. 2011. 'Migrants, Forests and Houses: The Political Ecology of Architectural Change in Hobeni and Cwebe, South Africa'. *Human Organization* 70 (3): 310–21.

Federal Council of Switzerland. 2018. *The Swiss Commodities Sector: Current Situation and Outlook*. Federal Council Report. Bern: Federal Council of Switzerland.

Federal Council of Switzerland. 2023. *Stand der Umsetzung der Empfehlungen aus dem Bericht «Rohstoffsektor Schweiz: Standortbestimmung und Perspektiven*. Bern: Federal Council of Switzerland.

Federici, Silvia. 2012. *Revolution at Point Zero: Housework, Reproduction and Feminist Struggle*. 1st edition. Oakland, CA: PM Press.

Federici, Silvia, and Peter Linebaugh. 2018. *Re-Enchanting the World: Feminism and the Politics of the Commons*. Oakland, CA: PM Press.

Ferguson, James. 1999. *Expectations of Modernity: Myths and Meanings of Urban Life on the Zambian Copperbelt*. Berkeley: University of California Press.

Ferguson, James. 2005. 'Seeing Like an Oil Company: Space, Security, and Global Capital in Neoliberal Africa'. *American Anthropologist* 107 (3): 377–82.

Ferguson, James. 2006. *Global Shadows: Africa in the Neoliberal World Order*. Durham, NC: Duke University Press.

First Quantum Minerals Ltd. 2002. 'First Quantum to Reduce Its Interest in Mopani Copper Mines Plc'. 22 April 2002. http://www.infomine.com/index/pr/Pa094754.PDF.

First Quantum Minerals Ltd. 2006. *Annual Information Form 2005*. Vancouver: First Quantum Minerals Ltd.

First Quantum Minerals Ltd. 2019. *Environmental and Safety Data Report 2019*. Toronto: First Quantum Minerals Ltd.

First Quantum Minerals Ltd. 2020. *Annual Information Form 2019*. Vancouver: First Quantum Minerals Ltd.

First Quantum Minerals Ltd. 2023a. *Annual Information Form 2022*. Vancouver: First Quantum Minerals Ltd.

First Quantum Minerals Ltd. 2023b. *Annual Report 2022*. Vancouver: First Quantum Minerals Ltd.

Fisher, J. L. 2011. *Pioneers, Settlers, Aliens, Exiles: The Decolonisation of White Identity in Zimbabwe*. Canberra: Australian National University E Press.

Fleischmann, Larissa. 2020. *Contested Solidarity: Practices of Refugee Support between Humanitarian Help and Political Activism*. Bielefeld: transcript Verlag. https://www.degruyter.com/document/doi/10.14361/9783839454374/html.

Förster, Till. 2001. 'Sehen und Beobachten: Ethnographie nach der Postmoderne'. *Sozialersinn* 3: 459–84.

Förster, Till. 2009. 'Limiting Violence-Culture and the Constitution of Public Norms: With a Case Study from a Stateless Area'. In *Non-State Actors as Standard Setters*, edited by Anne Peters, Lucy Koechlin, Till Förster and Gretta Fenner Zinkernagel, 324–47. Cambridge: Cambridge University Press.

Förster, Till. 2012. *Statehood in a Stateless Society: Political Order and Societal Memory in Northern Côte d'Ivoire*. Basel Papers on Political Transformations 4. Basel: University of Basel, Institute of Social Anthropology.

Förster, Till, and Carole Ammann. 2018. 'African Cities and the Development Conundrum: Actors and Agency in the Urban Grey Zone'. *International Development Policy | Revue Internationale de Politique de Développement* 10 (10): 3–25. https://doi.org/10.4000/poldev.2621.

Förster, Till, and Lucy Koechlin. 2011. *The Politics of Governance: Power and Agency in the Formation of Political Order in Africa*. Basel Papers on Political Transformation 1. Basel: Institute of Social Anthropology.

Franc, Andrea. 2021. *Im Austausch mit der Welt: Schweizer Unternehmen im 19. und 20. Jahrhundert*. Zürich: Hier+Jetzt.

Frank, Andre Gunder. 1967. *Capitalism and Underdevelopment in Latin America: Historical Studies of Chile and Brazil*. Revised edition. New York: Monthly Review Press.

Franke, Alexander, Roland Rechsteiner, and Graham Sharp. 2017. *The Endgame for Commodity Traders*. Zürich: Oliver Wyman.

Fraser, Alastair. 2016. 'Zambian Democracy: All Heat, No Light'. *ROAPE* (blog). 1 September 2016. http://roape.net/2016/09/01/zambian-democracy-heat-no-light/. Accessed 29 August 2024.

Fraser, Alastair, and John Lungu. 2007. *For Whom the Windfalls? Winners & Losers in the Privatisation of Zambia's Copper Mines*. Lusaka: Civil Society Trade Network of Zambia / Catholic Centre for Justice, Development and Peace.

Garrido, Marco. 2019. *The Patchwork City: Class, Space, and Politics in Metro Manila*. Chicago: Chicago University Press. https://press.uchicago.edu/ucp/books/book/chicago/P/bo40850773.html.

Gehriger, Res, dir. 2014. *Schweiz – Glencore-Xstrata und die Asthma-Toten von Mufulira*. https://www.srf.ch/news/schweiz/glencore-xstrata-und-die-asthma-toten-von-mufulira.

Gehriger, Res, dir. 2016. *Wirtschaft – Gericht in Sambia verurteilt Glencore-Kupferwerk*. https://www.srf.ch/news/wirtschaft/gericht-in-sambia-verurteilt-glencore-kupferwerk.

Gereffi, Gary. 2014. 'Global Value Chains in a Post-Washington Consensus World'. *Review of International Political Economy* 21 (1): 9–37. https://doi.org/10.1080/09692290.2012.756414.

Gewald, Jan-Bart. 2015. *Forged in the Great War: People, Transport, and Labour, the Establishment of Colonial Rule in Zambia, 1890–1920*. African Studies Collection 61. Leiden: African Studies Centre.

Gewald, Jan-Bart, and Sebastiaan Soeters. 2010. 'African Miners and Shape-Shifting Capital Flight: The Case of Luanshya/Baluba'. In *Zambia, Mining, and*

Neoliberalism: Boom and Bust on the Globalized Copperbelt, edited by Alastair Fraser and Miles Larmer, 155–83. Africa Connects. New York: Palgrave Macmillan.

Gill, Lesley. 2009. 'The Limits of Solidarity: Labor and Transnational Organizing against Coca-Cola'. *American Ethnologist* 36 (4): 667–80. https://doi.org/10.1111/j.1548-1425.2009.01202.x.

Ginsburgh, Nicola. 2020. *Class, Work and Whiteness: Race and Settler Colonialism in Southern Rhodesia, 1919–79*. Manchester: Manchester University Press.

Glencore. 2011. https://www.glencore.com/dam/jcr:268b58d2-61b8-44d1-997a-17e76bb66f93/Final-Prospectus-3-May-2011-lowres.pdf.

Glencore. 2018. *Annual Report 2017*. Baar: Glencore.

Glencore. 2020. *Annual Report 2019*. Baar: Glencore.

Glencore. 2023. *Annual Report 2022*. Baar: Glencore.

Glick Schiller, Nina. 2020. 'Solidarities of the Dispossessed'. *Anthropological Theory Commons* (blog). 2020. https://www.at-commons.com/2020/05/20/solidarities-of-the-dispossessed-response-to-julia-eckert-in-the-time-of-pandemic/. Accessed 29 August 2024.

Go, Julian. 2008. 'Global Fields and Imperial Forms: Field Theory and the British and American Empires'. *Sociological Theory* 26 (3): 201–29.

Godoy, Ricardo. 1985. 'Mining: Anthropological Perspectives'. *Annual Review of Anthropology* 14 (1): 199–217.

Gómez-Barris, Macarena. 2017. *The Extractive Zone: Social Ecologies and Decolonial Perspectives*. Durham, NC: Duke University Press.

Gómez-Barris, Macarena . 2019. 'A Dialogue on the Extractive Zone: Resistant Sensoriums'. *Cultural Dynamics* 31 (1–2): 151–4. https://doi.org/10.1177/0921374019838888.

Goodfellow, Tom. 2013. 'Planning and Development Regulation Amid Rapid Urban Growth: Explaining Divergent Trajectories in Africa'. *Geoforum* 48 (August): 83–93. https://doi.org/10.1016/j.geoforum.2013.04.007.

Goodwin, June, and Ben Schiff. 1995. *Heart of Whiteness: Afrikaners Face Black Rule in the New South Africa*. New York: Scribner.

Gordon, David M. 2021. 'Kingdoms and Associations: Copper's Changing Political Economy during the Nineteenth Century'. In *Across the Copperbelt*, edited by Miles Larmer, Enid Guene, Benoît Henriet, Iva Peša and Rachel Taylor, 155–78. Urban & Social Change in Central Africa's Borderland Communities. Suffolk: Boydell & Brewer. https://doi.org/10.2307/j.ctv199tj8b.13.

Graeber, David. 2011. *Debt: The First 5,000 Years*. Brooklyn, NY: Melville House.

GrantThornton. 2010. *Pilot Audit Report – Mopani Copper Mines Plc*. https://www.facing-finance.org/wp-content/blogs.dir/16/files/2012/03/2010_Report_audit_Mopani.pdf.

Greco, Elisa. 2020. 'Africa, Extractivism and the Crisis This Time'. *Review of African Political Economy* 47 (166): 511–21. https://doi.org/10.1080/03056244.2020.1859839.

Green, Erik, and Milja Norberg. 2018. 'Traditional Landholding Certificates in Zambia: Preventing or Reinforcing Commodification and Inequality?' *Journal of Southern African Studies* 44 (4): 613–28. https://doi.org/10.1080/03057070.2018.1461490.

Gross, Dominik. 2023. 'The Global Tax Rate Is Now a Tax Haven Rewards Programme, and Switzerland Wants in First'. *Tax Justice Network* (blog). 6 April 2023. https://taxjustice.net/2023/04/06/the-global-tax-rate-is-now-a-tax-haven-rewards-programme-and-switzerland-wants-in-first/. Accessed 29 August 2024.

Gudynas, E. 2018. 'Extractivism'. In *Reframing Latin American Development*, edited by R. Munck and R. Delgado Wise, 61–77. New York: Routledge.

Gupta, Akhil. 2015. 'An Anthropology of Electricity from the Global South'. *Cultural Anthropology* 30 (4): 555–68.

Hahn, Hans Peter. 2011. 'Antinomien kultureller Aneignung: Einführung'. *Zeitschrift Für Ethnologie* 136 (1): 11–26.

Haller, Lea. 2019. *Transithandel: Geld- und Warenströme im globalen Kapitalismus*. Frankfurt am Main: Suhrkamp.

Harvey, David. 1990. 'Between Space and Time: Reflections on the Geographical Imagination'. *Annals of the Association of American Geographers* 80 (3): 418–34.

Harvey, Penny, and Hannah Knox. 2015. *Roads: An Anthropology of Infrastructure and Expertise*. Expertise: Cultures and Technologies of Knowledge. Ithaca, NY: Cornell University Press.

Heintz, James. 2006. 'Low-Wage Manufacturing and Global Commodity Chains: A Model in the Unequal Exchange Tradition'. *Cambridge Journal of Economics* 30 (4): 507–20. https://doi.org/10.1093/cje/bei095.

Heisler, Helmuth. 1971. 'The Creation of a Stabilized Urban Society: A Turning Point in the Development of Northern Rhodesia/Zambia'. *African Affairs* 70 (279): 125–45.

Hendriks, Thomas. 2017. 'A Darker Shade of White: Expat Self-Making in a Congolese Rainforest Enclave'. *Africa* 87 (4): 683–701. https://doi.org/10.1017/S000197201 7000316.

Hern, Erin. 2020. 'Preferences without Platforms: How Voters Make Choices in Zambia's Elections'. *Democracy and Electoral Politics in Zambia*, May, 69–93. https://doi. org/10.1163/9789004430440_005.

Hertz, Ellen. 2014. 'On Bureaucracy: Excessively up at the International Labour Organization'. In *Up, Down, and Sideways: Anthropologists Trade the Pathways of Power*, edited by R. Stryker and R. Gonzales, 63–82. New York: Berghahn Books.

Hertz, Ellen . 2016. 'Pimp My Fluff: A Thousand Plateaus and Other Theoretical Extravaganzas'. *Anthropological Theory* 16 (2–3): 146–59. https://doi.org/10.1177/14634 99616654830.

Hertz, Ellen. 2020. 'Corporate Social Responsibility: The Great Shell Game'. *Journal of Legal Anthropology* 4 (2): 110–15. https://doi.org/10.3167/jla.2020.040207.

Hertz, Ellen, and Yvan Schulz. 2020. *Unternehmen und Menschenrechte: Die Grenzen des guten Willens*. Zürich: Seismo Verlag.

Hill, Matthew. 2024. 'Zambia to Start Trading Its Own Copper, Competing with Glencore'. *Bloomberg*, 25 February. https://www.bloomberg.com/news/articles/2024-02-05/ zambia-to-start-trading-its-own-copper-competing-with-glencore?embedded-check out=true.

Hobi, Anna-Sophie. 2017. 'Your Money Kills: Challenging Commodity Trading Giants: Anti-Corporate Activism in Zug, Switzerland'. Seminar paper, Basel: Institute of Social Anthropology, University of Basel.

Hobi, Anna-Sophie. 2019. 'Our Minerals, Our Wealth: Civil Society, Governance and Extractivism in the Minng Town of Solwezi, Zambia'. Master thesis, Basel: Institute of Social Anthropology, University of Basel.

Hoffman, Andy, and Catherine Bosley. 2020. 'Swiss Commodity Traders Up in Arms Over Bid at Foreign Liability'. *Bloomberg.Com*, 23 October 2020. https://www.bloomberg. com/news/articles/2020-10-23/swiss-commodity-traders-up-in-arms-over-bid-at-fore ign-liability. Accessed 29 August 2024.

Hollington, Andrea, Tijo Salverda, Tobias Schwarz and Oliver Tappe, eds. 2015. *Concepts of the Global South: Voices from around the World*. Köln: Global South Studies Center, University of Cologne.

Hönke, Jana. 2010. 'New Political Topographies: Mining Companies and Indirect Discharge in Southern Katanga (DRC)'. *Politique Africaine* 120 (4): 105–27.

Honneth, Axel. 1992. *Kampf um Anerkennung: Zur moralischen Grammatik sozialer Konflikte*. Frankfurt am Main: Suhrkamp Taschenbuch Verlag.

Honneth, Axel. 2003. *Unsichtbarkeit: Stationen Einer Theorie Der Intersubjektivität*. Frankfurt am Main: Suhrkamp Taschenbuch Verlag.

hooks, bell. 2001. *All about Love: New Visions*. New York: William Morrow.

Hopkins, Terence K., and Immanuel Wallerstein. 1977. 'Patterns of Development of the Modern World-System'. *Review (Fernand Braudel Center)* 1 (2): 111–45.

Huron, Amanda. 2015. 'Working with Strangers in Saturated Space: Reclaiming and Maintaining the Urban Commons'. *Antipode* 47 (4): 963–79. https://doi.org/10.1111/anti.12141.

Impala Terminals. 2016. *Impala Terminals Corporate Borchure*. Geneva: Impala Terminals.

Ingold, Tim. 2013. *Making: Anthropology, Archaeology, Art and Architecture*. London: Routledge.

IPC. 2020. 'IPC Acute Food Insecurity Analysis: July 2020–March 2021'. Issued in December 2020. https://reliefweb.int/report/zambia/republic-zambia-ipc-acute-food-insecurity-analysis-july-2020-march-2021-issued. Accessed 29 August 2024.

Interdepartemental Plattform on Commodities. 2013. *Report of the Interdepartemental Platform on Commodities to the Federal Council – Background Report: Commodities*. Bern: EDA.

Jacka, Jerry K. 2018. 'The Anthropology of Mining: The Social and Environmental Impacts of Resource Extraction in the Mineral Age'. *Annual Review of Anthropology* 47 (1): 61–77. https://doi.org/10.1146/annurev-anthro-102317-050156.

Jey Aratnam, Ganga. 2015. 'Glencore oder die Rhizome der Macht: Eine Spurensuche in Zug'. In *Geld und Macht in der Schweiz*, edited by Ueli Mäder, 395–425. Zürich: Rotpunktverlag.

Johnson, David S. 1980. 'A Note on the Population of North-Western Province'. In *Handbook to the North-Western Province 1980*, edited by David S. Johnson, 73–86. Zambia Geographical Association Regional Handbook Series 8. Lusaka: Zambia Geographical Association.

Jubilee Debt Campaign UK. 2020. 'Zambia Edges towards Debt Default, but Bondholders Could Make Millions'. *Jubilee Debt Campaign UK* (blog). 2 November 2020. https://jubileedebt.org.uk/blog/zambia-edges-towards-debt-default-but-bondholders-could-make-millions. Accessed 29 August 2024.

Kaaba, O'Brien. 2019. 'Kilolo Ng'ambi v Opa Kapijimpanga Appeal No. 210/2015 (Judgment of 9th October 2018)'. *SAIPAR Case Review* 2 (1). https://scholarship.law.cornell.edu/scr/vol2/iss1/7.

Kalaora, Léa. 2011. 'Madness, Corruption and Exile: On Zimbabwe's Remaining White Commercial Farmers'. *Journal of Southern African Studies* 37 (4): 747–62. https://doi.org/10.1080/03057070.2011.609341.

Kanton Zug. 2024. *Medienmitteilung: Zug investiert OECD-Mindeststeuer in Standortmassnahmen*. Zug: Kanton Zug. https://zg.ch/news/news~_2024_5_zug-investiert-oecd-mindeststeuer-in-standortmassnahmen~.html.

Kapesa, Robby. 2019. 'Solwezi Will Be the "New Copperbelt": Dashed Expectations, Collective Grievances, and Ethnic Tensions in North-Western Zambia – Robby Kapesa'. *Comparing the Copperbelt* (blog). 15 January 2019. http://copperbelt.history.ox.ac.uk/2019/01/15/solwezi-will-be-the-new-copperbelt-dashed-expectations-collective-grievances-and-ethnic-tensions-in-north-western-zambia-robby-kapesa/. Accessed 29 August 2024.

Kapesa, Robby, and Thomas McNamara. 2020. '"We Are Not Just a Union, We Are a Family" Class, Kinship and Tribe in Zambia's Mining Unions'. *Dialectical Anthropology* 44 (2): 153–72. https://doi.org/10.1007/s10624-019-09578-x.

Kapesa, Robby, Jacob Mwitwa and D. C. Chikumbi. 2014. 'Social Conflict in the Context of Development of New Mining in Zambia 2014'. *Southern African Peace and Security Studies* 4 (2): 41–62.

Keck, Margaret E., and Kathryn Sikkink. 1998. *Activists beyond Borders: Advocacy Networks in International Politics*. Ithaca: Cornell University Press.

Kesselring, Rita. 2017a. *Bodies of Truth: Law, Memory and Emancipation in Post-Apartheid South Africa*. Stanford Series in Human Rights. Stanford, CA: Stanford University Press.

Kesselring, Rita. 2017b. 'Disenclaving the Planners' Enclave: The Housing Project Kabitaka in Solwezi, Northwestern Zambia – Rita Kesselring'. *Comparing the Copperbelt* (blog). 21 August 2017. http://copperbelt.history.ox.ac.uk/2017/08/21/disenclaving-the-planners-enclave-the-housing-project-kabitaka-in-solwezi-northwestern-zambia-rita-kesselring/. Accessed 29 August 2024.

Kesselring, Rita. 2021a. 'Beware the Mineral Narrative: The Histories of Solwezi Town and Kansanshi Mine, Northwestern Zambia, c. 1899–2020'. In *Across the Copperbelt: Urban and Social Change in Africa's Borderland Communities*, edited by Miles Larmer, Enid Guene, Benoît Henriet, Iva Peša and Rachel Taylor, 122–52. London: James Currey Publishers.

Kesselring, Rita. 2021b. 'Zwei Minen für bloss einen Dollar'. *Die Wochenzeitung*, 28 January 2021. https://www.woz.ch/2104/glencore-in-sambia/zwei-minen-fuer-bloss-einen-dollar. Accessed 29 August 2024.

Kirsch, Stuart. 2020. 'Between the Devil and the Deep Blue Sea: Objectivity and Political Responsibility in the Litigation of the Exxon Valdez Oil Spill'. *Critique of Anthropology*, 40 (4): 403–19. https://doi.org/10.1177/0308275X20959420.

Kirshner, Joshua, and Marcus Power. 2015. 'Mining and Extractive Urbanism: Postdevelopment in a Mozambican Boomtown'. *Geoforum* 61 (May): 67–78. https://doi.org/10.1016/j.geoforum.2015.02.019.

Kiser, Edgar, and Audrey Sacks. 2009. 'Improving Tax Administration in Contemporary African States: Lessons from History'. In *The New Fiscal Sociology: Taxation in Comparative and Historical Perspective*, edited by Ajay K. Mehrotra, Isaac William Martin and Monica Prasad, 183–200. Cambridge: Cambridge University Press. https://doi.org/10.1017/CBO9780511627071.012.

Kragelund, Peter. 2020. 'Using Local Content Policies to Engender Resource-Based Development in Zambia: A Chronicle of a Death Foretold?' *Extractive Industries and Society* 7 (2): 267–73. https://doi.org/10.1016/j.exis.2019.09.006.

Krippner, Greta. 2012. *Capitalizing on Crisis: The Political Origins of the Rise of Finance*. Cambridge, MA: Harvard University Press.

Kvangraven, Ingrid Harvold, Kai Koddenbrock and Ndongo Samba Sylla. 2021. 'Financial Subordination and Uneven Financialization in 21st Century Africa'. *Community Development Journal* 56 (1): 119–40. https://doi.org/10.1093/cdj/bsaa047.

Laclau, Ernesto. 1977. *Politics and Ideology in Marxist Theory: Capitalism, Fascism, Populism*. London: New LEeft Books.

Laclau, Ernesto, and Chantal Mouffe. 2001. *Hegemony and Socialist Strategy: Towards a Radical Democratic Politics*. London: Verso.

Lahiri-Dutt, Kuntala. 2012. 'Race and Gender in Peripheral Resource Towns: Boundaries and Boundary-Crossings in Tanjung Bara Mining Camp in Kalimantan, Indonesia'. In *Company Towns: Labor, Space, and Power Relations across Time and Continents*, edited by M. Borges and S. Torres, 207–26. New York: Palgrave Macmillan.

Lamarque, Hugh. 2019. 'Night Drivers of the Northern Corridor'. *African Borderlands Research Network* (blog). 19 February 2019. https://www.aborne.net/afrigos-african-governance-and-space/2019/2/25/night-drivers-of-the-northern-corridor. Accessed 29 August 2024.

Lambek, Michael, Veena Das, Didier Fassin and Webb Keane. 2015. *Four Lectures on Ethics*. Chicago: HAU Books.

Lane, Barbara Miller, ed. 2006. *Housing and Dwelling: Perspectives on Modern Domestic Architecture*. Illustrated Edition. London: Routledge.

Lang, Josef. 2020. *Demokratie in der Schweiz: Geschichte und Gegenwart*. 2nd edition. Zurich: Hier und Jetzt.

Lannen, A., E. Bürgi Bonanomi, S. Rist and J. Wehrli. 2016. 'Switzerland and the Commodities Trade: Taking Stock and Looking Ahead'. *Swiss Academies Factsheets* 11 (1). Geneva: Swiss Academies of Arts and Sciences.

Lapegna, Pablo. 2009. 'Ethnographers of the World … United? Current Debates on the Ethnographic Study of Globalization'. *Journal of World-Systems Research*, 15 (10): 3–24. https://doi.org/10.5195/jwsr.2009.336.

Larmer, Miles. 2005. 'Reaction & Resistance to Neo-Liberalism in Zambia'. *Review of African Political Economy* 32 (103): 29–45. https://doi.org/10.1080/0305624050 0120992.

Larmer, Miles. 2007. *Mineworkers in Zambia: Labour and Political Change in Post-Colonial Africa*. London: Tauris Academic Studies.

Larmer, Miles. 2017. 'Permanent Precarity: Capital and Labour in the Central African Copperbelt'. *Labor History* 58 (2): 170–84. https://doi.org/10.1080/00236 56X.2017.1298712.

Larmer, Miles, Enid Guene, Benoît Henriet, Iva Peša and Rachel Taylor, eds. 2021. *Across the Copperbelt: Urban and Social Change in Africa's Borderland Communities*. London: James Currey Publishers.

Latour, Bruno. 1993. *We Have Never Been Modern*. Translated by C. Porter. Cambridge, MA: Harvard University Press.

Latour, Bruno. 2005. *Reassembling the Social: An Introduction to Actor-Network-Theory*. Oxford: Oxford University Press.

Latour, Bruno, and Carolina Miranda. 2017. 'A Dialog about a New Meaning of Symmetric Anthropology (with Carolina Miranda)'. In *Comparative Metaphysics – Ontology after Anthropology*, edited by Pierre Charbonnier, Gildas Salmon, and Peter Skafish, 327–45. London: Rowman & Littlefield. http://www.bruno-latour.fr/node/673.

Leap, Braden, Marybeth C. Stalp and Kimberly Kelly. 2022. 'Raging against the "Neoliberal Hellscape": Anger, Pride, and Ambivalence in Civil Society Responses to the Covid-19 Pandemic in the USA'. *Antipode* 54 (4): 1166–87. https://doi.org/10.1111/anti.12813.

Lee, Ching Kwan. 2014. 'The Spectre of Global China'. *New Left Review* 89 (September–October): 29–65.

Lee, Ching Kwan. 2017. *The Spectre of Global China: Politics, Labor, and Foreign Investment in Africa*. Chicago: University Of Chicago Press.

Levenson, Zachary. 2019. '"Such Elements Do Not Belong in an Ordered Society": Managing Rural–Urban Resettlement in Democratic South Africa'. *Journal of Agrarian Change* 19 (3): 427–46. https://doi.org/10.1111/joac.12310.

Li, Hangwei, and Xuefei Shi. 2020. 'Home Away from Home: The Social and Political Roles of Contemporary Chinese Associations in Zambia'. *Journal of Current Chinese Affairs* 48 (2): 7–23, 1868102620907224. https://doi.org/10.1177/1868102620907224.

Lochery, Emma, Thomas McNamara and James Musonda. 2024. 'Subsidising Extraction: Care at Work in Zambia's Copper Mines'. *Antipode* n/a (n/a). https://doi.org/10.1111/anti.13029.

Loimeier, Roman, Dieter Neubert, Cordula Weißköppel, Roman Loimeier, Dieter Neubert and Cordula Weißköppel, eds. 2005. *Globalisierung im lokalen Kontext: Perspektiven und Konzepte von Handeln in Afrika*. Vol. 20. Berlin: LIT-Verlag.

Lungu, John. 2008. 'Copper Mining Agreements in Zambia: Renegotiation or Law Reform?' *Review of African Political Economy* 35 (117): 403–15.

Luxemburg, Rosa. 1913. *Die Akkumulation des Kapitals*. Berlin: Paul Singer.

Maboshe, Mashekwa, Akabondo Kabechani and Grieve Chelwa. 2019. 'The Welfare Effects of Unprecedented Electricity Price Hikes in Zambia'. *Energy Policy* 126 (March):108–17. https://doi.org/10.1016/j.enpol.2018.10.041.

Macmillan, Hugh. 1993. 'The Historiography of Transition on the Zambian Copperbelt-Another View'. *Journal of Southern African Studies* 19 (4): 681–712.

Macmillan, Hugh. 2012. 'Mining, Housing and Welfare in South Africa and Zambia: An Historical Perspective'. *Journal of Contemporary African Studies* 30 (4): 539–50.

Magubane, Bernard. 1974. Review of *The Colour of Class on the Copper Mines: From African Advancement to Zambianization*, by Michael Burawoy. *American Journal of Sociology* 80 (2): 596–8.

Magubane, Bernard. 1975. 'The Colour of Class on the Copper Mines: A Rejoinder'. *American Journal of Sociology* 81 (1): 167–8.

Manley, David. 2017. *Ninth Time Lucky: Is Zambia's Mining Tax the Best Approach to an Uncertain Future?* New York: Natural Resource Governance Institute.

Marcus, George E. 1995. 'Ethnography in/of the World System: The Emergence of Multi-Sited Ethnography'. *Annual Review of Anthropology* 24: 95–117.

Martin, Isaac William, Ajay K. Mehrotra and Monica Prasad. 2009. 'The Thunder of History: The Origins and Development of the New Fiscal Sociology'. In *The New Fiscal Sociology: Taxation in Comparative and Historical Perspective*, edited by Ajay K. Mehrotra, Isaac William Martin and Monica Prasad, 1–28. Cambridge: Cambridge University Press. https://doi.org/10.1017/CBO9780511627071.002.

Martin, Carole. 2018. '*We Cannot Stick to One Language*': *Multilingualism in Solwezi, Zambia*'. Final Report of Guided Field Course in Anthropology. Basel: Institute of Social Anthropology, University of Basel.

Matthan, Tanya. 2020. 'Resource Politics and Entangled Lives in Extraction Zones: Review Essay'. *PoLAR: Political and Legal Anthropology Review* (blog). 14 September 2020. https://polarjournal.org/2020/09/14/resource-politics-entangled-lives/. Accessed 29 August 2024.

Mauss, Marcel. 2012. *Essai sur le don: Forme et raison de l'échange dans les sociétés archaïques*. 2nd edition. Paris: Presses Universitaires de France.

Mavhunga, Clapperton Chakanetsa. 2013. 'Cidades Esfumaçadas: Energy and the Rural-Urban Connection in Mozambique'. *Public Culture* 25 (270): 261–71.

McGregor, JoAnn. 2009. *Crossing the Zambezi: The Politics of Landscape on a Central African Frontier*. Harare: James Currey.

McIntosh, Janet. 2016. *Unsettled: Denial and Belonging among White Kenyans*. Oakland: University of California Press. https://www.ucpress.edu/book/9780520290518/unsettled.

Meillassoux, Claude. 1981. *Maidens, Meal and Money: Capitalism and the Domestic Community*. Cambridge: Cambridge University Press.

Meillassoux, Claude. 1992. *Femmes, greniers et capitaux*. Paris: Editions L'Harmattan.

Merry, Sally Engle. 1981. *Urban Danger: Life in a Neighborhood of Strangers*. Philadelphia, PA: Temple University Press.

Metal Bulletin. 2010a. 'Republic House Sets Up Metal Corp Trading Ahead of First Quantum Takeover'. https://www.metalbulletin.com/Article/2397816/Republic-House-sets-up-Metal-Corp-Trading-ahead-of-First-Quantum-takeover.html. Accessed 7 February 2019.

Metal Bulletin. 2010b. 'First Quantum Seeks to Buy Republic House'. https://www.metalbulletin.com/Article/2386951/First-Quantum-seeks-to-buy-Republic-House.html. Accessed 7 February 2019.

Mies, Maria. 1986. *Patriarchy and Accumulation on a World Scale: Women in the International Division of Labour*. London: Zed Books.

Mignolo, Walter D. 2000. *Local Histories/Global Designs*. Princeton, NJ: Princeton University Press.

Milberg, William. 2004. 'The Changing Structure of Trade Linked to Global Production Systems: What Are the Policy Implications?' *International Labour Review* 143 (1–2): 45–90. https://doi.org/10.1111/j.1564-913X.2004.tb00546.x.

Milisavljevic, M. 1978. *A Preliminary Report on Brick Clays of the Solwezi Area*. Economic Report of the Geological Survey 53. Lusaka: Ministry of Mines, Geological Survey Department.

Mineman. 2015. 'Training in London for Metalcorp Trading'. July 2015. http://www.mineman.com/News/2013-(2)/Training-in-London-for-Metalcorp-Trading.aspx. Accessed 29 August 2024.

Miroudot, Sébastien. 2017. 'The Servicifcation of Global Value Chains: Evidence and Policy Implications'. UNCTAD Multi-Year Expert Meeting on Trade, Services and Development. 18–20 July. Geneva: UNCTAD.

Mitchell, James Clyde. 1956. *The Kalela Dance: Aspects of Social Relationships Among Urban Africans in Northern Rhodesia*. Manchester: Manchester University Press for Rhodes-Livingstone Institute.

Mkandawire, Thandika. 2011. 'Running While Others Walk: Knowledge and the Challenge of Africa's Development'. *Africa Development* 36 (2): 1–36.

Mkandawire, Thandika. 2015. 'Neopatrimonialism and the Political Economy of Economic Performance in Africa: Critical Reflections'. *World Politics* 67 (3): 563–612. https://doi.org/10.1017/S004388711500009X.

Money, Duncan. 2017. 'Trouble in Paradise: The 1958 White Mineworkers' Strike on the Zambian Copperbelt'. *Extractive Industries and Society* 4 (4): 707–16. https://doi.org/10.1016/j.exis.2017.07.005.

Money, Duncan. 2022. 'Zambia's Copper Mines Hard-Baked Racism into the Workplace by Labelling Whites "Expats"'. *The Conversation* (blog). 22 August 2022. http://thec

onversation.com/zambias-copper-mines-hard-baked-racism-into-the-workplace-by-labelling-whites-expats-188751. Accessed 29 August 2024.

Money, Duncan, Hans Otto Frøland and Tshepo Gwatiwa. 2020. 'Africa–EU Relations and Natural Resource Governance: Understanding African Agency in Historical and Contemporary Perspective'. *Review of African Political Economy* 47 (166): 585–603. https://doi.org/10.1080/03056244.2020.1839876.

Money, Duncan, and Limin Teh. 2022. 'Race at Work: A Comparative History of Mining Labor and Empire on the Central African Copperbelt and the Fushun Coalfields, ca. 1907–1945'. *International Labor and Working-Class History* 101: 100–17. https://doi.org/10.1017/S0147547921000132.

Money, Duncan, and Danelle van Zyl-Hermann. 2020. 'Introduction: Rethinking White Societies in Southern Africa, 1930s–1990s'. In *Rethinking White Societies in Southern Africa: 1930s–1990s*, edited by Duncan Money and Danelle van Zyl-Hermann, 1–22. London: Routledge. https://doi.org/10.4324/9781003002307.

Moore, Henrietta, and Megan Vaughan. 1993. *Cutting Down Trees: Gender, Nutrition, and Agricultural Change in the Northern Province of Zambia, 1890–1990*. London: Heinemann.

Moore, Mick, Wilso Prichard and Odd-Helge Fjeldstad. 2018. *Taxing Africa: Coercion, Reform and Development*. African Arguments. London: Zed Books.

Moyn, Samuel. 2018. *Not Enough: Human Rights in an Unequal World*. Cambridge, MA: Belknap Press of Harvard University Press.

Mudenda, Dale, Maio Bulawayo and Manenga Ndulo. 2018. 'The Financialization of Commodity Markets: The Case of Copper in Zambia'. Unpublished paper.

Müller, Giorgio V. 2020. 'Glencore reagiert auf die Krise noch immer wie ein Rohstoffhändler'. *NZZ*, 6 August 2020. https://www.nzz.ch/wirtschaft/glencore-rohstoffhaendler-in-der-krise-ld.1570003. Accessed 29 August 2024.

Musambachime, Mwelwa C. 2016. *Wealth from the Rocks: Mining and Smelting of Metals in Pre-Colonial Zambia*. Bloomington: Xlibris Corporation.

Musonda, James. 2021a. 'Modernity on Credit: The Experience of Underground Miners on the Zambian Copperbelt'. *Journal of Southern African Studies* 47 (3): 1–16. https://doi.org/10.1080/03057070.2020.1864921.

Musonda, James. 2021b. 'Modernity on Credit: The Experience of Underground Miners on the Zambian Copperbelt'. *Journal of Southern African Studies* 47 (3): 369–85. https://doi.org/10.1080/03057070.2020.1864921.

Mususa, Patience, and Iva Peša. 2023. 'Making Mining Localities: Trajectories and Stories of Mining and Mobility in Zambia'. In *Mining, Mobility, and Social Change in the Global South*, edited by Gerardo Castillo Guzmán, Matthew Himley and David Brereton, 101–22. London: Routledge.

Mutale, Emmanuel. 2004. *The Management of Urban Development in Zambia*. International Land Management Series. Burlington: Ashgate.

Mutamba, Manyewu. 2007. *Farming or Foraging? Rural Livelihoods in Mafulira and Kabompo Districts of Zambia*. Grahamstown: Centre for International Forestry Research and Rhodes University.

Nader, Laura. 1972. 'Up the Anthropologist: Perspectives Gained From Studying Up'. In *Reinventing Anthropology*, edited by Dell H. Hymes, 284–311. New York: Pantheon Books.

Ndlovu-Gatsheni, Sabelo. 2017. 'Whither Dependency Theory?' In *On Dependency*, edited by Ushehwedu Kufakurinani, Ingrid Harvold Kvangraven, Frutuoso Santana, and

Maria Dyveke Styve, 34–41. Dialogues on Development 1. New York: Institute for New Economic Thinking.

Negi, Rohit. 2010. 'The Mining Boom, Capital, and Chiefs in the "New Copperbelt"'. In *Zambia, Mining, and Neoliberalism: Boom and Bust on the Globalized Copperbelt*, edited by Alastair Fraser and Miles Larmer, 209–36. Africa Connects. New York: Palgrave Macmillan.

Negi, Rohit. 2014. '"Solwezi Mabanga": Ambivalent Developments on Zambia's New Mining Frontier'. *Journal of Southern African Studies* 40 (5): 999–1013.

Niehaus, Isak. 2013. 'Anthropology and Whites in South Africa: Response to an Unreasonable Critique'. *Africa Spectrum* 48 (1): 117–27.

Nielsen, Morten. 2011. 'Futures within: Reversible Time and House-Building in Maputo, Mozambique'. *Anthropological Theory* 11 (4): 397–423. https://doi.org/10.1177/1463499611423871.

Ntarangwi, Mwenda. 2007. '"I Have Changed My Mind Now": U.S. Students' Responses to Female Genital Cutting in Africa'. *Africa Today* 53 (4): 87–108.

Nugent, Paul. 2018. 'Africa's Re-Enchantment with Big Infrastructure: White Elephants Dancing in Virtuous Circles?' In *Extractive Industries and Changing State Dynamics in Africa: Beyond the Resource Curse*, edited by Jon Schubert, Ulf Engel and Elísio Macamo, 22–40. New York: Routledge.

Nugent, Paul, and Isabella Soi. 2020. 'One-Stop Border Posts in East Africa: State Encounters of the Fourth Kind'. *Journal of Eastern African Studies* 14 (3): 433–54. https://doi.org/10.1080/17531055.2020.1768468.

Nyamnjoh, Francis B. 2012. 'Blinded by Sight: Divining the Future of Anthropology in Africa'. *Africa Spectrum* 47 (2–3): 63–92.

Obrist, Brigit, Veit Arlt and Elisio Macamo, eds. 2013. *Living the City in Africa: Processs of Invention and Intervention*. Berlin: LIT Verlag.

O'Callaghan, Margaret. 2019. *Copperfields: A History of the Impact of the First Decade of a Mining Boom in North Western Province, Zambia, circa 2002–2015*. Canberra, Australia: Self-published. https://margocall.wordpress.com/2020/03/28/copperfields-a-history-of-the-impact-of-the-first-decade-of-a-mining-boom-in-north-western-province-zambia-circa-2002-2015/.

OCHA. 2024. *Zambia: Drought Flash Appeal*. Geneva: United Nations Office for the Coordination of Humanitarian Affairs. file:///Users/ritakesselring/Downloads/Zambia%20Drought%20Response%20Appeal%20_06052024%20FINAL%20V2.pdf.

OECDWatch. 2011. 'Sherpa v Mopani Complaint'. https://www.oecdwatch.org/complaint/sherpa-et-al-vs-glencore-international-ag/. Accessed 29 August 2024.

Ogle, Vanessa. 2020. '"Funk Money": The End of Empires, The Expansion of Tax Havens, and Decolonization as an Economic and Financial Event'. *Past & Present* 249 (1): 213–49. https://doi.org/10.1093/pastj/gtaa001.

Olwig, M. F., C. Noe, R. Kangalawe and E. Luoga. 2015. 'Inverting the Moral Economy: The Case of Land Acquisitions for Forest Plantations in Tanzania'. *Third World Quarterly* 36 (12): 2316–36. https://doi.org/10.1080/01436597.2015.1078231.

OSISA. 2014. 'No Investigation of Corrupt Russia-Angola Debt Deal'. 5 February. http://jss.osisa.org/law/angola/no-investigation-corrupt-russia-angola-debt-deal.html. Accessed February 2019.

Oxfam. 2020. *Climate Finance Shadow Report 2020: Assessing Progress towards the $100 Billion Commitment*. Oxford: Oxfam.

Paremoer, Tamara. 2015. 'The New Masters of the Universe? Commodity Traders in the Age of Financialisation'. *Amandla!* 40 (August): 26–7.

Parker, Rachel, Stephen Cox and Paul Thompson. 2018. 'Financialization and Value-Based Control: Lessons from the Australian Mining Supply Chain'. *Economic Geography* 94 (1): 49–67. https://doi.org/10.1080/00130095.2017.1330118.

Parpart, Jane L. 1986. 'The Household and the Mine Shaft: Gender and Class Struggles on the Zambian Copperbelt, 1926–64'. *Journal of Southern African Studies* 13 (1): 36–56. https://doi.org/10.1080/03057078608708131.

Peša, Iva. 2019. *Roads through Mwinilunga: A History of Social Change in Northwest Zambia*. Leiden: Brill.

Peša, Iva. 2020a. 'Between Waste and Profit: Environmental Values on the Central African Copperbelt'. *Extractive Industries and Society* 8(4). https://doi.org/10.1016/j.exis.2020.08.004.

Peša, Iva. 2020b. 'Crops and Copper: Agriculture and Urbanism on the Central African Copperbelt, 1950–2000'. *Journal of Southern African Studies* 46 (3): 527–45.

Peša, Iva. 2020c. 'Mining, Waste and Environmental Thought on the Central African Copperbelt, 1950–2000'. *Environment and History* 28 (2): 259–84. https://doi.org/info:doi/10.3197/096734019X15755402985703.

Peters, Anne, Lucy Koechlin, Till Förster and Gretta Fenner Zinkernagel, eds. 2009. *Non-State Actors as Standard Setters*. Cambridge: Cambridge University Press.

Phimister, Ian. 2011. 'Proletarians In Paradise: The Historiography and Historical Sociology Of White Miners On The Copperbelt'. *Living the End of Empire*, January, 139–60.

Pieterse, Edgar, and Susan Parnell. 2014. 'Africa's Urban Revolution in Context'. In *Africa's Urban Revolution: Policy Pressures*, edited by Susan Parnell and Edgar Pieterse, 1–17. London: Zed Books.

Pieterse, Edgar, and AbdouMaliq Simone, eds. 2013. *Rogue Urbanism: Emergent African Cities*. Auckland Park, South Africa: Jacana Media.

Pilossof, Rory. 2012. *The Unbearable Whiteness of Being. Farmers' Voices from Zimbabwe*. Harare: Weaver Press.

Pirrong, Craig. 2014. *The Economics of Commodity Trading Firms*. Geneva: Trafigura.

Porta, Donatella Della, and Sidney Tarrow, eds. 2004. *Transnational Protest and Global Activism*. Lanham, MD: Rowman & Littlefield.

Pottier, Johan. 1988. *Migrants No More: Settlement and Survival in Mambwe District, Zambia*. International African Library. Manchester: Manchester University Press.

Preuss, Lena, and Daniel Schmidt-Eisenlohr. 2016. *Final Report Solwezi Urban Baseline Study*. Lusaka: GIZ.

Public Eye. 2016. *Dirty Diesel: How Swiss Traders Flood Africa with Toxic Fuels*. A Report. Bern: Public Eye.

Public Eye. 2017. *The "Paradise Papers", Switzerland and Commodities*. Bern: Public Eye.

Public Eye, and Andreas Missbach. 2017. *Alternative Facts from the Swiss Commodity Trading Lobby*. Bern: Public Eye.

Rajak, Dinah. 2011. *In Good Company: An Anatomy of Corporate Social Responsibility*. Stanford: Stanford University Press.

Rajak, Dinah. 2014. 'Corporate Memory: Historical Revisionism, Legitimation and the Invention of Tradition in a Multinational Mining Company'. *PoLAR: Political and Legal Anthropology Review* 37 (2): 259–80. https://doi.org/10.1111/plar.12074.

Ramge, Thomas, Jan Schwochow and Adrian Garcia-Landa. 2018. *Global Economy as You've Never Seen It*. New York: Melia Publishing Services.

Ranger, Terence. 1998. 'Europeans in Black Africa'. *Journal of World History* 9 (2): 255–68.
Redfield, Peter, and Erica Bornstein. 2010. 'An Introduction to the Anthropology of Humanitarianism'. In *Forces of Compassion: Humanitarianism between Ethics and Politics*, edited by Peter Redfield and Erica Bornstein, 3–30. Santa Fe: School for Advanced Research Press.
Reyes, Victoria. 2019. *Global Borderlands: Fantasy, Violence, and Empire in Subic Bay, Philippines*. Stanford, CA: Stanford University Press.
Ribas, Vanesa. 2015. *On the Line: Slaughterhouse Lives and the Making of the New South*. Oakland: University of California Press.
Ribeiro, Gustavo Lins. 2019. 'The Global/Local Tension in the History of Anthropology'. *Journal of Global History* 14 (3): 375–94. https://doi.org/10.1017/S1740022819000172.
Richards, Audrey R. 1939. *Land, Labor and Diet in Northern Rhodesia: An Economic Study of the Bemba Tribe*. Oxford: Oxford University Press.
Richards, Audrey. 1971. 'Introduction: The Nature of the Problem'. In *Councils in Action*, edited by Audrey Richards and Adam Kuper, 1–12. Cambridge: Cambridge University Press.
Robertson, Roland. 2012. 'Globalisation or Glocalisation?' *Journal of International Communication* 18 (2): 191–208. https://doi.org/10.1080/13216597.2012.709925.
Robinson, Jennifer. 2006. *Ordinary Cities: Between Modernity and Development*. London: Routledge.
Robinson, Jennifer. 2016. 'Inventions and Interventions: Transforming Cities – An Introduction'. *Urban Studies* 43 (2): 251–8. https://doi.org/10.1080/0042098050 0495812.
Rorty, Richard. 1989. 'Solidarity'. In *Contingency, Irony, and Solidarity*, 189–98. Cambridge: Cambridge University Press. https://doi.org/10.1017/CBO9780511804397.
Ross, Fiona C. 2010. *Raw Life, New Hope: Decency, Housing and Everyday Life in a Post-Apartheid Community*. Cape Town, South Africa: UCT Press.
Rubbers, Benjamin. 2013. *Le paternalisme en question: Les anciens ouvriers de la Gécamines face à la libéralisation du secteur minier katangais*. 1st edition. Tervuren: Editions L'Harmattan.
Rubbers, Benjamin. 2019. 'Mining Towns, Enclaves and Spaces: A Genealogy of Worker Camps in the Congolese Copperbelt'. *Geoforum* 98 (January): 88–96. https://doi.org/10.1016/j.geoforum.2018.10.005.
Rubbers, Benjamin. 2020. 'Company Brokers: Human Resources Managers in Foreign Mining Projects in the Congolese Copperbelt'. *Ethnography*, September, 1466138120948911. https://doi.org/10.1177/1466138120948911.
Rupp, Stephanie. 2016. 'Circuits and Currents: Dynamics of Disruption in New York City Blackouts'. *Economic Anthropology* 3 (1): 106–18.
Rutherford, Blair. 2001. *Working on the Margins: Black Workers, White Farmers in Zimbabwe*. Harare: Zed Books.
Said, Edward W. 2007. *Orientalism*. 25th Anniversary Edition. London: Penguin Books.
Salverda, Tijo. 2019. 'Between Access and Critique'. *Journal of Business Anthropology* 8 (1): 35–40. https://doi.org/10.22439/jba.v8i1.5714.
Sánchez, Felipe, and Philipp Hartlieb. 2020. 'Innovation in the Mining Industry: Technological Trends and a Case Study of the Challenges of Disruptive Innovation'. *Mining, Metallurgy & Exploration* 37 (5): 1385–99. https://doi.org/10.1007/s42461-020-00262-1.

Sanogo, Aïdas, and Carole Ammann, eds. 2017. 'Secondary Cities – the Urban Middle Ground'. In *Secondary Cities – the Urban Middle Ground*, 36–46. Basel Papers on Political Transformation 11/12. Basel: Institute of Social Anthropology.

Saunders, Richard, and Alexander Caramento. 2018. 'An Extractive Developmental State in Southern Africa? The Cases of Zambia and Zimbabwe'. *Third World Quarterly* 39 (6): 1166–90. https://doi.org/10.1080/01436597.2017.1409072.

Schmid, Luzia, dir. 2020. *Der Ast, auf dem ich sitze: Ein Steuerparadies in der Schweiz.* DOK: Gesellschaft & Politik. First Hand Films. https://www.3sat.de/film/dokumentarfilmzeit/der-ast-auf-dem-ich-sitze---ein-steuerparadies-in-der---schweiz-100.html.

Scholvin, Sören. 2020. 'Endogenous Obstacles to Development in Global Value Chains: Insights From the Oil and Gas Sector'. *Africa Spectrum*, July, 0002039720937024. https://doi.org/10.1177/0002039720937024.

Schramm, Katharina. 2009. 'Negotiating Race: Blackness and Whiteness in the Context of Homecoming to Ghana'. *African Diaspora: Transnational Journal of Culture, Economy & Society* 2 (1): 3–24. https://doi.org/10.1163/187254609X430795.

Schroeder, Richard A. 2012. *Africa after Apartheid: South Africa, Race, and Nation in Tanzania*. Bloomington: Indiana University Press.

Schubert, Jon, Ulf Engel, and Elísio Macamo. 2018. 'Introduction: Boom and Bust: Extractive Industries and African States in the 21st Century'. In *Extractive Industries and Changing State Dynamics in Africa: Beyond the Resource Curse*, edited by Jon Schubert, Ulf Engel and Elísio Macamo, 1st edition, 1–21. New York: Routledge.

Scott, James C. 1985. *Weapons of the Weak: Everyday Forms of Peasant Resistance*. New Haven, CT: Yale University Press. http://archive.org/details/weaponsofweakeve0000scot.

Sennett, Richard. 2012. *Together: The Rituals, Pleasures, and Politics of Cooperation*. New Haven, CT: Yale University Press.

Sibanda, Octavia. 2018. 'Wounded Citizenship: The Post-Colonial City and Poor Whites'. *Anthropology Southern Africa* 41 (1): 15–24. https://doi.org/10.1080/23323256.2017.1406809.

Silver, Jonathan. 2015. 'Disrupted Infrastructures: An Urban Political Ecology of Interrupted Electricity in Accra'. *International Journal of Urban and Regional Research* 39 (5): 984–1003. https://doi.org/10.1111/1468-2427.12317.

Simone, AbdouMaliq. 2004. *For the City yet to Come: Changing Urban Life in Four African Cities*. Durham, NC: Duke University Press.

Simone, AbdouMaliq. 2010. *The Social Infrastructures of City Life in Contemporary Africa*. Discussion Paper 51. Uppsala: Nordic Africa Institute. https://www.files.ethz.ch/isn/123515/51.pdf.

Simutanyi, Neo. 1996. 'The Politics of Structural Adjustment in Zambia'. *Third World Quarterly* 17 (4): 825–39. https://doi.org/10.1080/01436599615407.

Sitko, Nicholas J. 2010. 'Fractured Governance and Local Frictions: The Exclusionary Nature of a Clandestine Land Market in Southern Zambia'. *Africa* 80 (1): 36–55. https://doi.org/10.3366/E0001972009001259.

Sitko, Nicholas J., and T. S. Jayne. 2014. 'Structural Transformation or Elite Land Capture? The Growth of "Emergent" Farmers in Zambia'. *Food Policy*, Boserup and Beyond: Mounting Land Pressures and Development Strategies in Africa, 48 (October):194–202. https://doi.org/10.1016/j.foodpol.2014.05.006.

Smal, Daniela. 2015. *Zambia's Dependability: Imports and Exports*. Lusaka: Privately printed.

Smith, Constance. 2019. *Nairobi in the Making: Landscapes of Time and Urban Belonging*. London: James Currey Publishers.

Solifonds. 2018. 'AnwohnerInnen in Mufulira Fordern Sauberes Wasser Jetzt!' *Solifonds Informationsbulletin* 106 (February): 1–3.

Southern Africa Resource Watch. 2020. *First Quantum Minerals Corporate Governance and Social Responsibility: Kansanshi Mine*. Johannesburg: Southern Africa Resource Watch.

Sparks, Stephen John. 2012. 'Apartheid Modern: South Africa's Oil from Coal Project and the History of a Company Town.' Thesis. University of Michigan. http://deepblue.lib.umich.edu/handle/2027.42/91528.

Spencer, Paul. 1971. 'Party Politics and the Processes of Local Democracy in an English Town Council'. In *Councils in Action*, edited by Audrey Richards and Adam Kuper, 171–201. Cambridge: Cambridge University Press.

Spittler, Gerd. 2001. 'Teilnehmende Beobachtung als dichte Teilnahme'. *Zeitschrift für Ethnologie* 126:1–25.

Spittler, Gerd. 2002. 'Globale Waren – Lokale Aneignungen'. In *Ethnologie der Globalisierung: Perspektiven kultureller Verflechtungen*, edited by Brigitta Hauser-Schäublin and Ulrich Braukämper, 15–31. Berlin: Dietrich Reimer Verlag.

Spittler, Gerd. 2009. 'Contesting The Great Transformation: Work in Comparative Perspective'. In *Market and Society: The Great Transformation Today*, edited by Chris Hann and Hart Keith, 160–74. Cambridge: Cambridge University Press.

Statistik Kanton Zug. 2023. 'Bevölkerungsstand'. 2023. https://www.zg.ch/behoerden/gesundheitsdirektion/statistikfachstelle/themen/01bevoelkerungszahlen/bevoelkerungsstand. Accessed 29 August 2024.

Steyn, Melissa. 2001. *Whiteness Just Isn't What It Used To Be: White Identity in a Changing South Africa*. Albany: State University Press of New York.

Steyn, Melissa, and Don Foster. 2008. 'Repertoires for Talking White: Resistant Whiteness in Post-Apartheid South Africa'. *Ethnic and Racial Studies* 31 (1): 25–51. https://doi.org/10.1080/01419870701538851.

Straube, Christian. 2020. 'Speak, Friend, and Enter? Fieldwork Access and Anthropological Knowledge Production on the Copperbelt'. *Journal of Southern African Studies* 46 (3): 399–415. https://doi.org/10.1080/03057070.2020.1770512.

Suchman, Lucy. 1987. *Plans and Situated Actions: The Problem of Human-Machine Communication*. Cambridge: Cambridge University Press.

Suchman, Lucy. 2007. *Human-Machine Reconfigurations: Plans and Situated Actions*. Cambridge: Cambridge University Press.

Táíwò, Olúfẹ́mi O. 2020. 'An African Case for Carbon Removal'. *Africa Is a Country* (blog). 29 September 2020. https://africasacountry.com/2020/09/an-african-case-for-carbon-removal. Accessed 29 August 2024.

Tembo, Bernard. 2018. 'Strategic Investment Decisions in Zambia's Mining Sector under a Constrained Energy System'. Doctoral Thesis University College London. https://discovery.ucl.ac.uk/id/eprint/10048151/.

Tembo, Bernard, Rabecca Hatoongo-Masenke and Chama Bowa-Mundia. 2020. 'Energy Poverty in Zambia'. 42. Working Paper. Lusaka: ZIPAR.

Thörn, Håkan. 2009. 'The Meaning(s) of Solidarity: Narratives of Anti-Apartheid Activism'. *Journal of Southern African Studies* 35 (2): 417–36. https://doi.org/10.1080/03057070902919959.

Tille, Cédric. 2017. 'The Changing International Linkages of Switzerland: An Overview'. 12176. *CEPR Discussion Papers*. CEPR Discussion Papers. C.E.P.R. Discussion Papers. https://ideas.repec.org/p/cpr/ceprdp/12176.html.

Tilly, Charles. 1999. *Durable Equalities*. Berkeley: University of California Press. https://www.ucpress.edu/book/9780520221703/durable-inequality.

Tischler, Julia. 2013. *Light and Power for a Multiracial Nation: The Kariba Dam Scheme in the Central African Federation*. Cambridge Imperial and Post-Colonial Studies Series. New York: Palgrave Macmillan.

Tischler, Julia. 2014. 'Cementing Uneven Development: The Central African Federation and the Kariba Dam Scheme'. *Journal of Southern African Studies* 40 (5): 1047–64.

Trafigura Group Pte. 2018. *2017 Annual Report: Advancing Trade*. Singapore.

Tsing, Anna. 2005. *Friction: An Ethnography of Global Connection*. Princeton, NJ: Princeton University Press.

Udelsmann Rodrigues, Cristina, Patience Mususa, Karen Büscher and Jeroen Cuvelier. 2021. 'Boomtown Urbanization and Rural-Urban Transformation in Mining and Conflict Regions in Angola, the DRC and Zambia'. *Sustainability* 13 (4): 2285. https://doi.org/10.3390/su13042285.

UNRISD, dir. 2018. *The Swiss Commodity Trading Hub and Its Impact in the Global South*. Graduate Institute of International and Development Studies, Geneva. https://www.youtube.com/watch?v=i0UM8eCVsPE. Accessed 29 August 2024.

URS Scott Wilson Zambia. 2013. 'Access Road to Kansanshi Copper Smelter: Final Environmental Impact Statement'. URS Scott Wilson Zambia, Kitwe.

Van Alstine, James, and Stavros Afionis. 2013. 'Community and Company Capacity: The Challenge of Resource-Led Development in Zambia's "New Copperbelt"'. *Community Development Journal* 48 (3): 360–76.

Wahman, Michael. 2020. 'Violence and Money: A Constituency-Level Survey of Pre-Electoral Manipulation'. In *Democracy and Electoral Politics in Zambia*, edited by Tinenenji Banda, Kaaba O'Brian, Marja Hinfelaar, and Muna Ndulo, 283–310. Leiden: Brill. https://brill.com/view/title/57421.

Walsh, Andrew. 2019. 'The Ordinary Ethics of Charcoal in Northern Madagascar'. *Journal of the Royal Anthropological Institute* 25 (S1): 108–23. https://doi.org/10.1111/1467-9655.13017.

Welker, Marina. 2014. *Enacting the Corporation: An American Mining Firm in Post-Authoritarian Indonesia*. Berkeley: University of California Press.

Werthmann, Katja, and Tilo Grätz, eds. 2012. *Mining Frontiers in Africa: Anthropological and Historical Perspectives*. Mainz: Rüdiger Köppe Verlag.

Wikileaks. 2005. 'Public Library of US Diplomacy: South Africa: Minerals and Energy Newsletter *The Assay*, Issue 2', February. https://wikileaks.org/plusd/cables/05PRETORIA1099_a.html.

Wilkin, Paul David. 2012. 'UNZA in the NWP: 1975–79; New Chapter in My Life'. *The Northwestern Province of Zambia: Professional and Personal Reflections of Paul David Wilkin and Friends* (blog). 2012. https://davidwilkinnwpzambia.com/davids-story-photographs/unza-in-nwp-1975-79/.

Williams, Christine L. 2021. *Gaslighted: How the Oil and Gas Industry Shortchanges Women Scientists*. 1st edition. Oakland: University of California Press.

W.I.R.E., Nicholas Bornstein, Stephan Sigrist and Senem Wicki. 2015. 'Stadtidee Zug: Ein Leitbild für Politik, Wirtschaft und Bevölkerung zur Gestaltung der Zukunft in Zug'. Zürich.

Wolpe, Harold. 1972. 'Capitalism and Cheap Labour-Power in South Africa: From Segregation to Apartheid'. *Economy and Society* 1 (4): 425–56. https://doi.org/10.1080/03085147200000023.

Wright, Chris F. 2016. 'Leveraging Reputational Risk: Sustainable Sourcing Campaigns for Improving Labour Standards in Production Networks'. *Journal of Business Ethics* 137 (1): 195–210. https://doi.org/10.1007/s10551-015-2552-1.

Wu, Di. 2020. *Affective Encounters: Everyday Life among Chinese Migrants in Zambia*. London: Routledge.

Wylie, Sara Ann. 2018. *Fractivism: Corporate Bodies and Chemical Bonds*. Durham, NC: Duke University Press.

Yeung, Henry Wai-chung, and Neil Coe. 2015. 'Toward a Dynamic Theory of Global Production Networks'. *Economic Geography* 91 (1): 29–58.

Zambia Chamber of Mines. 2018. 'Trafigura Group Helps Re-Establish Historic African Trade Route'. *Zambia Chamber of Mines* (blog). 28 September 2018. http://mines.org.zm/trafigura-group-helps-re-establish-historic-african-trade-route/. Accessed 29 August 2024.

Zambia EITI. 2017. *Extractive Industries Transparency Initiative (EITI) Eighth Report for the Fiscal Year Ended 31 December 2015*. Lusaka: EITI.

Zambia EITI. 2020. *Extractive Industries Transparency Initiative (EITI) Eleventh Report for the Fiscal Year Ended 31 December 2018*. Lusaka: EITI.

Zambia EITI. 2023. *Extractive Industries Transparency Initiative (EITI) Fourteenth Report for the Fiscal Year Ended 31 December 2021*. Lusaka: EITI.

Zeller, Wolfgang. 2019. 'Drivers of Regional Integration: Blood and Solidarity on the Road and Online with the SADC Truck Drivers Association'. Paper presentation at the 8th European Conference on African Studies, Edinburgh, 11 June.

Zyl-Hermann, Danelle van. 2021. *Privileged Precariat: White Workers and South Africa's Long Transition to Majority Rule*. Cambridge: Cambridge University Press.

INDEX

www.ingramcontent.com/pod-product-compliance
Lightning Source LLC
LaVergne TN
LVHW021259080425
808019LV00003B/74